SPOTS OF A
LEOPARD

on being a man

AERNOUT ZEVENBERGEN

Published by
LAUGHING LEOPARD PRODUCTIONS
Cape Town, South Africa

www.laughingleopard.co.za

Publication © Laughing Leopard Productions 2009
Text © Aernout Zevenbergen 2009
Cover photo © Aernout Zevenbergen 2009

Originally published in 2007 in the Netherlands by
Mets & Schilt Uitgevers as 'Vlekken van een luipaard'

Translated, edited and revised © Aernout Zevenbergen 2009

Editor: Elzanne Roos
Logo running man: Adam Carnegie

ISBN 978-0-620-43311-2

Dear Esther and Stuart,

For Wisse Amani,
An audacious traveller

Wow! Still in every muscle!
But amazing to get back
into my body ;)

Herewith, as gratitude,
something for the mind

So, then, the double-edged sword of wounding. There are wounds that crush the soul, distort and misdirect the energy of life, and those that prompt us to grow up.

James Hollis – graduate of C.G. Jung Institute, Zürich

To be modern is to find ourselves in an environment that promises us adventure, power, joy, growth, transformation of ourselves and the world – and, at the same time, that threatens to destroy everything we have, everything we know, everything we are.

Marshall Berman – professor of Political Science,
City University of New York

CONTENTS

Preface ix

CONCEPTION 1

LAWS OF THE ANCESTORS 3
    Rejected by forefathers 5
    Majestic silence 17
    Lessons from the past 33

NEVER FORLORN IN AFRICA 43
    'You have to be able to love yourself' 47
    No more longing for ouzo in Kisangani 61
    Chasing the wind 75

LOVE IN TIMES OF AIDS 87
    Teeming Zululand 91
    Flammable spirits 103
    Do it yourself 123

TO PROCREATE, PROVIDE, AND PROTECT 137
    A respectable throng on barren lands 139
    Coffee is a gentleman 153
    Waiting for the kola nut 169

FATHER'S PRIDE 183
    Heroes of oblivion 185
    The rusty insides 195
    A *zwerfkei* behind a dike 213

EPHEMERAL 227
    Royal rags 229
    Emptiness 243

Acknowledgements 247
Literature 249

MAP OF AFRICA

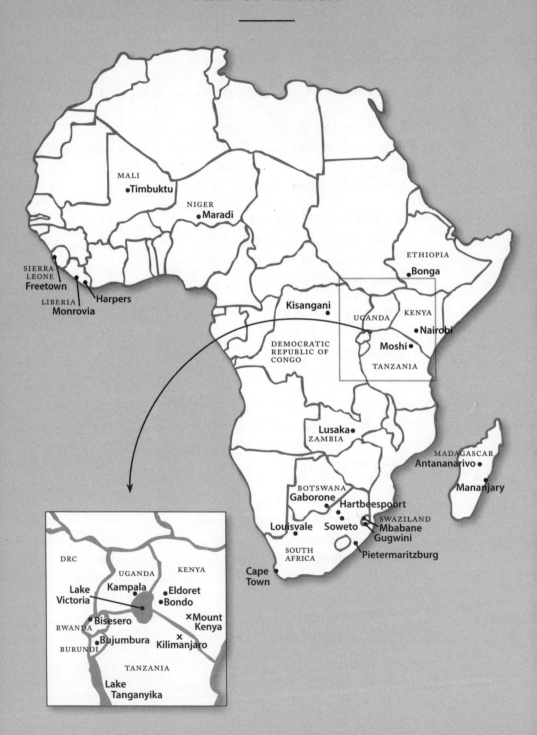

MALI
•Timbuktu

NIGER
•Maradi

SIERRA
LEONE
Freetown
•Harpers

LIBERIA
Monrovia

Kisangani

ETHIOPIA
•Bonga

UGANDA   KENYA
•Nairobi

DEMOCRATIC
REPUBLIC OF
CONGO

Moshi•

TANZANIA

Lusaka•
ZAMBIA

MADAGASCAR
Antananarivo •

BOTSWANA
Gaborone•
•Hartbeespoort   Mananjary

SWAZILAND
Louisvale•   Soweto•   •Mbabane
                        Gugwini
SOUTH
AFRICA   •Pietermaritzburg

Cape
Town

Inset map

DRC

UGANDA   KENYA

Lake
Victoria   Kampala•
                •Eldoret
                •Bondo

•Bisesero   ×Mount
RWANDA   Kenya

•Bujumbura   ×
BURUNDI   Kilimanjaro

TANZANIA

Lake
Tanganyika

PREFACE

The origin of this book lies at a meeting, one day in 2001, in a slum in Nairobi. It was an ordinary event. Nothing big. No drama. No sweeping statements. Nothing extreme. Just a meeting between an AIDS activist, infected with the virus herself, and a group of men. Through games that visualised how HIV spreads, a lot of laughter, a few serious notes and a fake penis, the assembled spoke of the pandemic that has affected tens of millions of people all over the planet – approximately thirty million individuals in Africa alone.

No dying patients, no suffering. On the contrary. People joked and people laughed. And, of course, the sun beamed its light – a the cruel sun: *jua kali*.

Yet the conversation that day put me on a journey that still continues today. What happened?

Let me take you to Kayole, almost eight years ago now.

NAIROBI – Her pair of glasses gives Hilda Ochieng (29) a stern look. Her smile though, disarms. The men opposite Ochieng know intuitively that although jokes are welcome, ridicule is not. Listen to Ochieng, and she'll listen to you.

'What do you want to know about sex?' she asks, not restrained by any of the many taboos still doing the rounds in Kenya, in November 2001. 'Everything,' answers one of the men in Ochieng's audience. 'I'd like to know what HIV is, and how to prevent getting it,' says another.

Around fifty men have gathered in the Mayaka International Club – a bar near the slum of Kayole in Kenya's capital, Nairobi. Most of them wear rags or overalls. They have put down their tools, which they work 'under the cruel sun', jua kali in Swahili. All make a living in the informal sector. Some are welders, others are spray painters, carpenters or plumbers. Most are 'everything that helps make a living'.

The men have reached an age at which they want to start families. An abundance of love and sexuality awaits exploration.

'Be open, Hilda,' says one.

'Name things as they are, otherwise what you say becomes too complicated,' says a second man in the audience.

'How dangerous is anal sex?' a third wants to know. 'That is as good as it gets, so how dangerous is it?'

A shy man dares ask if 'romantic cuddling is risky too?'

Ochieng works for Woman Fighting Aids in Kenya (WOFAK), one of many AIDS organisations in the country. Her purpose today is to show the men the risks of untamed, unbridled lust.

'Talking of abstinence so far hasn't worked,' Ochieng has learned. 'Some men always need to have a go at it.' For many men, monogamy is not a serious option. 'The best I can hope for is to persuade them to use condoms.'

In the Kenya of 2001, Ochieng fights an uphill battle. All churches explicitly forbid their members to use the latex barrier. President Daniel arap Moi himself set alight a stack of condoms, only three years earlier. The born-again president did not feel comfortable about informing the population of the risks of AIDS.

Estimates of the prevalence of HIV amongst the largely unprotected and ill-informed sexually active population of Kenya reaches as high as 15 per cent. It is reported that seven hundred people die daily of AIDS–related diseases, with the City of Nairobi itself losing up to twenty experienced and educated staff per week. Confronted by these figures, and after pressure from civil society and international donors, Moi agrees to import three hundred million condoms that year to be distributed freely. But the myths around condoms have by then already grown roots. It is those myths that Ochieng has to fight.

'My pastor tells me that the virus is smaller than the smallest of pores in the latex,' objects one of the jua kali workers. 'He also tells me that wearing a condom is therefore useless. He says I should have sex without one. What do you think of that, Hilda?'

Ochieng takes on the challenge, and names the facts as she knows them.

'And what about the rumour that it's the fluid that keeps the condoms moist that actually contains the virus?' Ochieng laughs. 'The condom protects you. It is the only kind of protection you can find.'

'I was told my balls will explode if I always make love with a condom. Is that true?' For the first time Ochieng is too stunned to speak. It is this question that opens the floor to a whole lot of other questions.

Ochieng needs to understand, some men say, that urges aren't only supposed to lead to pleasure but also to procreation.

'If we were to throw away our seed, how then do we make babies?'

And: 'Aren't we sinning against God's word by wasting our seed?'

Or: 'It is our duty as men, Hilda, to plant our seeds in as many flower pots as possible. Condoms prevent us from doing that.'

Ochieng replies, 'Is it really God's will for you to sleep around? If you are monogamous you don't need condoms. But you have to ask yourself how many children you can raise on your income…'

In a short demonstration Ochieng shows how to use a condom; she rolls the latex off on a black penis, cut from wood.

'What a tiny one, Hilda – come on, you have to be realistic.' Raucous laughter.

At the end of the meeting Ochieng hands out condoms. She has brought boxes full of them. But most men politely refuse to accept, before they return to their tools and their sheds.

'No wrapper around my sweetie – sorry, Hilda.'

This was not the first piece I wrote on AIDS, and many articles were still to follow. The elements of the story are hardly the stuff of headlines. Many, if not all journalists working in Africa, will have written similar things.

For some reason though, the questions and comments made at the meeting, that one morning in Kayole's Mayaka International Club, are etched in my memory. The conversation raised a great deal of questions about how the participants saw themselves individually as 'men' – how they relate to themselves, to other men, to women, to their own sexuality, and to their roles as (potential) fathers, lovers and husbands.

'It is our duty as men, Hilda, to plant our seeds in as many flowerpots as possible. Condoms prevent us from doing that.'

What did this remark say about manhood? About masculinity? About life? About the links between being a father, being a man, being a sexual creature, being human?

'I was told my balls will explode if I always make love with a condom. Is that true?'

Where did this rumour come from? What did it say about the man who was honest and courageous enough to share it with a group? What did the statement say about the way forward, in the struggle against HIV/AIDS?

What did the comments indicate about the abyss between scientists far away, who think of mechanical solutions, and normal people whose main challenge of the day is how to make it to the next?

How did the questions fit into the clean, scientific approaches and the political agendas of organisations trying to tackle the pandemic?

Since I began to cover Africa as a journalist in August 1997, I have written many pieces on HIV/AIDS, on awareness campaigns, on the disaster that the epidemic has unleashed on individual lives. I have also written extensively about sexual and domestic violence, on rape in times of war, and fists in times of alcohol abuse.

The themes of HIV/AIDS and violence against women have made a lasting impact on me. For me, the two plagues point at a breakdown of the most intimate of relationships human beings can have with each other.

Of course, I spoke to those who had made careers of fighting these scourges. I listened to grand explanations about cultures, traditions, rites and rituals, and how – once Africa was 'developed' – all would work out for the best. This conservative, rightwing approach said, 'If only they "modernised", all would be well.'

On the other side of the ideological spectrum, I met those who stated in a wide variety of discourses that all of Africa's present-day woes (AIDS and violence included) are rooted in colonialism, racism and the malfunctioning of the global economy. 'If only society was transformed, all would be well.'

My problem with these explanations is that each portrays human beings as machines. Individual choice does not exist. Individual accountability appears to be a joke. Individual dissent seems impossible. Individual wisdom is denied. Individual fallibility and perfection – and the leeway between these two extremes – are negated.

The 'theories' unsettle me.

How come domestic violence in Kibera, Nairobi's worst slum, is so much worse than in the rural areas in the north of Kenya, where life is much harsher, much poorer, much more devoid of 'comfort'? How come AIDS is so much more widespread in relatively wealthy Botswana than in dirt-poor Burkina Faso (meaning: The Land of The Honourable Men)?

The 'rightwing' reference to cultures, traditions, rites and rituals that were seen as 'primitive', and therefore responsible for both HIV/AIDS and violence against women, seems too simplistic. Surely, on a continent where *Homo sapiens sapiens* have roamed, lived and loved for close to a hundred thousand years, people must have found ways of living and relating that are efficient. It can't all be bad, can it?

Healthy cultures do not tend to self-destruct, and culture, whatever its form, is only one aspect of existence and therefore cannot in itself be the only source of the problems.

The 'leftwing' reference to the excesses of capitalism, to racism, and to poverty also seems insufficient. Not every poor man rapes, and rich men too can molest wives or children. Poverty is always part of a much larger context, and is hardly ever absolute. Poverty, whatever its form, is always relative and is only one aspect of existence, and therefore cannot in itself be the only source of the problems.

Some men in times of poverty grab a gun, kill, loot and rape. Other men, however, don't. They work, share a beer with friends, and converse with relatives. Some men in times of HIV/AIDS grab, seduce or force a woman into unprotected sex. Other men don't. They relate to loved ones as loving, caring relatives do.

Fuelling the flames

What makes a man think his balls will explode were he to use a condom? It can't be based on fact, because balls don't explode that easily. Could it be fear? If so, what then did he fear? The real-life explosion of testicles, or the explosion of a sense of manhood?

What makes it so crucial, if that were indeed the case, for some men to plant their seed 'in as many flowerpots' as they can? What is it with semen, that some men love to scatter it about – but only if it's directed at a fertile womb? Why this urge to procreate with a seeming disregard for negative side effects?

I could not find answers to these questions. Not in libraries, not in the offices of non-governmental organisations, not on the Internet. I tried for over a year to find openings. I read some of the classics of feminism, but found in hundreds of pages only studies, quotes and opinions on the 'how' of patriarchy but never on the 'why'.

Only one paragraph in Susan Faludi's standard work *Backlash* (1991), for example, describes how men's fears of no longer being the sole provider fed a harsh response to any policy that intended to free women from the yoke of patriarchy. But Faludi never explained *why* men have that fear.

Although she focused on the situation in the United States during the last decades of the previous century, her reasoning appears to be shared by most gender activists around the world. Gender studies, the field of social science that examines the relationship between men and women, does so mainly in terms of power dynamics.

I don't think that approach suffices. Is the desire to be 'the sole provider', for no other reason than to be the 'boss', indeed all there is to manhood? Or is there something more substantial beneath the surface? What male need is satisfied by being in charge? What does he gain by exclusively holding the reigns? Is a man's quest for power – if that is truly all a man's life is about – a purpose in itself, or does that 'power' lead to something else? If so, what?

What is power, apart from a deep desire for control over the outside world, driven by fears of the unknown? Power satisfies a deep psychological need. Exactly what that need is seems to be irrelevant to most gender activists. And this is something I don't understand.

Surely if a fire rages and one wants to stop it from further destroying individuals or even society as a whole, it is not enough merely to describe the flames. It is crucial to get to the heart of the fire and see what could be feeding it.

What fuels the man who feels this urge to plant his seed in as many flowerpots as possible? What motivates him? What drives him? What defines the choices he makes?

Answers to these questions do not lie exclusively in political science, which happens to be my own background. They do not lie in economics, sociology or anthropology. Those fields describe the landscape, the soil, the surroundings and the influences to which no person is invulnerable. But on their own they seem insufficient. It is not the economy per se that determines the choices a person makes, neither is it the society nor the political arena in which he or she exists.

The answers to the questions above lie in the hearts of men, in their minds and souls. The answers speak through hands that either caress or hit, through feet that either dance or kick, through mouths that either speak words of support or those of destruction.

A war

It is a September evening in a plebeian neighbourhood in Cape Town. The year is 2008. A grandfather and his grandson have an argument. The eighteen-year-old Mr. W. junior wants to fetch the clothes that he left at his grandfather's house months earlier. The 79-year-old Mr. W. senior refuses to open the door. He wants nothing more to do with his grandchild.

Eight months earlier, Senior told Junior and his sisters to leave. They had been stealing his stuff: socks, clothes, food, money. They returned late at night or in the wee hours of the morning, breaking windows and damaging doors. Senior felt he could no longer cope with his grandchildren's lifestyle: unemployed, broken, off-track, leaning to a life of drugs and crime.

Junior does not accept the closed door. He climbs a drain pipe and breaks in, grabs a broomstick and starts beating his grandfather on the head, demanding the old man's retirement money – a mere two hundred rand.

Mr. W. senior retreats to his bedroom, where he sits down on his bed. Junior follows him.

The young man later confesses in a written guilty plea, 'I […] turned him around onto his stomach. I opened my pants and put my penis in his mouth. I then took a broomstick and put it in his anus. When I was done I put my penis in his anus. After finishing I left the complainant there and fled the house.'

After the assault, the grandfather fled to a neighbour, dressed only in a T-shirt and underpants. 'Full of blood, full of blood,' Senior tells the court.

The prosecutor would like to know how he feels.

'Very angry with him, yes.'

'How is your heart?' asks the prosecutor.

'Very hurt.'

Senior wants his grandson punished, severely. 'Something has to happen to him. I've been hurt badly. I will never forget, never forgive. Ever.'

Junior's defence lawyer tells the court that the accused is one of five siblings. 'My client also informs me that he has never really had a father figure.' He lived with his grandfather until he was thrown out, and has a child himself, 'a little boy who resides with his mother. [S]he is however unemployed, her family supports the child.'

Money ran out for schooling when Junior reached Grade Seven. Just like his brother, Junior has always been unemployed. 'He previously had a drug problem, but [...] he left that lifestyle four years ago.'

The defence continues: 'My client is eighteen years old. He is young, very young, your Worship. He has his whole life ahead of him. [...] [H]e is still a good candidate for rehabilitation.'

The judge is stern in his verdict: 'He vented his rage in an inhumane and abhorrent way on his grandfather. He purposefully humiliated him. There is no trace of remorse whatsoever. [...] Apart from the physical wounds, the events were very traumatic for the victim. He has been humiliated repeatedly through sexual acts [...] committed by his own grandson.'

He continues, 'The present levels of violence and serious crimes in South Africa are such that when sentencing, emphasis needs to be placed on the deterring effect of a sentence.'

Junior gets life.

Violence in South Africa is a serious problem. In the case of Senior versus Junior, a grandson beat up his grandfather and stole his money. The clash escalated into a power struggle through sexual violence for no other purpose than humiliation.

No one knows how many men rape other men in South Africa – victims don't easily report the crimes inflicted on them. Even amongst inmates of the harshest of South Africa's jails, where rape is instrumental in establishing the hierarchy, reports of sexual violence are rare. Victims fear retribution.

The same applies to ordinary girls and women who, after having been raped, often choose not to go to the police. Sexual violence in South Africa has taken on epic proportions. By some estimates, every twenty-six seconds a man in South Africa rapes a woman – and often, the women in question are infants or elderly. Every six hours a man kills his life partner.

'The South African Police Service reports that 36 190 cases of rape and 6 763 cases of indecent assault were reported between April and December 2007,' writes Kopano Ratele, a psychology professor at the University of South Africa. 'While there has been a decline from numbers reported for April-December 2006, this is a country still in the middle of a war against its women and children. Add to these figures the 18 487 cases of murders, 18 795 cases of attempted murder, 210 104 cases of assault with the intent to inflict grievous bodily harm, and 198 049 cases of common assaults reported between 1 April 2007 and 31 March 2008, South Africa is a leader amongst the most unsafe countries in the world for its citizens and guests, most of whom are the very people in need of protection and care from the state, organisations, families and all of us.'

'Macho attitude fuels alarming brutality of young males,' is the headline of a news story in the South African newspaper *The Times*, on 5 October 2008. Ratele is quoted in the article: 'Our men can't walk away from a challenge. Parents need to teach their children it is okay to walk away from a conflict, instead of fighting with their fists.'

South Africa is not the only country in Africa faced with a problem of masculinity. During the conflict in the Democratic Republic of Congo, rape was labelled 'a weapon of war' by both human rights and aid organisations. That 'war' did not end when the armed groups signed a peace agreement, and hasn't let up since the country went to the polls in 2006. Rape in the DRC is now no longer a 'weapon of war' – it is simply rape, on a massive scale, with thousands of victims annually.

Post-war sexual violence in Liberia is so widespread, it can only be termed an epidemic.

In Kibera, Africa's biggest slum, located in the heart of Nairobi, uncles increasingly rape nieces, and grandfathers assault granddaughters.

'Women in villages around Korhogo, northern Côte d'Ivoire, dare not walk to their fields alone for fear of rape,' writes *IRIN news* on 30 March 2009.

It is extremely difficult to say with absolute certainty how bad 'the war against [the] women and children' is in the wide variety of African societies. As said earlier, many assaults go unreported.

South Africa is one of the few countries with the financial means to do independent scientific research. A report by the Medical Research Council, published in June 2009, sent shock waves through the country when it revealed that over a quarter of the 1 738 men asked about their experiences with non-consensual sex admitted having forced a girl or woman into intercourse.

According to the researchers, most important for the likelihood of a man being a rapist were psychological factors. 'Rape was associated with significantly greater degrees of exposure to trauma in childhood.' More specifically, those who rape were themselves made outcasts while growing up, or made others to feel cast out. Relationships while young were for most rapists based on power plays. And rape, at times, is part of a bonding ritual between teenage boys.

'Teasing and harassment, or bullying, were reported by many of the men in their childhood. Over half of the men had experienced this themselves (54%) and somewhat fewer (40%) had teased and harassed others. Both experience of bullying and being bullied was much more common among men who raped.'

That power play does not just show up in the way rapists force girls and women into sex, but seems a dominating view of life. 'Delinquent and criminal behaviour were more common among men who raped. Men who raped were much more likely to have been involved in theft and, with the exception of legal gun ownership, they were very much more likely to have been involved with weapons, gangs and to have been arrested and imprisoned.'

Justice Malala, columnist at *The Times*, responded to the findings on June 22. He wrote, 'A conversation is needed among South African men. We need to start defining what we mean when we say that we are men. There is a problem with the way we perceive ourselves, and the way in which we present ourselves to the world: to our brothers, our sons, our sisters, our wives and our partners. We are not men; we are broken beings.'

Years before Malala wrote this, a young man in Soweto told me about this sense of befuddlement. 'Men are confused, I think. We don't know where we stand any more. We copy life as we see it on TV, in American soap operas. Sometimes I think that we are all a bunch of bad actors; we play roles and characters. But that is not who we really are, what our genetic make-up and history tell us to be, or what our social and natural surroundings demand of us. We are leopards who are trying to wipe away their spots.'

Honour and respect

A news article on the front page of the *Cape Times* tells of an amicable superintendent in the South African Police Service who suddenly blows a fuse. He empties his service pistol into his girlfriend, colleagues, two women and a toddler. His name is Chippa Mateane. He is eventually shot by his own mates who chase him and in doing so accidentally kill an innocent pedestrian.

Before Mateane went on his shooting spree, he wrote a farewell note to his girlfriend who had just left him:

I am not to blame. I am important – I deserve to be loved by you. I deserve to be treated with respect. And I will still love you forever.

The superintendent saw his girlfriend's decision to leave as unacceptable, and interpreted it as a rigorous denial of his standing in society.

If Mateane had been a lone wolf, and the bloodbath he caused an exception, then his story would have been no more than a ripple on the surface of ordinary life. However, Mateane is not the only man going on a killing spree because of unrequited love – he is not even the only South African police officer to use violence as an outlet for his harsh confrontations with life. And Mateane's girlfriend is not the only victim of bruised male pride.

What is this 'respect' Mateane wrote about in his farewell letter?

Respect is a stamp of approval, received from the outside – a sign that a person's existence is considered worthwhile to others. Honour creates freedom of movement, ease of contact, peace of mind.

Respect is closely related to self-esteem, with one fundamental difference: respect comes from outside, whereas self-esteem has its origins within. A person with healthy self-esteem relies little on how others perceive him or her, whereas a person with poor self-esteem will do almost anything to gain a sense of honour through they eyes of others.

John Iliffe, professor of History at Cambridge University, was the first scholar to write a book about the meaning of 'honour' and 'respect' in Africa's history. Iliffe sees both as keywords in understanding contemporary Africa. His book *Honour in African History* (2005) opens as follows: '[U]nderstanding African behaviour, in the past and present, must take account of changing notions of honour, which historians and others have neglected.'

How important then is honour? Iliffe writes, 'Until the coming of world religions, honour was the chief ideological motivation of African behaviour. It remained a powerful motivation even for those who accepted world religions.'

Viewing contemporary Africa from this angle, Iliffe does not see AIDS in Africa as primarily a sign of poverty, a lack of responsibility or even as a lack of knowledge. For Iliffe the pandemic is essentially a matter of wounded masculine honour having turned against women, expressing an unconscious desire to kill and a flight from reality. Iliffe ends his book in a very outspoken way: 'If the AIDS epidemic displayed heroic masculine honour at its most self-destructive, it also displayed female honour at its most heroic.'

The issue of 'respect' also lies at the root of domestic and sexual violence. These days, no reasonable person perceives rape as an attempt to find sexual pleasure. Sexual violence or the excesses of war and crime are phenomena in which perpetrators take what they are unable to get in any other way. 'Respect', however twisted or illusionary, is the ultimate goal – extorted or commanded.

Who's on top?

Are the HIV/AIDS epidemic and the widespread violence against women really, as some dare suggest, the consequence of culture – of traditions, rites and rituals? Does a healthy culture allow for its daughters and women to be raped? Do healthy traditions demand of men to rape fellow citizens?

Or do (sexual) violence and the scale on which it happens indicate the opposite: societies that are crumbling, individuals who cannot deal with the stresses of life?

There is a saying that Africa survives on the strength of its women. They lug the water, cook the meals, till the land and send the children to school. Women give birth, they nurture, they show the way and they keep families together under the pressures of modern times.

Where are the men in all of this?

At the risk of generalising - and keeping in mind the existence of over four thousand different ethnic groups on the whole of the continent - traditional family life in Africa is a complex system of networks, fluid roles, rights and duties. But most of these diverse cultures assign identical core tasks to men: to procreate, provide and protect. In exchange for these services, a wife bears offspring that will honour her husband and continue his legacy after his death. Every day a meal awaits him, prepared by his wife or his daughters.

The nuclear family as the cornerstone of society is a Western concept. The strict boundaries of social life in the West seem unfathomable elsewhere. Outside Europe and North America, people tend to think in terms of extended families. The family as a social unit containing only a father, a mother and their offspring is quite untenable and practically unknown in Africa.

Until quite recently, the ideologies of materialism and individualism were unthinkable in Africa. For millennia, the individual survived here thanks to the benevolence and strength of the collective, and the collective survived due to the energy invested by each individual. Even today, in the last bastions of traditional life, an aunt can breast-feed a baby if the mother is away; any uncle will discipline youngsters if the biological father is out working; a neighbour can explain the ins and outs of life as a married man; a cousin can teach a younger relative the tricks of seduction.

And so it has been for a very long time. But things are changing.

Africans are now generally poorer than they were four decades ago. Globalisation has brought few advantages to the continent. It is hard, indeed often impossible, for Africa to compete in the global race. Serious industrialisation of the continent has yet to take off. The agricultural sector has not been able to compete with subsidised production from the United States or the European Union, nor can it comply with the strict bureaucratic import regulations of the economic superpowers.

These processes, combined with the introduction of both materialism and individualism, have had a profound effect on the relationship between the sexes, as well as on Africa's rich and diverse customs, traditions and value systems.

Development organisations from abroad and African women's groups have been working for decades to empower women. In their programmes men are, at best, seen as irrelevant; at worst they are adversaries.

There is an inherent problem with that approach. Most African societies are patriarchal in nature – nothing will really change unless men endorse the renewal that is being sought.

'AIDS is about who's on top,' says Gethwane Makhaye from the AIDS-ridden province of KwaZulu-Natal in South Africa. For years she had been informing women in her province about their rights, with unforseen consequences. Women whom she had informed of their right to demand a condom or to say 'no' to sex returned to her offices days later, with bruises and black eyes.

Makhaye: 'A woman may insist on a condom, but that doesn't mean that the man will want to use one. If we want to succeed in the fight against AIDS, we have to change men's behaviour as well.'

Working with men, however, is far from common and appears to be an uphill battle that, apart from changing the politics between men and women, needs to include some serious soul-searching. Mbuyiselo Botha, active in Sonke Gender Justice, says, 'It is all about choices. If we [men] want to save our souls, we have to face our demons. But it is difficult to take responsibility, because then we become accountable for our actions.'

A talent for indifference

Many men in Africa find themselves on pedestals. Some describe the role of the man as 'the bull leading the herd.' Many men give orders, beat women, shoot sperm and, occasionally, also a bullet. Nothing, or so is the assumption, will get them off that pedestal – no laws, no mores, no virus.

Sometimes these images cause a maddening itch deep inside me; sometimes they merely irritate me. At other times I feel a strange mixture bubbling beneath the surface, a combination of boiling anger, dark hopelessness and the urge to laugh out loud. And then doubts set in.

Why should I care if some of the most powerful politicians in Africa so often choose to look the other way?

Why should I care when a man with presidential ambitions thinks it's perfectly okay to have unprotected sex with an HIV-positive friend of his family, less than half his age, supposedly for no other reason than that she wore a short skirt? Why should I care if his supporters, including numerous women, hold banners outside the court room where his rape case is being heard, shouting 'Burn the bitch!' – referring to the complainant?

Why should I care when women in Congo explain in detail the rape they had to undergo at the hands of self-proclaimed 'rebel fighters'?

Or when a Rwandan man complains of his male compatriots' drinking beer on the side of the road while their women carry forty kilogram loads of bananas or potatoes on their heads to markets to earn a buck?

Or when I read about mass rapes of girls in Liberia by neighbours, grandfathers and uncles?

What am I to do? Practise a talent for indifference; hiding behind my shield of 'impartial journalism'?

Look the other way?

Snort and splutter about excesses of masculinity, and then get on with my own life?

Chained to a yoke

My umbilical cord was cut by a nurse in a hospital in Lusaka, but I was educated in schools and universities in the Netherlands. I am a child of Erasmus and Hugo Grotius, of Luther and Calvin, of the Enlightenment and the welfare state. Of Willem (a development worker) and Bertie (a primary school teacher).

As an adult I settled in Africa for its riddles and its smells – the smell of the air, the aromas of the savannah, the desert, the *fynbos* of the Western Cape, a rainforest and a shanty town. A melange, a dash of rotting garbage, a hint of flowers blossoming, smouldering fires, and tinges of days-old sweat. The flavour of the earth under a sweltering sky, and soil hungry for seeds and rain. I have only found this mixture in Africa. It's the smell of my earliest youth, a vague reminiscence, a subconscious sense of nostalgia: This place smells safe.

On my travels as a correspondent in Africa, I've stumbled upon an increasing number of stories that, at first glance, seem unrelated to the major news events making headlines in Europe. They are not primarily on the price of copper or coffee on the global market, nor on bloody civil wars with repressed groups and 'rebels' fighting for 'liberation.' While rummaging through material for those headline articles, I came across stories from inside homes, with thin threads leading to bedrooms and to what happens once the curtains have been closed and the doors have been shut.

An illusive war – hardly noticed; a war that is barely reported in a coherent, sensible way. A war chalking up millions of casualties, year after year. It is the struggle between men and women. What are we as men to do with this battle? What am I to do with it?

I too am a man. And at times I resonate with the words of the Chilean poet Pablo Neruda in his poem *Walking Around*: 'It so happens I am sick of being a man.'

Behind the impersonal statistics of HIV/AIDS or domestic violence, and beyond the gruesome stories of some of the latest armed conflicts, I have come across expressions of a type of masculinity gone horribly astray – it is a kind of masculinity I have no sympathy for whatsoever. A type of masculinity that, if looked at directly, raises questions about honour, self-esteem and perceptions of reality.

Those topics, in turn, highlight issues of love, friendship, loneliness, fatherhood, commitment, and the right to be imperfect versus the urge to succeed in everything. They point to a degrading definition of success, which is increasingly measured only by the ability to gather possessions, at whatever cost.

These issues started screaming for attention in my own life. A few months before I met the men in Mayaka International Club in Nairobi in 2001, my house of cards had collapsed. We were about to get married later that year and were planning a modest ceremony. Until I found the letter she'd written to him, her lover.

A relationship that had lasted for more than a decade had ended, and that ending threw me back into myself. What hit me hardest was the realisation that I would no longer become a father in the foreseeable future.

The avalanche of consequences of a love lost did not stop there. I started dating again, and found myself in circumstances stranger than fiction. Nothing seemed similar to the dating scene I remembered from more than ten years earlier. It was a different place, a different time, and I had grown into a different man.

An abyss of insecurity opened up. It seemed dating was stripped of everything I knew. There were no agreed rules, no agreed codes, no agreed guidelines – a jungle of lust, love, disappointment, fear, anger, desire, expectation and demands, popularly known as 'baggage'. My return to dating felt like a slide into an obscene landscape, governed by futilities.

One woman would be insulted if I kept a door open, another would feel incensed if I didn't. I myself couldn't care less about the door or the veneer of either chivalry or misogyny it was supposed to represent.

If I ever wanted to feel comfortable in this bush of contemporary 'romance', I would have to first figure out what mattered to me, what I needed, and what I could very well do without. I could not afford to define my essence on codes or guidelines from outside which were extremely confusing at best. It became clear that only through a descent to the core of my own being could I make sense both of the world around me as well as my place in it.

I found myself surrounded by questions millions of other men worldwide are struggling with. Questions that have become urgent since women started liberating themselves from the yoke of patriarchy, and so paved the way for men to do the same.

Patriarchy doesn't limit only women's freedom. This system is seen to be a man's best guarantee for staying on top of things, and for being placed on a pedestal in his own backyard. But at the core, patriarchy undermines the right of half the globe's population to have emotions and express them. In its most extreme form, it denies men the right to be compassionate and to be of service to others.

The price a man has to pay for the privilege of remaining on his pedestal, is the amputation of large chunks of his own humanity. Is there a way out?

Steel chains lie on the ground, under a lean-to in a small courtyard of a mental asylum. The first link is anchored in concrete. Attached to it are rusty links, one after the other. The complete chain is probably two metres long and has a large ring at the other end to attach the prisoners to.

I cannot call them 'patients'; patients are cared for. Here humans are fed and scrubbed clean once a month. That's all. The mentally ill are merely kept alive.

I wander through the asylum of Freetown, Sierra Leone, from the courtyard where the insane are bound to chains, through a ward with more chains, towards the isolation cells. I open the latch of one of the steel doors. Startled eyes stare at me: wide open, beastly, inhuman and without a glimmer of expectation.

Behind him I read a few words scratched onto the brown wall. 'To be a man is not easy.' The man who scratched these words onto the wall of an isolation cell of the asylum in Freetown has a story unknown to me.

The simplicity of his words stays with me. It is devoid of drama, of heart-rending pain. A dry observation, like talking about the weather.

Wounding, healing and journeying

'Men's lives are violent, because their souls have been violated.' James Hollis wrote these words in his book *Under Saturn's Shadow* (1994). Hollis is an archetypal psychologist, who picked up the theme of masculinity during a period when men's groups sprouted like mushrooms in the United States. It was a trend he did not particularly appreciate for he feared that the group processes would not allow individual men to take personal responsibility for healing their own individual wounds.

'If men are to heal,' Hollis wrote, 'they must activate within what they did not receive from without. Unless men can emerge from darkness, we shall continue to wound women and each other, and the world can never be a safe or healthy place.'

Does this analysis – coming from an American psychologist trained in the tradition of Carl Jung, psychology's European founding father – have any bearing on contemporary Africa? Or does it merely deserve to be dismissed as 'alien' and therefore 'useless'?

What is the nature of the wound that turns an eighteen-year-old boy into his grandfather's rapist? What is the nature of the wound that makes wife-beaters out of potentially compassionate men? What wounds cause a man to refuse responsibility for his own choices and behaviour? What causes so many men to hide behind mountains of arguments against either using condoms or sufficiently adjusting their sexual conduct in times of AIDS?

More importantly: What can be done about these wounds?

Hollis formulates an answer that rings true for me: 'Our wounds are to the soul, and only that which reaches it can heal.'

To reach the soul requires a new journey. 'The hero quest today is not through the physical world but through the badlands of the soul. The evil men must engage is not the barbarian at the gates but the darkness within, the fear from which only boldness may bring delivery.'

It slowly dawned on me that, if I were to make sense of reality around and inside me, I would have to journey into some of the darkest corners of my own soul. What are my shadows, what are my deepest fears, what are my greatest weaknesses and strengths?

Slowly, the first outlines of a new voyage became visible.

I would have to ask but one simple question to find clues that could help me rebuild the simplest of foundations, one that would enable me to construct my own path forward.

What does it mean to be a man, today?

Cape Town, July 2009

CONCEPTION

March 1996 – in the desert of Mali, between Bamako and Timbuktu

Tracks run in a northerly direction through the hills. Thorny bushes blossom here and there in the desert. It is empty, inhospitable. Hot. Dusty.

The emptiness of the desert has taken hold of me. In the void of the indescribable open plains, life revolves around trifling things and the art of observation – looking without knowing, being astounded without needing an answer.

In the distance I see a boy walking. He wears a coat, browned by sweat and grease, reaching just above his knees. I estimate him to be around thirteen years old.

He comes from the east and walks westward, assisted by a walking stick. Along a path I cannot distinguish.

His gait is determined; a well-paced stride that could last for hours. Who is he?

The sun shimmers above the Sahara. And the boy pushes along. With his head bowed down, he stares at the earth passing beneath him.

He crosses the tracks leading to Timbuktu; looks neither right nor left. Where does he come from?

Bare feet. Hot sand.

At times he looks up, staring at the horizon. Most of the time though, he just plants his stick in front of him and simply walks.

The boy disappears in quivering, hot air. Where is he heading?

LAWS OF THE ANCESTORS

Traditions are weird things.

Traditions are the answers to questions of purpose and direction. They are the habits, customs, rituals and legends that tell a person who he is, where his roots are and where he can go in life. Traditions, however, also safeguard the perks of the privileged.

Some speak of them as static and permanent – the everlasting and untouchable rules as laid down by ancestors. Traditions seem written in stone, but when one looks at them from a different angle they appear fluid and malleable, and the stone itself undergoes constant erosion. They change with time.

In traditional Africa, almost all objects have meaning. Belief in witches and the spirits of ancestors, in mysticism and the healing magic of crushed herbs and animal organs, is still alive.

From the oldest inhabitants of the continent, the Bushmen[*], to some of the last to arrive (the white Africans), each people has its own stories, myths, heroes and legends. The Afrikaner *Boere* constructed their holy shrine in Pretoria, to commemorate the Battle of Blood River in 1838. There, every year on 16 December, the sun shines on their Covenant with God. According to legend, Afrikaners killed over three thousand Zulus during this

---

[*] The term Bushman resonates with years of racism and is therefore officially no longer used. These days the Bushmen (officially referred to as the San) are grouped together with another ethnic group: the Khoikhoi. Historically speaking, however, it is incorrect to combine the Khoikhoi and the San into one word, since they never perceived themselves as one and the same ethnic group. Most of the Bushmen find the word 'san' distasteful; it was a derogatory term used by the Khoikhoi. It means 'thief', 'rogue' or 'outsider'.

battle, and this was only possible, it is claimed, through a direct intervention of their God. Victory in this battle was proof, or so the Afrikaners chose to believe, of a divine calling to rule over the lands and the peoples of Southern Africa.

For the Bushmen, a people of hunters and gatherers, there was no difference between the world of the five senses and spiritual existence. Their shamans travelled easily from one realm of reality to another, and back. In the South African Drakensberg, over thousands of years, the Bushmen made 3 500 paintings in which they depicted their spiritual connection to nature, and especially to the eland. In those mountains, one doesn't ridicule nature. Here, man is a guest, vulnerable and dependent on his environment. Live and let live. Hunt and honour. Gather and grace. Know the rules of the relationship between man and nature. Most of these rules have been laid down in the rock paintings of the Bushmen.

For many thousands of years these hunter-gatherers were able to withstand the pressures, limitations and dangers of the Drakensberg. Until, with the arrival of white settlers in the 19th century, they lost their prey. The settlers shot most of the game, and so eliminated the Bushmen's primary means of existence in the area.

The last Bushman in the Drakensberg was seen in the 1880s. Fifty years later hikers found a few arrows and a bow, left behind on a ledge as if only moments ago their owner had disappeared. This same type of weapon was, for millennia, the most important means of survival for the Bushmen.

These days the last of the Bushmen survive mostly in the Kalahari desert, a area without rocks, and therefore devoid of places to paint. For many a Bushman, Spirits these days are found in spirits.

The art of rock paintings faded into oblivion halfway in the 19th century. When an older Bushman was asked to explain the meaning of some thousand-year-old paintings in the private game park Kaga Kamma, he shook his head.

'It is a coded message from my ancestors,' he said.

'But we've lost the key to decipher it.'

REJECTED BY FOREFATHERS

Johannes Julius speaks in a gentle and composed way. His seat is a pot, turned upside down on the earth. Orange light from a huge lamppost shines on his face. He is twenty six years old, has short curly hair and a moustache. Smoke from a smouldering charcoal fire repeatedly forces Johannes to close his eyes.

Wanda (21) walks up and down, goes inside and comes out again. Three candles light up their shed, made of corrugated plates, all nailed to bent wooden sticks. Pieces of cardboard keep out the worst cold from corners where it is too hard to beat steel into shape. Inside, a wooden partition separates the living quarters from the 'dining room'. It all measures three metres by five.

Wrapped around her head, Wanda wears a cloth to cover her hair. She listens intently when an older woman explains the basics of housekeeping. Her mentor shows her which pots to use for which meal, explains the purpose of cutlery and indicates how much fat to use when cooking.

An old man comes strolling along, greets his company, grabs a chair and makes himself comfortable. From one of his pockets he takes a pipe and some tobacco. He looks around, stands up, whispers something into Wanda's ear, and sits down again.

Johannes has freshened up after a hard day's work at the tannery, located somewhere between the provincial capital of Upington in the Northern Cape and the township, Louisvale. His task is to sprinkle salt on the skins of slaughtered sheep. It's a 'contract' job, which means he only gets paid when the tanner has skins to work on. When there are none, he waits.

It is a life of slogging away, but Johannes has dreams. Big dreams. He wants to be deacon in his charismatic church, which he joined only a few weeks ago. He wants to earn enough money to offer his future wife, Wanda, and their daughter Tshepang a decent life. Gone are the days of booze, drugs, fights, girlfriends and 'confrontations with the law'.

Johannes and Wanda are preparing for their wedding. Brothers from his church teach him how to be a responsible man; sisters teach her how to do her housekeeping.

A puppy walks through a hole in the fence. The wind picks up and gusts blow into Johannes's face. The old man in his chair moves restlessly. He grabs the neighbour's toddler and starts playing with the infant, on his knees.

Johannes speaks of the changes he and Wanda are going through. It started in the week before his birthday, in March. Johannes had ended up with broken facial bones when someone hit him with a stone. 'I thought, I am heading for my death. One more thing and that will be it; one more fight and my time has come. This has to stop.'

One night, recently, Johannes had a dream. Wanda had caught two fish. Reverend Daniël Willems had told him good times were in the making. Fish are signs of good things to come. According to the Bible, and to Reverend Willems.

'It burns inside me,' Johannes told Wanda that night. 'I want to change. Booze creates too many problems. If we both change our lives, we might get it together.'

While Johannes tells me his story, the old man stands up again and silently walks towards Wanda. The two of them no longer whisper – their tone now reveals rage. He wants something, and she is not willing to give it to him.

Johannes remains silent, observes what happens before him, and stares into the light of the lamppost. He plays with the laces of his shoes and repositions himself on his upturned pot. 'Wanda is my inspiration. Of the two of us, she is the most determined to turn life around.' Missing her baby Tshepang scorches her insides, more so than his.

The conversation between Wanda and the old man is spinning out of control. He yells while he grabs her. 'This is all because of that damned baby of yours.' She screams back, like a haunted woman.

The old man pulls his hat over his head, and stumbles away as only drunkards do. Wanda watches him go. Her eyes spew fire.

He wanted money. 'My reputation has gone to smithereens because of that bloody baby of yours.' He makes a fist and clasps his pipe.

Oupa Jan was one of the first suspects the police arrested for the rape of baby Tshepang. One of the other six suspects was Johannes.

Earlier on that Saturday morning in October 2001 Johannes was woken up by his brother. 'Your baby has been raped!' Johannes was recovering from a night of hard liquor and drugs.

Louisvale was outraged about Tshepang's ordeal, about her bloodstained dress and her torn vagina and anus. The masses wanted revenge, and they wanted it fast. *Oupa* Jan and the other six men were suspected of a gang rape. They had to give blood to be compared with DNA found in the sperm on Tshepang's body. Tests showed none of the men had been involved in the assault.

Oupa Jan was awarded seventy-eight thousand rand in damages for his arrest. Most of the compensation is gone by now, left at the liquor store in small increments, one bottle at a time. With no more money left, *Oupa* Jan needs a new source.

Who else to approach but the mother of the 'bloody baby'?

The rape of baby Tshepang unleashed a shockwave in South Africa. Newspapers started publishing stories about sexual violence against children and babies – a topic they had all but ignored before. Some spoke of the 'moral bankruptcy' of post-apartheid South Africa. Then deputy-president Jacob Zuma, responsible for a campaign for the Moral Regeneration, labelled his country 'ill'.

The rape of children was neither a new phenomenon nor proof of the moral bankruptcy of the 'new' South Africa. What was new in the days after the rape of Tshepang, was the massive attention it received by the media, the police, the judiciary and even politicians. In the darkest days of apartheid (a heavily theocratic ideology), the rape of children went mostly unreported – any news of this kind would have tainted the 'good name' of the blissfully ignorant and god-fearing white minority.

The country faced a rough wake-up call when confronted with the unknown elements of its own reality. The first 'experts' to shine their light on baby and child rape referred to some old African tradition, which states that sex with a virgin would heal a man of all illnesses. In modern-day Africa that would also include the contemporary disease of HIV/AIDS.

But of all the cases brought to trial, none of the accused ever mentioned this myth in his defence. Child rape in South Africa had little, if not nothing, to do with alleged old African traditions.

Even in the trial against David Potse (23 in those days), not a word was uttered about a possibly healing ritual of sex with a virgin. Potse had finally been arrested in March 2002 in Cape Town, more than nine hundred kilometres from Louisvale, six months after the torn and bloodstained Tshepang was found. His wife Lya Booysen put him in the pillory.

A reconstruction of events, based on statements made in court, shows how Wanda left her baby in the care of her own mother on that fateful Friday evening. Wanda went shopping but did not return. Instead, she went out drinking with a friend – it was a Friday evening after all, and that is what one does in Louisvale on a Friday evening.

Wanda's mother, worried about her daughter, set out to find her and left Tshepang on her own. When both returned home, they found the girl on the floor of their shed.

Following the rape, inhabitants of the township want to see blood. Confronted with this rage, the perpetrator flees Louisvale, fearing for his life.

The only witness to the crime is Lya Booysen. She saw her husband, Potse, rape the baby, but for months does not dare make a statement. She had felt his fists before, repeatedly. He is a violent man. Wanda too, Potse's mistress, regularly felt his anger when things were not going to his liking, or whenever he had been drinking too much.

Johannes, Tshepang's biological father, had just been released from jail. He spent three months behind bars for contempt of court, for not showing up at a trial where he was supposed to have been a witness. While he was in jail, his relationship with Wanda cooled off; Potse became her new lover.

Revenge was Potse's motive. He suspected Wanda of having an affair and was enraged, seething with anger, livid. He felt he had to put Wanda in her place, and chose Tshepang as his means to do so.

In his verdict on 26 July 2002 Judge Hennie Lacock openly regrets the abolition of the death penalty, and condemns Potse to a life in jail. Tshepang by then is undergoing her seventh corrective operation on her genitals and anus.

Johannes and Wanda see their daughter twice, after the rape. During their last visit to the town where Tshepang lives in a children's home, the police are put on high alert. Popular fury has not faded yet.

From his kitchen, Reverend Johannes Stuurman has a view over the semi-desert behind his home. One day he might build a veranda, he says. It would make a nice place to take a deep breath, he explains, and regain balance after a hectic day.

His voice has a softness, which seems out of place here, and hardly fits his words. 'Every week we have a case of rape, usually by a group. One could see it almost as a ritual in which men proclaim their brotherhood, and show their "proof" of masculinity.'

Stuurman moved into Louisvale eight years ago, to lead his flock. Apart from being a reverend, he is actively involved in the provincial administration. Being an integral member of his community, he is aware of a huge sense of insecurity amongst the men of Louisvale, mostly inspired by major problems around issues of identity.

'Those group rapes are linked to an inferiority complex, if you ask me. No one ever taught the perpetrators how to engage with a girl or a woman in a respectful way. They lack the guts to chat or go out on dates. They join a gang so they can survive, socially speaking. And to survive is more important than being "good" or "evil". The only place they feel at ease is on the streets. That's where *they* rule.'

Stuurman takes a break, and gets up to make some tea. 'Remember one thing: the worst of the worst is "normal" here. Alcohol abuse. Abuse of women. If that is what you see every day of your life when you grow up, that is what you do when you are an adult. No one ever taught you anything different.'

If I want to understand the rape of Tshepang, Stuurman explains, I will need to look at the living conditions in Louisvale – *all* of the living conditions. He mentions poverty, nihilism, unemployment, and warns me, 'Poverty does not necessarily lead to murder, death, rape or theft. More is needed to turn someone into a cold-blooded character.'

Stuurman paces up and down his living room, and dismisses the myth of 'sex with a virgin'. 'I do not see how this could have anything to do with African traditions. Africans care for the weakest of their community. In this case, the weakest became a carefully chosen target.'

The reverend sits down again, folds his hands as if preparing to pray. He stares at our teacups on the coffee table. 'Someone made a conscious decision to rape Tshepang. It all revolves around that particular choice. What made the short-circuit happen in the brain of the perpetrator, David Potse? Why was he as enraged as he clearly was? What fuelled that rage?'

Many experts explain sexual abuse of women in the townships of South Africa as the result of poverty. I have trouble accepting that as the sole reason for the nihilism I can taste, smell and feel while walking through Louisvale. I have experienced poverty more often than I care to remember – poverty that strips away every layer of human dignity, until there is nothing left.

But here in Louisvale I do not see it. Apart from, maybe, the most recent additions to the township – shacks which Johannes and Wanda call 'home'.

Maybe I am pulling the wool over my own eyes, blinded by the electrical wiring to almost all the houses and the blooming roses of Tannie Hennie's garden. Maybe my memory of poverty in Africa's biggest slum – Kibera – plays tricks on me. Kibera comes as close as humanity can ever come to its own rectum.

Maybe I have become too hardened, but in my perception, Louisvale is not the poorest place. Not in South Africa, not in Africa, not on earth.

Jackie Greeff (53) rebukes me. His father was one of the first to come to Louisvale; he built a church and opened a school. Greeff Jr. is one of the very active members of his community.

While he shows me around, he shares his opinion. 'Poverty is going to bed hungry, not having decent clothing to wear, walking barefoot to school. Not having a roof to protect you from the rain. But don't get confused: poverty is *not* being dirty – being dirty comes from being lazy.'

The Indian Nobel laureate, Amartya Sen, describes poverty as being both absolute as well as relative. Poverty in an absolute sense is the absence of housing, food, clothes and clean water. But poverty is also, if I understand Sen correctly, the absence of dignity.

And dignity is what is lacking in Louisvale. The 'other side' of South Africa, of wealth and splendour is a virtual reality here – but one that is still visible to each and every person in Louisvale. Every day, when the people of Louisvale roam around the town centre of Upington, they see comfort and a luxurious lifestyle floating by in air conditioned vehicles and 4X4s.

In Louisvale, I do not see abject poverty. What stares me in the face is the futility of life, an existence filled with idleness and nihilism.

I ask Greeff for his opinion. 'Abject poverty,' he responds, 'is the loss of every sense of self-respect. Totally wiped out. Nothing remains. That, my friend, is poverty.'

Outside the store, 'Overseas', a group of men hang out around a wooden picnic table. They roll their cigarettes with newspaper and tobacco and bide their time. Look around. Few words are spoken. Silence seems most appealing. Once in a while one of them stands up, paces around, then sits down again. Young men in their early thirties. Unemployed. Idle.

'A man is supposed to take care of himself, his kids, his wife, his home. That is your primary responsibility. That is how you earn respect. Through the roles you play at work, and at home.' Dirk Johannes Meyers chooses his words carefully, while playing with a blade of grass between his teeth. 'But fulfilling your roles is simply impossible here,' he adds subtly, after a long silence.

From his breast pocket he takes a lottery ticket, and ticks it rhythmically on the table. He has won seven rand. A poster behind him on the wall announces the Miss Winter beauty pageant: 'Nice Babes 4 u 2 c'.

'Still, that is what you are supposed to do: to take care. How can I take care if I can't earn money? How do I control my anger if I see sugar daddies taking all the girls from Louisvale, in their fancy cars and their fancy clothing? They got the jobs, the income; they get the girls. Sure, that's when I feel inferior. Jealous.'

Meyers and his friends do not mince their words about domestic violence. About anger. About men who drink the child benefits, and about women who molest their husbands. About women in a drunken stupor who sleep in their own vomit. About men who abandon their families, because they can't support them on forty rand a day.

They talk of women who treat their men as docile imbeciles, because they make more money than the guys do. They also talk of women demanding things, for no other reason than to make men feel incompetent.

'She demands that you have a job, whereas she damn well knows jobs are not available. Women like that make you disrespect yourself.'

According to the young men outside Overseas, their township Louisvale is hanging by a thread. Jeremy de Weer (32) clears his throat – up to then he had only been listening. 'We have nothing to build on. We have no elders, like blacks do – we are coloureds. Who disciplines the individual? Who knows the rules? Who knows the traditions?'

His friend Meyers has been with the same woman for the last fifteen years – quite the exception in Louisvale. The couple have three kids; they share a home and every secret. 'I'd say it is a good, warm, loving relationship.' But he knows the rage his friends have been talking about. He has felt it within himself, and has witnessed it amongst his friends. An outrage stemming from sheer impotence. 'I start shaking, and something crawls in my belly.'

Sometimes a comrade will invite him to share a drink. At other times he goes down to the river to fish. 'I do my best to control that anger. Trust me, it isn't always easy.'

Liquor, crime and unemployment are Louisvale's three biggest problems. The township is home to eight thousand people. The houses closest to the main road were constructed first; some go as far back as the 1930s.

The government of the day in Pretoria had to formulate a plan to confront the increasing poverty amongst white Afrikaners in the region. The desert, it was decided, had to start producing grapes. Water from the Orange River and cheap labour from the Cape Province were to lay the foundation for development.

The first rows of homes these days house the descendants of the first inhabitants. Reverend Stuurman: 'They feel at home here. The further you get from the main road, the newer the people. The further you go, the less connected people are to this place and to each other.'

The influx of newcomers has been huge over the past couple of years. They left farms where previously they had livelihoods. When the post-apartheid government withdrew its financial support for white farmers, many farms collapsed. Bankruptcies forced commercial farmers to lay off staff by the thousands; workers had to find new means of survival. For those who came to Louisvale, the major place for employment is a company that exports raisins and other dried fruits, as well as a cotton factory down the road.

Katrien Willems is a representative in the community council, an active member in her church and involved in many social activities in Louisvale. She earns a living in the raisin factory. Willems wants me to meet her manager.

Her hair is neatly tucked under a cap. Forklifts drive around carrying loads of raisins. 'You need to talk to someone here. Something is going horribly wrong, and only if we're willing to face the facts can we change them.' She leads the way to the office of manager Rudel du Preez.

He explains how the company gets most of its workers from Louisvale. His litany is long and depressing. The company loses thousands of man-hours a month due to people not showing up. 'Abnormally high,' says Du Preez.

In April 2004 he lost 2 817 man-hours. His 198 employees submit hundreds of sick leave requests per month. Funerals keep workers away, as do other personal problems. AIDS, drugs, peer pressure, divorce. 'Suddenly someone simply doesn't show up anymore. No explanation – just a vacancy. They will not resign, because if they resign they won't get unemployment benefits. I need to fire them.'

Du Preez continues, reading from his computer screen the reasons for absenteeism. Court cases because of drunken and disorderly behaviour, prostitution, theft or break-ins. 'Last Tuesday a forklift driver was arrested on an accusation of raping an eight-year-old girl. It really baffles me, I knew him well. He had a good job, a good salary. Now this…'

Du Preez would prefer to work exclusively with women. Men, he says, do not have the same sense of responsibility. 'But there's no escaping the need for men. Who will do the hard physical labour?'

Alcohol abuse is Du Preez' biggest management problem. In a few cases the company sent employees to Cape Town to clean up their act in therapy. The directors intervened. 'We don't do public welfare,' Du Preez was told.

For the coloured community in South Africa, alcohol abuse is one of the greatest challenges, especially in the wine producing regions. Foetal Alcohol Syndrome flourishes because so many mothers continue drinking while pregnant, denying the foetus the chance to develop naturally.

For centuries, farmers paid their staff partly in wine. It made for docile workers, and because it came from their own cellars the costs were minimal. This so-called *dop* system has been banned, but workers still flock to the liquor store at the end of the last working day. Being drunk from Friday to Sunday evening is perceived 'normal'.

'Booze and being drunk are far from helpful "traditions",' Greeff explains. He himself was an alcoholic for years. He lost his first wife because of it, and saw his options in life evaporate. 'When I drank, all that was wrong seemed right. Every stupid decision seemed to be the right one. Every problem disappeared all by itself. Any doubts I had, vanished.'

In Louisvale, one person after another tells me the same thing. The head master of a school. Reverend Daniël Willems. Johannes' mentor. Jackie Greeff. Frank. Tannie Hennie.

'I used to be a drinker.'

Greeff walks with me through Louisvale. The rape of Baby Tshepang made him look at his own community, trying to understand how things could have gone so horribly wrong.

For Greeff one thing is clear above all else: David Potse made a choice. Greeff himself knows what it means to be an alcoholic; he was one once. Potse's lifestyle was his own choice, as was his act of raping a baby.

Greeff mentions some of the limitations a man has to face in Louisvale. 'We find fewer rules to live by. When I grew up, a man was the head of the household. That's how the Afrikaners educated us. "The woman stays at home, the man is in control." But not any more. And many men are unable to adjust.'

We stroll beside houses with smashed windows and continue past other houses with neat curtains and sayings on the wall. We pass gardens with flowers, and gardens filled with garbage.

Greeff continues. 'A man has to earn respect; it is not something given for nothing. You can't just go about killing people for no reason and then expect to be respected.' Self-respect is a rare commodity in Louisvale, says Greeff. The coloured population of South Africa has had to do without it for generations.

'Coloureds' became the label for everyone deemed neither black nor white. When there was doubt, a simple test was used. If a pencil was stuck into the hair of a person whose skin colour was not very dark, and the pencil did not fall out, that person was 'coloured'. Many coloureds are the descendants of whites, often men who had sex with their staff or with slaves or with a girl they picked up somewhere in a village. The women were black, Khoisan or Asian.

Hardcore racists saw anyone of mixed descent as a few steps down on their ladder – bastards who did not deserve any of the perks life reserved for 'pure whites'. Only blacks were deemed more 'inferior' than coloureds.

Being labelled a 'coloured' is a hot issue, even today. The classifications invented by whites supposedly gave coloureds some kind of preference over blacks. Some black South Africans therefore feel as if 'the new dispensation' owes the coloured communities nothing.

An official in Upington lectured me during my visit to his office. 'So-called coloureds do not exist,' he told me. 'We are blacks.' Before me sat a man behind his desk who had all the characteristics of a man from Italy, or Greece. Why the need to call himself a 'black man'?

I ask Greeff, 'Are you black, or are you coloured?'

'I am proud. I am proud of who I am. I am proud of the group I belong to. I am a coloured man. Not a "so-called" coloured man, but one of flesh and blood. Those who speak of the "so-called" coloureds do us no good. They increase confusion. They seemed to be ashamed of who we are.'

Greeff touches the core question of life in Louisvale. Reverend Stuurman has spoken of it, as have the boys outside Overseas.

Coloureds do not have 'tribes'; they have no elders. Their religion was brought by white settlers; church-going ancestors who would reject their own sons and daughters. Those same forefathers would pay for labour in liquor, and defined the identity of their offspring through a trick with a pencil.

'All this alcohol abuse,' muses Greeff, 'is a total lack of self-respect. Nothing moved me. Nothing interested me. The smell of a flower meant nothing to me. I drowned my sorrows. But those sorrows would never really go away. Inside, my life was dark and empty. I could not handle that darkness.'

Greeff greets the owner of a shop, who serves customers from behind bars, to protect his goods from people he knows by name, nickname and personal weakness.

Greeff seeks answers that might help to fill the vast emptiness around him. 'We should educate our own people about their roots; create some kind of pride about who we are and what we had to go through to arrive where we are today. It is a huge problem. We know so little, have no material to fall back to. We need stories, stories that make sense. Where do we come from? Who are we? Where do we go to?'

It is a peaceful Friday evening. Louisvale prepares itself for the weekend. Queues are lengthening in front of the liquor store. Inside the homes and behind shower curtains girls apply their make-up and boys wash the sweat off their torsos. The bartender of the illegal shebeen counts his crates of beer and his bottles of liquor. On the streets young men throw the dice. Today was payday.

'Women Against Crime' walk to the police station. They will take care of the victims of the night, and will keep a close watch on the officers in charge when suspects are treated in too rough a manner. Other volunteers – again only women – prepare their cakes and mix the fruit juice they will sell on the streets of Louisvale. The corfball club needs funds.

Inside her kitchen, Katrien Willems cuts kilo after kilo of chicken legs, while steam escapes from pots and pans with beetroot and potatoes. Her kitchen itself has become like an oven. A friend bakes muffins. Whatever they sell tomorrow will be for the benefit of the school.

Katrien's husband steadies himself against the refrigerator. His eyes are red and hazy. 'Look,' says Katrien, 'this is what *I* have to deal with.' She nods in his direction. 'Friday night, and I am sweating to make some money for the community school. I have a full-time job, I am a councillor, I am active in my church, and I take charge in my community. *This* is what I have to put up with. A man who drinks like a fish.'

A sigh.

Greeff and I approach Johannes and Wanda in the darkening dusk. Johannes talks of his battles with his demons, and with Wanda. They are trying to swing their existence into a new direction, less hectic and more stable. The main aim is to create a life in which they could take care of Tshepang again, now a young girl.

Jackie prepares to leave, after Oupa Jan and Wanda have their collision. Just before we depart, Johannes brings his upturned pot back inside, and takes me aside. 'I realise that *I* make my own life. I decide where to go: either deeper into the darkness or slowly away from it. I can accept that now. It won't do to lie on my back and stare at the sky or at the stars – waiting for magic to happen. Life is now. Life is mine.'

Post Script
David Potse refuses to comment. On 2 August 2005, the governor of his jail in Upington, Mr. J.F. Massyn, sent a fax stating: 'Mr. Potse has indicated to have no interest whatsoever to be interviewed by anybody.'

Three months after my first visit to Louisvale, I knock on the door of the shed where I met Johannes and Wanda, again on a Friday afternoon. A friend of the family washes himself behind a screen. The garden looks well tended. No, Johannes and Wanda are not at home. And no, things are not going well at all. Both have started drinking again, have left their church and fight each day. Their wedding has been postponed, indefinitely.

Pictures hang on the wall just above the dining table of Josiah Lushaba (72) and his wife Selina (60). The youngster in the first picture has a gentle smile; his gaze seems somewhat insecure. He looks into the camera, in a candid way. Red feathers adorn his hair. Next to it hangs another picture, old, black and white, scratched and torn. This one is of an older man, also smiling. His expression is one of self-assurance. He appears to fear nothing.

A father and his son: King Sobhuza II and King Mswati III.

Outside the home of the elderly couple, a bull breaks loose from a rope, and charges the fence. Inside Selina sits serenely in an easy chair close to the window, her arms relaxed. On a goatskin at her feet lies a thin foam-rubber mattress. On the table stands a high-pressure paraffin lamp next to a gas bottle and a heater. The cold period is about to start, and high up on the hills of Gugwini in the southwest of Swaziland, the evenings can be chilly.

Josiah looks respectfully at the portraits of his ruler and points at details in the royal dress. 'I love him. I am a Swazi; it is my duty and my privilege to obey my monarch.'

King Mswati III of Swaziland is the *ngwenyama*, the lion of the nation. Shortly after he was born he was named Makhosetive, Lord of Nations. During his coronation in 1986 he was renamed after the ancestor who had doubled the territory of Swaziland in the mid-19th century. He is one of 210 children, fathered by Sobhuza II (1899-1982). In the narratives of his subjects, Mswati is the undisputed leader. He protects the nation; he leads her, feeds her, dresses her and houses her.

He is the only head of state in Africa who descends directly from leaders who held sway long before European powers carved up the continent. Mswati is also the only remaining autocratic sovereign. Since his ascent to power he has been steady as a rock, he governs by decree and enjoys his entitlements. He was eighteen at his coronation; fresh from a high school in Dorset in the United Kingdom, where – rumour has it – his lackeys had walked around with suitcases on their heads.

Selina has difficulty breathing. Her arms are brittle, her cheeks hollow. Josiah sighs deeply as he settles in a chair opposite his wife. He straightens his back and stammers. 'I have this wound on my back, which hurts badly.'

The path to the home of the elderly couple leads down a hill, through a stream and up another hill. Too much for either of them. They rely on their children and the village volunteer. Most Swazi's live on hills like this elderly couple. Electricity does not reach this far. Water has to be collected from the neighbour's well.

Gugwini is miles away from the capital, Mbabane. A gravel road through mountains and valleys ends a few hundred metres outside the village. A handful of houses are stuck against the steep hills. Maize grows in some of the fields.

The skin of Selina's hands pulls tight over her knuckles, her fingers grip the armrest. She breathes deeply. The mattress is ready at her feet. If she wants to sleep, she only has to glide down from her chair, and slide under a sheet and blanket. 'Half an hour more,' she says. Then she'd like to take a nap.

Josiah: 'The first time I heard of AIDS must have been some time in the late eighties. It scared me, because I did not understand how a disease like that could do the rounds.' He had already sown most of his wild oats in those days. He had girlfriends when he was young – many girlfriends. Josiah smiles waggishly. 'The more girlfriends, the stronger others consider you. Having many women is proof of power and success. People look up to you – respect you. That was how things were when I grew up, and that is how they still are… When a woman appreciates a man, that man will feel strong and content.' Condoms did not exist when he was young and virile. 'They are quite new here.'

When Josiah felt it was time to settle down, he asked Selina to marry him. She gave him three sons. One wife was enough, he always thought. More women would increase the need for income, which he would never be able to earn at the department where he was employed. He'd need money for dowries and sustenance. It would be a waste of his hard-earned and meagre income.

Josiah calls for a granddaughter to straighten up the pillow behind his back, and orders her to make some tea. 'I am so tired… A nurse told me I'm infected, last year. I was plagued by all sorts of pains. She tested my blood for this AIDS thing. How I got it, or when, or who gave it to me, I don't know. I have it; that's all I need to know.' He gazes straight ahead for a while, then looks his wife in the eye.

'You know, this AIDS is a slow-working poison. You don't realise it until it is way too late. Once it is too late, you see how it destroys everyone you love. AIDS does not make any distinction; it does not do a background check on you, to see how you behaved over the past thirty years. Were you gentle? Did you do what you had to do for the community? It does not check if you paid your taxes – nothing. One wrong move, one wild night and you're done. Finished.'

'This thought of the old days, that a man needs many girlfriends, that thought is no longer valid. Strong men become weak men. They even become too weak to feed their families. What used to be a sign of strength, power and manhood has turned into nothing less than a disaster.'

A generation has been lost in Josiah's village. Gugwini has too few adults left who, blessed with physical strength, can take care of children. AIDS has hit Swaziland hard – very hard. Statistics are only available for women, who have to go for testing once they fall pregnant. Of all the tested women in 2005, 42.9 per cent were infected with HIV. In the age group between twenty and thirty the rate of infection shoots up to 56 per cent. Men hardly ever get tested. They perceive hospitals and clinics to be the domain of the weaker sex. A real man does not consult a doctor, because a real man is never sick. If he happens to feel weak, Swazi culture tells him that a woman is to blame, and he should give her a beating.

The causes of the high HIV/AIDS figures for Swaziland are many. Labour migration to South Africa separates spouses. The epidemic in Swaziland is assisted by the transformation of the old custom of polygamy with its fixed set of rules and obligations into the new habit of polyamoury – a lifestyle with many different, concurrent lovers. Intercourse often takes place without protection.

Josiah's vision of the future is dark and pessimistic. In his nightmares he sees his country devoid of human beings. Corpses lie spread out on hills and in valleys. It is impossible to point fingers at the perpetrators of the slaughter. Most people in Swaziland had heard about HIV/AIDS, they were warned – but only few heeded the alarm bells.

I ask him if the monarch, the lion of the nation, the man whose word is law, the king that could make a difference – if that man leads by example. Josiah takes his time. He looks at me and sends his eyes out on a quest through the living room, to finally find peace at the regal pictures on the wall.

Early in 2006, Mswati had twelve wives, one fiancée and many girlfriends. Collectively they gave birth to twenty-five children. Having many kids is seen as safeguarding the future of the nation.

Josiah smiles mysteriously. 'I am only a simple Swazi. It is neither my task nor my right to judge my king. He shows us the way, we must follow.'

The wind plays with leaves in their yard. On the slopes, the high grass waves rhythmically. Sunlight plays with the panicles. The bull has been reined in again, tied to a tree. The chants of an invisible herdsman echo through the hills. Josiah closes his eyes. It is nearing noon. He would like to rest now.

In his home, each Swazi man is the mirror image of the monarch. In each village every man is the commander of all who are younger than him. Sizakela Nhlabatsi was twelve when she attended a funeral nearby. Both her parents were bedridden. As the eldest in the family, it was her duty to be present. Staying away from a funeral could be construed as a sign of complicity in a person's death.

The demise of a fellow villager demands booze to ease the process of mourning. So the invitees drank. Among them was the man who would rape her later that day, as Sizakela walked home under the cloak of night.

A few months later the girl noticed how her belly started to grow and she asked her sick mother for advice. 'What have you done? Who stuck his member inside you?' It was only then that Sizakela realised the connection between her belly and the assault that fateful night. She conveyed her secret, which forced her fragile mother to call for a meeting of the village committee. The perpetrator appeared as well, summoned by the village. He defended himself. 'I cannot remember a great deal of what happened that evening. I was drunk.'

He acknowledged he had had intercourse with the girl, but disagreed with her being a minor. 'How can she be, when her body can get pregnant? If a woman can get pregnant, she is mature enough to have sex.'

The accused refused to take care of her and their son.

'How could I possibly marry her? I don't love her …!'

A tiny sweater hangs on a line in Sizakela's farmyard, 'No 14' printed in large letters on its belly. Sizakela's brothers play around, with anything they can find. She's almost sixteen now, and in charge of the household.

A plough rusts away in a corner of the grounds. Neither she nor any of her brothers are strong enough to drive the ox-pulled plough. A couple of strong hands would do the trick for the orphans. Just a few square metres, so they can grow their own food.

'However,' says Cebile Dlamini, 'there are no more spare men available to cut open the fields. Too many deaths. Too many uncles or aunts have departed. The old social networks have crumbled, too many relatives are dying.'

Dlamini wears a T-shirt with a clear message: 'Stop violence against women'. She leads a delegation from Amnesty International through Swaziland. Far away from home and in the backwaters of her own nation, she knows every story behind every front door: the orphans, the AIDS patients. She sees which women take a beating from husbands, boyfriends, fathers, brothers and neighbours, and which don't.

Dlamini speaks passionately – this young woman in her early twenties. She has lively, mischievous eyes. They remind me of the picture of the old king Sobhuza II: noble eyes, an unflinching look that states clearly how she gets what she wants.

'Justice. So the voice of women will be heard.'

Dlamini has a mission and she follows it in a slightly militant way. Only after one of her colleagues points out her family name do I see the connections. Every Dlamini in Swaziland is, somehow, related to king Mswati.

'You're a princess?' I ask.

'Yes, the king is my uncle.' Her role here, far away from Mbabane, surprises me. A niece of the monarch in a campaign for women's rights and AIDS prevention? Dlamini only laughs.

For a while it seemed her uncle would take the lead in the struggle against HIV/AIDS. In 2001, Mswati declared the HIV epidemic a 'national disaster', which freed money and manpower to fight it. The pith of this campaign was a series of decrees. Mswati commanded women to wear skirts longer than knee-high. He forbade girls under eighteen to have sex. And he pleaded for moderation.

In doing so, he laid the main responsibility for fighting HIV/AIDS in the laps of women, thereby ignoring the fact that Swazi women hardly have a say over their own sexuality. Mswati did not wish to thwart men in any way.

His campaign was a non-starter. He broke his own law when he added a teenage girl to his harem, and easily paid the fine he had decreed: one cow. His own minister for Public Information – one of the leading characters in the national information campaign against AIDS – lost his credibility the day he got caught on the streets of Mbabane in the company of a prostitute, with his trousers around his ankles.

Mswati's niece says shyly that it wasn't easy to get the family's approval for her campaigning, adding quietly, 'I cannot afford to sit still; you see, even the royal family has not proven invulnerable to the virus.'

―――――――

Mswati is an easy target for anyone out to ridicule African leaders. His court gladly helps him to maintain his dubious position by remaining silent and aloof, at all times. The extravagant lifestyle of the sovereign, for example, is a popular topic for the international media.

The King of Swaziland is the proud owner of the world's most expensive vehicle: a Maybach limousine, that sells for over half a million euros. The king also owns two Mercedes bolides and a few BMWs. The costs of building residences for his wives are higher than the country spends annually on health care. Mswati also regularly rents a private jet to be flown to South Africa's gambling paradise of Sun City. He wallows in luxury, bathes in the privileges extended to him by Swazi traditions and then bows his head to his elders.

Mswati countered criticism of his spending habits by issuing a decree which forbade anyone to take snapshots of him getting in or out of his cars. His court is convinced that the best policy to handle all criticism is to remain silent. However, their silence opens the way for any observer to intensify the mockery and caricature Swaziland's royalty makes of itself.

For over a year, I tried getting in touch with the court. First to check facts and ask for comments, later because I wanted to interview the king. He can hardly be as appalling as he is being portrayed, or can he?

The offices of the monarch and his servants are surrounded by an impenetrable fog. Phone numbers for his Cabinet are nowhere to be found, and neither are those of the Prime Minister nor those of the Ministry of Foreign Affairs. Emails bounce.

One number works: that of Ludzidzini, the palace of the Queen Mother. The phone rings and rings. After numerous attempts, someone finally answers – an employee of the kitchen services. He has no idea where I can find Mswati or any of his advisors.

Mswati rules through vetos and decrees. His father taught him the art of absolutism. Sobhuza himself tore up the constitution in 1973 and monopolised power. Sobhuza also trained Mswati in hunting and traditional dancing, and taught his son how to fulfil the role of a king.

'Just because the world preaches democracy, it does not mean we have to follow,' the monarch once said in a meeting with hundreds of priests. He was dressed in a loincloth made of the skin of an antelope. 'Democracy is not good for us. God gave us other ways to organise things.'

Mswati's polygamy worries some of his wives. Two of them have already left, reportedly fearing HIV infection.

Queen Matsebula has to juggle her position as Mswati's wife with her own moral conviction, as well as her profession as a specialist in family planning. She campaigns for men to be monogamous, while herself married to a man with multiple wives. 'Think carefully before you plant your seed in every bit of fertile ground you might find, and save yourself for the one you really love,' she once said.

Of all his marriages, only the one to LaMbikiza seems to be grounded in romance. The two dated long before they got married. It was LaMbikiza who birthed Mswati's first child. She is also the only queen to have graduated from university, as a lawyer. However, even the love of his life had to fight for her right to work. Mswati believes most contemporary problems are caused by women wearing pants.

In a rare interview in 2001 the king complained of stress. 'I am overworked,' he said, 'because I need to do all I can to alleviate the suffering of my people.' Since then, the United Nations have had to feed large parts of the Swazi population, while the HIV infection rate has climbed from 32 per cent to almost 43 per cent.

Ted Reilly is a white Swazi who, since 1961, has been the pivot of wildlife management in the kingdom. He meets the monarch regularly to debate issues of tourism. Reilly knows Mswati as a sober, human, modest and rational man.

'It is very easy to get stuck on the details,' says Reilly on the veranda of a restaurant in one of his parks. Two hippos are playing in the quagmire behind him. A crocodile lies half hidden in the water, its eyes focused on an impala by the waterside.

'Why this obsession of the West and western journalists with the royal fleet of cars? By focussing on that, you'll be unable to see the meaning and importance of this king for the one million Swazis who have a deeply traditional outlook on life. For them, he is the crux of the nation.'

I try my best to explain how those subtleties quickly get lost in the media, especially if a journalist spends days or hours amongst the poorest of the nation and then observes a regal limousine pass by. Why are the palace gates as tightly closed as they are? What's to hide?

'The king is the king through his subjects. You need to understand that. It has little to do with good or bad. This is about the structure of a nation, in which the king plays a key role. His position, more so than his person, is nearly sacrosanct.'

Whereas all the other peoples in Southern Africa were overrun by white settlers, the Swazi retained their autonomy, their identity and their culture, thanks to Swaziland's sovereign rulers. More than any other leader in Africa, Mswati's father, Sobhuza II, managed to safeguard his nation from oblivion by staying true to the Swazi culture.

'The dilemma the king and his court find themselves confronted with,' Reilly stresses, 'is how to keep the traditions alive; how to hold on to customs and habits while at the same time facilitating modern, Western concepts and ideas of development and growth; how to hold on to who the Swazi are, while creating space for new ideas, new norms and new values. What stays? What goes?'

Reilly studies my face to see if I understand what he has just said. 'Mswati has burnt himself too often, giving interviews to journalists who were not interested in hearing the other side of the story, but who wanted sound bites to fill the gaps in stories they had already written in their heads. Some have torn him to pieces. No one in Lozitha Palace will warmly welcome another reporter.'

Reilly picks up his cell phone and walks away to make a phone call to the court in privacy. 'Mswati's adviser Sam Mkhombe is glad to receive you tomorrow,' he tells me when he returns. 'Plead your case with him. That's all I can do.'

The next day, men and women sit in the shade of a lean-to at Lozitha Palace, awaiting an audience. It's Wednesday, the one day in the week on which the gates of the royal offices are open to citizens who need royal assistance. Cars come and go – some with a police escort, others without. A man in a blue overall mows the lawn. Soldiers play a game of cards.

A young man dressed in a tracksuit with an iPod in hand, stands out from the crowd. A clumsy attempt at being cool.

'A prince,' whispers a man in a three-piece suit. He jokes subserviently with the teenager and greets him as he has seen people do on MTV.

Sam Mkhombe leads me to his desk, which has one virginal dossier on it. The royal coat of arms graces its cover. Mkhombe interrogates me extensively on my motives for wanting to meet the king. I explain as best I can that I would like to interview Mswati on his role as symbol of a nation plagued by HIV/AIDS. Mkhombe listens, but his eyes are glazed. I see no indication whatsoever that he has even the slightest interest in the agenda I have just presented.

'Send us your detailed proposal, including all of your questions. Where can our intelligence services find your stories, so we can get an idea of your writing? Fax it all to this number. We might then invite you for a meeting with a council of advisors. This will probably take a few months but, hey, who knows? You might get somewhere…' His voice carries a dash of sarcasm.

The moment I leave the building, I feel as if I am drowning in protocol. Mkhombe said everything he wanted to say in his opening line, even before he started making notes in a new file on the meeting that he will make sure will never happen.

'King Mswati is accountable to no one.'

On a previous visit to Swaziland, someone told me about a mountain range where members of the royal family are buried inside caves, sitting up, with legs bent. The caves are guarded by the shepherds roaming around the slopes.

'You must be talking of Zombodza, near Lozitha Palace.' Historian Richard Patricks grabs a map from a stack of paperwork in his office at the national museum, unfolds it next to an ancient computer and an ashtray full of cigarette butts. He points. 'That's where the princes are buried.'

Patricks introduces me to one of his colleagues, Dzeliza Dlamini. 'She is the daughter of Masitsela, one of the most powerful princes in the kingdom.' Dlamini gives me her phone number. She loves to talk about her nation.

'Let's have tea.'

With Patricks's map imprinted in my memory, I try to find my way to Zombodza. I slither up on a dirt road past farmyards with classical trucks leaning on boulders, braving the elements.

Geese guard the yard of *motsa*, the father-in-law of Miriam Thandekile. Hers is the first house on his grounds. A dozen or so more buildings are spread out. Thirty people inhabit the yard: sons and daughters, women and men, concubines, and grandchildren. Thandekile sits down on her fake leather sofa in the living room. She crochets tablecloths to earn extra cash. Her main source of income is her teaching – but educating the future seems like scraping a living on barren soil.

Yes, her father-in-law is indeed the sexton here, on this part of the Mdzimba Mountains. She considers it an honour to live this close to the mortal remains of noble blood.

'Having a monarch gives me a sense of being part of something bigger, and that is what I tell my pupils: "Follow the king." He is the highest man in the land. His relatives are buried up there, in the mountains. Their spirits float around here. Spirits are important. They guide the way. Royal spirits are the most powerful spirits one could wish for.'

With the assistance of three employees, Thandekile's father-in-law takes the corpses up into the caves. Once there, they need to break the legs so the body can be positioned sitting up straight. In extensive rituals they brew a concoction resembling beer. A full burial takes two to three days.

Thandekile: 'The first thing he does once he's back home, is to grab some hard liquor. He needs to forget that, only hours earlier, he broke the bones of a dead man.'

I cannot see him today, Thandekile explains. 'It's too late in the afternoon. He has this bad habit of drinking all day long. If you want to get something sensible out of him, you need to come back in the wee hours of the morning.'

A few days later Miriam Thandekile takes me by the hand to visit her father-in-law's home. Dressed in a loincloth of goatskin, he appears in the doorway. From behind the door he takes a thick, woollen coat and puts on his huge, red shoes. From another corner he grabs a walking stick. I see old age in his legs.

'Eighty-two,' he says proudly, 'and still as chirpy as a cricket.'

He has no secrets, he tells me. 'But now is not a good time.' His breath carries the smell of alcohol and his eyes are bloodshot. 'Come tomorrow and we'll have a beer.'

Black clouds skim over the Valley of Heaven, at the foot of the mountain range. Lighting shoots into the ground.

Thandekile once peered through a hole in her curtain, she confides, as the men prepared a burial. One spotted her. 'Mind your own business, you woman! Don't you know that watching us can make you infertile?' However, her curiosity won over the intimidation. She has never seen the insides of the caves, she admits. Rascals who ignored all the warnings and threats once told her of their visit to the blue-blooded corpses. Decaying remains in pieces of cloth, falling apart. Around them they saw jars with Swazi beer.

I ask Thandekile how often she sees her father-in-law go up the mountain, to bury remains. When was the last time? A few months ago, a few years, a few weeks?

'Ha, are you crazy? They come here every week, sometimes even a few times a week. Usually in a black van. The ceremony has by then already taken place, at home. Only the van arrives, with the corpse. They either come here, or go to a place a few miles down the road. As far as I know, the dead are also getting younger.'

'AIDS,' I ask?

Thandekile shrugs her shoulders. 'When someone dies of AIDS, everyone will keep it a secret. Especially when it relates to someone in the royal family...

'You know, as a wife you see your husband go out every night and you see him come back drunk. Or he doesn't come back at all, until the next evening. He beats you up and tells you he loves you. Then, one day, you wake up and you just know that something has hit you. That you are sick. I am sorry to have to say this, but men just have no clue of what they do most of the time.'

She looks at her geese, and shouts when some of them charge each other. 'How do we know if the women the king sleeps with are HIV negative? What would happen to the Swazi if he were to die of AIDS? Yeah, I can be honest about that: it worries me. Especially because he hardly ever says anything about it. At times it seems as if AIDS does not exist in Swaziland. Still – I hear all these awful things about it... It makes you wonder...'

Thandekile promises to make an appointment for me with her father-in-law. Once he is sober, just after dawn. She calls me the next morning. 'He has gone back into the mountains. Another van came, just after you left. A white one this time.'

A quick exercise in adding and subtracting: Mswati's father Sobhuza married seventy women, who gave him 210 children. Of these 180 made it into adulthood. In 2004, ninety of them were still alive, according to the historian Patricks. Sobhuza probably had 1 200 grandchildren. They alone are part of the royal family and are entitled to use the title Prince or Princess. Of these, only the men are given a burial on the mountain; women are buried on the land of their husbands.

If burials take place as often as they do in the caves of Zombodza, it is credible to assume the AIDS epidemic rages with a vengeance within the royal family.

And still, Mswati remains silent.

———————

Dishes line the kitchen table in the residence of Prince Masitsela. Rice, beans, maize, chicken, peanut paste and a jug of *emaganu*, a fermented juice from marula. 'Get yourself a plate and eat as much as you can,' invites Prince Masitsela. He is Dzeliza Dlamini's 74-year-old father. Our appointment for tea had evolved into a meeting with her dad. His house lies hidden in a forest, high up on the mountain near the capital, Mbabane.

Portraits adorn the kitchen walls. Most are of Masitsela's father – Sobhuza – taken at various stages of his life. One photo in particular is Masitsela's favourite. A close-up, taken from a low vantage point. 'Look at his eyes... Courageous, hopeful, trustworthy and trustful. The look of a hunter who knows where to find what he's looking for.'

Princess Dzeliza guides me to the living room, where I get to meet five of her brothers and a toddler. 'My youngest sister.' She caresses the girl and pinches her cheeks. The young girl later uses her elderly father as a jungle gym.

'Welcome, please find yourself a spot and join us.' Masitsela's sons sit on the floor, with their plates between their legs. They use their hands for cutlery, and speak Swazi to each other. Only when they review the football games on TV, do they speak English.

One son wears traditional clothes; another is dressed in a shirt with the colours of the national flag. A third one had a tailor design his suit. I'm asked for my reasons for visiting Swaziland, and the moment I answer, the man in the flag-shirt starts moving restlessly. His voice radiates irritation. I ask what disturbs him.

'Why all this fuss about AIDS? It is all heavily exaggerated. Okay – I grant you that according to some statistics, 42.9 per cent of pregnant women tested positive in 2005. You do know that this figure doesn't say anything about the women that were not tested, or about the men?' His brothers cheer him on.

'Exactly!' says one. 'Tell him what this really is all about,' comments another. 'Imperialism!' the first one continues, encouraged by his brothers. 'Some say the solution is a condom. Nonsense.'

Having said what needed saying, that's the end of it. Another game of football starts somewhere in the United Kingdom, as broadcast on satellite tv.

Prince Masitsela joins his sons, observing the fruits of his loins as the proud father he is. Most of them graduated from private schools in Great Britain.

'Let's move one room further,' he suggests. 'With a game on, it is impossible to talk here.'

Habits, customs, traditions and the invasion of Western values – he sums up how his daughter explained to him what I want to talk about.

'The environment is crucial in shaping a human being. What you see adults do teaches you how to act. However, our surroundings are changing rapidly. More and more Swazis see Western values as the ideal way of life. I think that's twaddle. Western values are good for people in the West. Not for us.'

Masitsela describes life as he knew it – an existence in which everyone had his own chickens, goats and cattle, and grew his own maize through the muscle power of wives and children. A life in which oxen pulled ploughs in exchange for grass. People walked for hours to meet relatives or friends, and to hear what transpired in the village on the other side of the hill.

'At the end of the day we drank a mug of *mielie* beer. Sugar-free and nutritious. These days people drink till they drop. Boundaries have disappeared.' He takes a deep breath. Masitsela sips at his glass of fermented marula juice, straightens three feathers in his silver-grey curls and tightens his cloth.

'Much of this is lost for good, I fear. We stepped away from our way of life and will never get back what has disappeared. My father resisted change heavily. He found the elders on his side. "Forget who you are and you'll lose track of yourself," they had told him. It kept us on the straight and narrow.

'In this day and age, we Swazi, and especially our king, are under fire because we choose to maintain our identity. Our way of life, our values, are under threat. The international media are at war with anything they find strange and uncomfortable. Believe me, the pen really is mightier than the sword.

'Our biggest mistake was to bring education to Swaziland. The problem is not education itself, but what we actually teach our children. They have lost pride in who they are, where they come from and what defines them. A new philosophy has been hammered into our youngest, with great admiration for individualism and materialism. Understand that those things gnaw at the roots of who we are as Swazis and as Africans. We are first and foremost members of a community. What we are about to lose is what made us survive for millennia: we eat together, we work together, we talk together, and we fight together. Here in Swaziland, we call that *lilima*. A human can *not* survive without his community.

'If you want to destroy someone, then destroy his roots. No tree can survive without roots, no bush, no plant. Still, that is what is happening to the Swazi nation: our roots are disappearing.'

Masitsela has spoken for an hour, he has said what he wanted to say, corrected an image of Swaziland where he felt it needed correcting. We haven't spoken about AIDS – the scourge that is wiping away his fellow countrymen, hollowing out the economy from within, and flushing away all remaining collective structures.

According to the prince it's not AIDS that is the biggest threat to the nation, but foreigners who do not understand the essence of Swaziland. Foreign media especially.

Journalists.

Like me.

At night I drive through the Valley of Heaven lit by a waxing moon. I think back on the conversation with the brothers in the living room, and the HIV/AIDS statistics they dismissed off-hand. Earlier that day, I had spoken to their sister Dzeliza about AIDS, as two cups of tea steamed on her desk. She remembered how, as a young girl, she had observed her father packing his condoms whenever he went travelling.

'He protected himself – I respect that.'

In a rare display of openness, she confessed how one of her brothers suffers from AIDS. He is in his early thirties. 'He was drunk one night and ignored the warnings the girl gave him, about her status. Although she pleaded with him, he refused to use a condom. He was convinced AIDS couldn't be that bad.'

Princess Dzeliza fell silent behind her desk in her office, and with the back of a pen ticked on files in front of her. 'He almost died, last year. For six weeks I cared for him at home. I fed him, washed him. I was convinced he wouldn't pull through. Now he seems better. He has gone back to live on his own. He won't take ARVs. "That is pure poison," he says. "An invention of Western pharmaceuticals to enslave Africans." I know it's all a load of crap, but that is what he chooses to believe, just as he chose to believe that AIDS is not as bad as people say it is.

'Seeing him fall ill one more time? Taking care of him one more time? I don't think my poor heart will survive that.'

LESSONS FROM THE PAST

Friday evening: two headlights search for a road along thorny bushes and agaves, across a field and over narrow paths. It is pitch-dark. A wafer-thin moon shines behind the lazy clouds. A horn breaks the silence of Bondo, West Kenya. Rhythmical, inviting. On the roof of the Peugeot station wagon is the coffin, tied up and covered in thick black plastic. It looks ominous among colourful water barrels.

For kilometres nobody dares to join the funeral procession consisting of two cars. Then, suddenly, there is a terrifying scream. Aggressive and angry. A man takes the lead of the procession. His features are sharply outlined in the harsh glare of the headlights. With a tree branch, he chases away the evil spirits in front of him. One by one, children, wailing women and bold men join him to help keep the demons at bay.

Jarred Apamo returns to the land of his ancestors. Nobody knows the cause of his death. He collapsed early one morning on his doorstep after a night of heavy drinking. He was forty years old. Nairobi was his city, the slums of Korokocho his home. That is where he worked, like so many other Luos. Outcasts of an earth that became too dry to feed her children any longer.

In Nairobi, he fathered four children by his wife, Dorcas. He was born in Bondo and it is in Bondo where he will return to the soil. Such is the law of tradition. A corpse buried in foreign ground feeds evil spirits.

On the late Jarred's small piece of land, an oil lamp is passed from hand to hand. From the five-seater Peugeot emerge ten people, two hens and a rooster, sacks of maize and a bag of coal. The night fills up with sorrowful cries. Dorcas screams from the depths of her lungs. The 28-year-old widow has no choice. If she were to mourn in private, people would say she's a witch, a lesbian, a loveless woman, a prostitute; maybe she has even caused her husband's death.

Hurricane lamps are hung from trees. The crowd now focusses on Dorcas. 'Her panties are dirty,' sings a woman. The widow cries.

'Nobody needs her panties.'

A man joins in. 'She is a filthy woman.'

A melodious voice suggests, 'It is not good to be alone.'

Dorcas is the centre of attention. No one seems interested in the deceased. Jarred's earthly life is over, hers goes on. The crowd is preparing her for the observance of the traditions. She is 'filthy' and has to be cleansed. She will need a new man too. The outline of Dorcas's future is roughly visible, even before the first spade cuts into the earth to bury her old life.

The coffin is taken from the roof and placed near the shrubs. Someone opens the hatch. Curious bystanders take a look at the deceased. He looks amazingly well after a month in the morgue.

Dorcas's son Victor complains, 'I don't know this place – what are we doing here?' His eyes search for something to hold on to in this strange night. Silence again. The smell of herbs mixes with that of decomposition, a stench that one cannot escape.

In Nairobi, traditions rule the reality of Dorcas Akinyi Apamo. They provide an anchor in the metropolis, where life runs according to the indefinable rules of modern times. Rituals and traditions give meaning and direction to her existence.

Korokocho, Dorcas's district, is one of the toughest slums in Nairobi. Somalian gangs with *Kalashnikovs*, the African fundamentalist sect, Mungiki, charismatic churches and alcohol all compete for the favour and money of the estimated two hundred thousand inhabitants. Survival is the basic instinct they all share, in the midst of rotting waste and black, stinking mud. Discarded plastic bags will long outlast the humans in the area.

Dorcas lives deep in Korokocho. In front of her house, goats roam the streets for food. A man repairs a cracked plastic bucket with a glowing bar. Young men drink any kind of alcohol that will help them escape from reality. In a churchyard, torn flags blow in the wind. A man kneels there to pray.

'No way I can work now,' Dorcas says emotionless. Her house is made of mud and twigs. Canvas keeps out the wind and moisture. Calendars of years long gone adorn the walls. Between them hangs a cock's feather. Her children are out playing, but she doesn't know where. Under normal circumstances Dorcas would be packing beans in a nearby factory for seven cents a kilo. On a good day she can make up to 1.75 euros.

Since her husband's death, she has spent all her energy raising money for the funeral. She figures it would cost the equivalent of about 680 euros. She has to budget for transport to Bondo, which is 350 kilometres from Nairobi: 225 euros. Keeping the body in the morgue: 270 euros. A coffin: 135 euros. Food for the guests: 45 euros.

'It is all about traditions,' Dorcas explains. 'Rituals, traditions and taboos of my people, the Luos. No Luo can escape these rules. If he is not buried at home, there will be no place for us, his surviving relatives, to be buried. We will no longer be welcome, even if we were to starve in Nairobi.'

Three weeks after Jarred's death, Dorcas manages to raise 70 euros at a couple of *harambees*, fund-raising parties held on Sunday afternoons and attended by friends and acquaintances. With this amount of money, Jarred may end up in a mass grave just outside Nairobi. Unacceptable. 'It would be like throwing him away, like garbage.'

'You know what it is?' Dorcas seems lost in thought. 'There are too many dead, in too many families, among too many friends. And there are too many acquaintances that can't cope. Everybody is mourning someone. Diseases, accidents, murders, hold-ups. So many dead. So many causes.'

The Virus stalks the city and causes carnage. Few talk about it, and even fewer take precautions. So many die that the relatives just cannot afford any more funerals. Nobody will blame a death on AIDS. It seems as if the word itself is infectious.

Florence Akinyi, a close friend of Dorcas and AIDS volunteer, knows the dead and sick in her district by name. She visits the bedridden at home. Her most conservative estimate states that one fifth of all people between fifteen and fifty-five is infected.

In a narrow alley just outside Akinyi's tiny office in Korokocho lies Vivian (20) – emaciated and perpetually drained of energy. Black eyes stare into space. Vivian is too weak to sit up. Her sister Maureen takes care of her every day. A cup of porridge in the morning, a wash, and then she rubs her with soothing oil. Maureen has very capable hands. She sees her sister dying and gives her all the love she deserves. Vivian will live two more weeks.

Akinyi (HIV-positive herself) trained Maureen as well as many others to care for the sick, and in the prevention of further infections. Swimming against the tide. Akinyi recalls a visit to a dying woman. A man entered the room 'with an urgent need.' Could Akinyi please leave the room for a moment, the sick woman requested. Akinyi understands. 'She needs the money. She has to eat, buy medicine for TB and ointment to soothe the pain of her ulcers. But him? He sees AIDS in a dying woman's eyes, yet he still wants to have sex with her.'

Dorcas also carries the virus. She has never been tested, she just knows. 'I already have all the symptoms. If I go for a test, I'll die sooner.' Her husband gave it to her, after one of his many drunken escapades. 'Alcohol made Jarred aggressive. He quickly went out of his mind.' She shrugs. It is too late now. Nothing can change the past. Only the future matters.

By torchlight Joseph Opiyo Ochieng attaches electric wires to the poles of a car battery. He checks the lights on his ghetto blaster and looks through a pile of cassette tapes. Ochieng begins with pious music, fitting the wake. It will be a long night. The elders must decide on the proper burial procedures for Jarred.

The problem is clear. Jarred never built a house. His father – old and confused – also has no roof over his head. Without a house, according to Luo traditions, he cannot be buried. More importantly, the vicar has no time on Saturday. 'Too many funerals,' says Joseph Ochieng.

Ochieng is Jarred's first cousin. Jarred's two older brothers died before him. Luo culture puts Ochieng in charge of Dorcas and her children. He has to advise her, protect her from pitfalls – and if the elders so decide, he is also to marry her.

It was Ochieng who went from the West Kenyan province of Nyanza to Nairobi in order to make preparations for the funeral. But Dorcas didn't give him a cent. 'Joseph drinks – and I need all the money for the funeral.' She gave the responsibility to John Onyango, a distant acquaintance with a steady job in an international hotel. Someone who earns enough money himself would not take hers.

Here in Bondo, Joseph Ochieng is the man on duty, the centre of the wake. His choice of music is bewildering: Congolese *Lingala* instead of the earlier religious hymns. The volume is deafening. Ochieng's eyes are no longer looking straight, his hips are moving. He wants children and women to dance with him until dawn. He makes fun of the dead man, who never constructed a dwelling on his native land but sought refuge in Nairobi. Joseph has few worries in life; he easily sneers at Jarred's spirit.

Dorcas sits among her friends, aunts and nieces by marriage. Her children are nearby. She looks resigned. Ignores the coffin completely. Ignores Joseph as well, despite his ogling. She doesn't share his impatience; Dorcas knows the rules.

First the funeral, then four days of seclusion, waiting for the elders' verdict. They will determine her future just before the burial, inform her of it, and then never mention it again. Dorcas's cleansing will follow, after which she'll be able to marry again.

In Nairobi Dorcas had been determined. Despite opposition from AIDS counsellors and members of her clan in the big city, she wanted to undergo all the rituals. Neither the deadly virus in her, nor the many deaths around her would stop Dorcas.

Those more enlightened in Nairobi urge Dorcas to think carefully. Also John Onyango, the organiser of the funeral and treasurer of the *harambee*, hammers, 'It is her life – and no one else's. But these days you must be crazy to allow old-fashioned traditions to play with your life. In an age of HIV/AIDS, cleansing and marital inheritance belong on the rubbish dump of history.' Onyango's words fall on deaf ears.

The custom of widow cleansing is as old as the Luos themselves. The ritual is to determine whether a curse rests on the widow or not. If the so-called cleanser dies shortly after the act, the woman is dangerous territory. If he lives, the coast is clear. In order not to put Luos or even members of the clan itself at risk, the elders search for a suitable outsider who gets handsomely rewarded for taking the plunge. After the cleansing he hangs his shirt somewhere outside the woman's house and her hair gets shaved.

The ritual is set by the Luo culture, explains Luo elder Joanna Ogutu. If a widow died before her cleansing, the elders would get in touch with an 'unstable' person to have sex with the corpse. If the man lives, a normal funeral can be held. If the 'volunteer' dies, however, the cursed corpse has to be taken far away from her own land to be buried somewhere else and return to dust.

Widow cleansing and marital inheritance by a brother of the deceased are the main forces driving the HIV/AIDS epidemic in Nyanza where the Luo live. If the deceased husband was infected, so is his wife. If he wasn't infected, then the cleanser can infect the widow. She will infect her brother-in-law, and he in turn his wife, and possible mistresses.

In 2001, with an estimated one third of its sexually active population infected, Nyanza province has the highest HIV infection rate in Kenya. All the money the provincial authorities have spent over the years on information campaigns and free condoms has been to no avail. 'People just don't change their behaviour,' sighed the provincial director in a radio interview not too long before Dorcas's husband died. Widow cleansing and wife inheritance are too deeply rooted to go away any time soon.

'We receive so much information here,' laughs elder Joanna Ogutu, 'that even a newborn baby knows what AIDS is. Our problem is that we cannot change ourselves. Cancel or change a ritual or a tradition and our system of laws and customs will collapse like a house of cards. Then, suddenly, everything goes wrong.'

In 2000, a group of intellectual Luos organised a debate in which many severely criticised the traditions that threaten their people – the second largest group in Kenya – by spreading HIV. It was an outstanding debate. However, it remained within the 'ivory towers' where it was held and thus had little impact on the wider public.

Ogutu: 'Such talk has no influence in the bush. These intellectuals are modern and liberal, we are conservative.'

'I have to share a bed with the widow cleanser; that is cast in stone,' Dorcas says resolutely. 'I put my future as well as that of my children at risk if I refuse to be cleansed.' She has not yet chosen the man. 'Maybe I'll go to a bar, get a man drunk and let him take me.'

Dorcas knows that she is infected. She will not insist that her cleanser uses a condom. After all, she has nothing to do with him. He is not from her own clan and is of no concern to her. She also knows he will cleanse many others when he is done with her. 'Let's face it: that is how he makes his money.'

Saturday afternoon. The sun is blazing without mercy above Bondo. Only Jarred's coffin is in the shade, thanks to a few mats and cloths hung around it. They will be moved throughout the day, to stay ahead of the scorching sun.

By daylight Bondo is a hilly region, with small fields spread as far as the eye can see. Most of these lie fallow: no rain, no crops.

The wake has attracted men and women from far away. On a path nearby a woman is sleeping off the drinking bout of the night before. The booze had no mercy.

Further away, an old man is running as fast as he can, holding his stick menacingly up in the air. Suddenly he stops, shouts a few threats at no one in particular and then resolutely attacks the evil spirit that was apparently hanging around.

Behind some bushes, food is simmering in an immense pan. A woman calls out, 'The dogs are eating the maize porridge,' and then continues with a litany. Nobody pays any attention – it is just one of many exorcisms.

Husband-candidate Joseph and his brother are building a temporary house for the late Jarred. A male voice is singing in the distance. An ox is brought in. 'This morning you saw your last sunrise,' laughs Joseph.

Didacus Kola Orwa (77), the father of the deceased, helps wherever his old body allows him to. He was once an important man, and intelligent too. He used to work for the colonial administration and was well respected. The death of his first son, ten years before, robbed him of his life's joy. The second died a few years later. Since then Didacus has been drifting.

'Only Didacus still understands Didacus,' says an old friend. He adds in a whisper, 'He now cleanses the widows of other clans.'

Didacus: 'I have no idea why my sons died before me. All of them were sickly. Explain to me how a man as strong as me can produce such weak children?'

He knows about AIDS, others have been talking about it. But he has never seen an AIDS patient. The epidemic can therefore not be all that serious, he thinks. A lot of fuss about nothing. Didacus pulls his goatee. 'Young people call everything AIDS. We, the older ones, don't – we have more brains.'

Didacus admits that the new husband has been selected already. Dorcas may choose her cleanser. The elderly widow cleanser has no doubts; daughter-in-law Dorcas must be cleansed. 'She has to prepare herself for her future life. Without a cleansing her existence will stop here and now.' Will he advise Dorcas to use a condom? Didacus sees no relevance to the question. In all his life he has never seen a real condom in Bondo – he thinks it's one of the jokes of modern times. 'On these hills everything has its own pace, its own laws and its own rules.'

The sun sets; the shadows are getting longer. Twigs stick out of the ground and form the skeleton of a house that will never be completed. Joseph is nowhere to be found. The cynics say, 'He's gone off with the bottle.'

Dorcas's friends rest in the shelter of a bush. Dinner is simmering on a wood fire. The widows among them have all been cleansed, and swear by it.

Alice Akon (49): 'Our ancestors wrote the laws. We have no choice but to follow them. Even our grandchildren have no alternative. You can't be just a little bit traditional. It's all or nothing.' The rules are many and all-embracing. The ladies name a few.

If you are born third in the family, you cannot get married first. As soon as the first-born is married, he can no longer share anything with anyone. Sex with a sister will kill you. If you, as a widow, are not cleansed, you are not allowed to cook for your children – they might die. Even the children's actions are regulated. The first-born, for example, may not marry as long as the mother is not cleansed.

'Traditions,' Joyce Omolo (43) summarises, 'open the way to your future. They show you where to go and what to do. Abolish them and you lose your way.'

But what if something 'new' such as AIDS appears – a disease that didn't exist when the ancestors wrote the laws? A disease that has already claimed so many Luo lives. The women are slightly confused at this point.

'AIDS? Oh well, catching AIDS is just bad luck,' sneers Alice Akon. 'Hey, you can get robbed, or struck by lightning. The traditions are more important.'

'You must keep the new out,' claims Nderea Atieno (50). 'Give it not even a chance.' This is why most Luos rejected the Church and Christianity. They knew these "two things of the white people" would cause a rift within the clan because the church wanted to ban traditions.

'The Church wanted us to choose between our identity and that of an outsider,' says Alice Akon. 'To choose between the familiar clan and the unknown Church. The Church lost.'

Traditional she may be, but Dorcas still needs the church's benediction for her husband's grave, and for the funeral. Even though many Luos rejected the church, her clan prefers to be on the safe side. 'Suppose God really exists, you'd better bet on Him too.'

While thunderbolts announce a storm on the horizon, the church choir sings, accompanied by drums. The priest blesses the place where the third grave will be on Didacus' land. Men start digging. Tomorrow morning the hole will be deep enough.

Sunday, just before dawn. The chickens and rooster from Nairobi are the first to be killed, and then the goat. The ox is the last animal whose blood will flow.

Dorcas: 'Rules are rules.'

Joseph is still digging in the hard ground. He didn't sleep all night.

The women are changing their clothes behind a bush. Off with the peasant robes, on with the city clothes. A cloth is tightened between trees and benches arranged. Neighbours, friends and family members begin to trickle in. The elders are not there. They are meeting under a secret tree where they will make firm plans for Dorcas's future.

A select company praises the deceased in short speeches, each one completed with a song by the choir. Joseph is the last to make a speech before the vicar's sermon. He speaks incoherently with heavy gestures. Again this morning he could not resist the bottle. He has everybody laughing. 'Even if Dorcas decides to walk back to Nairobi, I will carry her cases.'

With a few stern words thrown at Joseph, the female vicar takes over the reigns of the service. She's fed up with his drunken mood. From a notebook she delivers her message of comfort. She keeps the holy water in a *Lady Gay* shampoo bottle, and sprinkles it whenever she thinks it is appropriate. But her strict, pedantic tone does not tempt anyone to listen. Hell and damnation make no impression anymore. Heads are nodding, eyelids heavy after an exhausting two-night wake.

'She is not worth a straw,' whispers Joseph. 'Her husband died years ago. Afterwards she chose the church. She has not even been cleansed yet. Just imagine, and here she is telling us what we should think … What has she got to do with it? Nothing at all.'

The choir sings. The church women walk in procession to the grave. The guests follow. Dorcas grabs her four children and pushes them to the front. A Ugandan man stands noticeably close to the grave. John Bataza is the widow cleanser of the neighbourhood. He will cleanse Dorcas; that much everybody knows. There is no alternative. Bataza has never seen a condom in his life, he admitted earlier.

Didacus watches as his third son's coffin disappears under the sand. Joseph sweats heavily, but cannot stop himself. He toils to fill the hole, and dances on the grave. A beautiful female voice praises the Almighty in high tones.

Jarred is in heaven now.

Dala mamalon dala – 'There is a village near God; the right place.'

Dressed in white, Dorcas looks on.

One lone and uncertain tear falters down her cheek.

NEVER FORLORN IN AFRICA

Wherever one goes in Africa, people are on the move. They walk on the side of the road with tables, suitcases or bags of potatoes on their heads. Eyes looking nowhere in particular, a mind put on hold so as to concentrate on walking for miles and miles on end. Tightly packed in minibuses passengers race along South Africa's straight and wide highways. Seated in long-distance busses, they travel at death-defying speeds along the gravel roads of Tanzania or the mountain passes of Ethiopia.

Chickens, goats and cabbages are tied to the roof, next to rolled-up mattresses and heavy-duty bags full of clothes and merchandise. Plastic containers and jerry cans are fastened to the corners of roof racks; in the next village they are worth a few pennies more.

Always travelling from Y to Z. Leaving family behind in Y, finding family in Z. A cousin, thrice removed, an 'aunt' or a 'niece' who happens to be the daughter of a stepsister.

I have found it almost impossible to be lonely in Africa, and very difficult to be alone. On the endless plains, in overpopulated cities or inside thick forests where insects buzz, lonesomeness evaporates as a useless emotion. Life is all around, in every possible shape and form.

I am far more likely to experience loneliness at a chic dining table, behind silver cutlery and amidst tall tales of adventure and the jokes of fake personas keeping up appearances.

Loneliness is not a lack of others; loneliness is being unable to be content with my own company.

Friendship, desire, home, sex, being alone, love, offspring – every topic I discuss with someone else, I see mirrored in myself. Observing from a safe

43

distance, scribbling down notes in my notebook, staring 'independently' into other people's existence – all this is no more than scratching the surface. Fascinating to the mind, and meaningless to the heart. If I really want to delve into some of the core issues of modern-day life, I need to let go of what is keeping me safe from scrutiny.

How far dare I go?

A small, faded piece of paper hangs on a board I have at home. One finger long, two fingers wide. 'Bar', I wrote on top of it, but the time and place have slipped my mind.

Notes from a watering hole – God knows which one.

'Food: chicken, goat.'

'An Abba record plays.'

'Woman sings along, out of tune, breaking.'

'Cuddling carefully – dancing cheek to cheek.'

'Not really moving. Bums – hips – hands – arms.'

It could have been anywhere. A bar with coloured light bulbs, where blown speakers still vomit sounds. One of those places somewhere in a forgotten village between two cities. Too far from the one, too far from the other. A place where beer flows and the smells of fried meat tease the appetite.

It could have been Uganda, on my way to Kigali in Rwanda. It just as well could have been a bar somewhere in Ethiopia, where the fourteen-year-old girl had her ass slapped by a chauffeur while Aster Aweke sang – 'Bitchengna' (loneliness), a melody that cuts straight through the soul.

Curfew is about to start. Two young women sit opposite me in the garden of the hotel. Each has a beer bottle in front of her on the table. When, minutes later, I open the door to my room, I find them behind me.

'Wanna fuck?'

'No thanks.'

'Can I use your toilet then?'

'Sure, be my guest.'

I hear the toilet being flushed, and see her standing in front of me. She left her zipper undone. 'You sure you don't wanna fuck? You can have us both.'

The other woman too slowly unzips her pants.

'Curfew is about to begin. Now is not the time to send us away. Where can we sleep? Look at all this beauty we're offering you.'

'Will you close the door behind you on your way out?'

They don't want to go.

'We give you warmth, attention. Two women. Let us rub your loneliness away.'

———————

'Where are you from? Who is your family? How many children do you have?' The questions people ask me the moment I close my notebook, lay bare *their* priorities: origin, home, children, connection.

'I didn't ask you what you do for a living.' The young man in Zanzibar looks me straight in the eye. 'I asked you to whom you are connected. Who is your family, who are your friends? To whom do you go, when life is tough?'

His question is sharp, to the point. His eyes are not yet ready to give up. 'When I ask you who you are, you answer by telling me how you make a living. When you ask me who I am, I will tell you who my father is, and who my mother, my uncles, my aunts and my cousins are. Do you see the difference?'

I toy with his remark, and tell him that in the country where I now reside, South Africa, his comparison walks another mile. There I am neither what I do for a living nor who I know. There I am first and foremost valued by what I own.

Africa awaits a chilly wind, picking up from the south.

'YOU HAVE TO BE ABLE TO LOVE YOURSELF'

The first rays of sunlight mix with the green of fluorescent lighting as well as with a warm yellow from the streetlights. The signs of a filling station contrast with a dark blue sky. The rising sun has chased away the deepest black of the night. Now is the twilight zone, filmmakers call it the 'magical hour', a multi-hued time of day.

In Africa the magical 'hour' lasts about fifteen minutes, at most. On the equator the sun rises as if someone just switched on the light. Day comes like the blow of a hammer. The chill of the night disappears rapidly.

Jua kali – the cruel sun. During the day he will shine without mercy, drying crops and exhausting the body. Too bright to gaze around, too hot to do anything.

Africa's biggest hunters shun him. Lions and leopards prefer to hunt in the evening hours. Hyenas follow in their footsteps, laughing. At midday they rest in the shade of bushes or trees. Only a fool works under a cruel sun.

Man is such a fool.

Touts wash their minibuses, known as *matatus*, in a corner of the filling station. They wipe the dust off chrome rims and mirrors, and clean the benches. The adolescents – uniformed in baseball caps and sneakers – show an unfamiliar side of themselves.

During the magical morning hour they show care, affection and an eye for detail. In the early hours no tout has an appetite yet for the crudeness of the day. Their source of income – the *matatu* – has to be prepared for hours in traffic.

During the day they rule the roads of Nairobi, indifferent to God, laws and fellow human beings. Their only traffic rule is that might is right, decided by strength, size and rudeness.

Acid House rumbles in the background. The louder the thundering bass, the more the drivers and touts feel at home in their money-making monsters. The rhythm of Africa's heartbeat, performed by American descendants of black slaves, hammers through downtown Nairobi from buses that pack passengers like sardines in a tin. The bellboy, the civil servant, the secretary, the domestic worker and the gardener all are on their way to work. Toiling under the sun. Sweating, sighing, groaning – for the children's school fees, the rent for the tiny flat and the twelve weekly rides in a *matatu*.

Fabien rubs the sleep from his eyes. A small man, pitch-black. His pair of trousers has been ironed stiff, with a sharp crease. He wears his immaculate shirt tucked tightly into his trousers. His sleeves are buttoned around his wrists. Shining loafers fit the style of his entire outfit. In the days that follow Fabien will take a checked handkerchief from his pockets to wipe sweat from his hands, dust from in-between his fingers and tiny drops of perspiration from his neck.

'*Bonjour. Bien dormi?*' His eyes are honest, but seem to have lost their expressiveness. His voice, I will come to realise as the days pass, does not give any hints of either his thoughts or his feelings.

Fabien does not wait for me to answer his well-wish, and disappears. Together with his 'tank boy', Wambua, he checks his truck and trailer. Wambua appears to be everything his boss is not. Cheerful eyes, and quick-witted. He combines cynicism with a wide smile.

'Africa,' he will say repeatedly while shaking his head. 'It will take a long time before we'll get it right.' Or: 'Africa? Allow us one more generation to get our act together. My kids might have a better life.'

Sad is only sad if you allow setbacks to throw you off your balance. Wambua cannot afford to be thrown off balance.

A kick against each tire. Six axles, twenty tires. Fabien points out one tire, and tells Wambua to change it with the one behind it. A simple trick to hoodwink hungry traffic officers. 'Hyenas work harder for a living than your average police officer. He just holds up his hand, begging for "something small". Grousers.' Wambua smiles one of his cynical smiles, follows it up with yet another of his aphorisms on Africa.

Bujumbura, Burundi's capital, is our destination. The journey could take eight days. 'Or twenty – depending on the mood of the red tape,' Wambua grins. Three borders, thousands of litres of fuel, many dinners, gallons of tea. Sunsets and sunrises. Hookers, girlfriends, flirting shop owners. Flat tires, cracked engine blocks. Willing tarmac will precede asphalt as pockmarked as the face of an acne sufferer, followed by corrugated dirt roads.

The route from the Kenyan port of Mombassa to the Great Lake Region is the aorta of East Africa. Coffee, tea and commodities like gold and diamonds find their way to the global markets in exchange for luxury products, building materials, emergency aid and weapons.

Close to a hundred million people rely on what the truckers collect and deliver. The Congolese woman buys her piece of Kenyan soap. The Rwandan man sells his coffee. The displaced child in Burundi gets a blanket from an overseas aid organisation. The Ugandan driver uses fuel which was refined abroad and shipped to his doorstep via Mombassa and Nairobi.

Some segments of the route are infamous. Rebels there act as if they were 'vampires', as Wambua calls them. On other stretches, robbers await their chance for a 'hit and run'. Truckers constantly have to assess what's ahead, and make their decisions accordingly. Wait for a convoy? Take a detour? Go as fast as his old engine will allow him?

Just before Eldoret in East Kenya, a five to ten kilometre haul is heavily damaged. Deep potholes scar the road. White lines are drawn together on the tarmac, making a mosaic of the surface that needs to be replaced. They were painted years ago, and are now slowly fading.

Fabien cruises along fast enough not to allow robbers to cut the ropes that keep his cargo neatly packed, yet careful enough not to wreck his truck in the crater-sized potholes. Often during the day, entire cargos disappear into the bush – thrown there box after box by gang members who jump on trailers out of sight from the rear-view mirrors, and slowly suck away the freight. Henchmen collect the goods.

At night, they resort to more violent ways of loot collection: shotguns, *Kalashnikovs* and anything else that will silence a driver.

Fabien has been ploughing this route for the last eighteen years. He knows the risks of muggings, hijackings and theft. He knows the smell of a civil war - Uganda in the eighties, his own Rwanda in the early nineties and Burundi. He doesn't talk about any of it – not a word.

'Burundi is our Chechnya,' sneers a tank boy somewhere along the route, to add a while later, 'You must be nuts and weary of life! No one can send me into Burundi. You would not go into Chechnya, would you?'

Europe's hotbeds are well known in Africa. We pass canteens with names like Sarajevo or Croatia. Passing buses display names like 'Bosnia Express' and 'Kosovo Convoy'. One of the express services between Uganda's capital

49

Kampala and Nairobi is named after the Serb dictator Milosevic; another is called Karadzic or even Lockerbie. Names of internationally indicted war criminals are famous, and can easily be replaced by those of movie stars like Stallone, Schwarzenegger or Jean-Paul Belmondo. But who knows those movie stars, far from television and cinema, in an area devoid of tabloid magazines?

Radio, on the other hand, brings the news every hour. Whatever makes headlines makes memories, and inspires those who need to think of a catchy name for a bus or a restaurant.

Hussein, Ghaddafi, Mladic. For bus owners they are no more than exotic names, used as easily as Walt Disney used Timbuktu to mean the end of the earth.

Malaba, on the border between Kenya and Uganda, at nightfall. Fabien searches for a hotel room. Tomorrow morning he will have to queue at 7 a.m., to get his paperwork going. Pencil pushers will be his fate. Clearing his goods will take a day. At least. 'It takes a long time to get a stamp, and I need many stamps to cross.'

Like a captain leaving his bridge, Fabien walks away from his truck. Wambua takes the keys to the truck, and takes over the guard duty. To kill time the tank boy grabs his bag of potatoes from their hiding place between one of the axles, and starts peeling.

From a little cupboard he lifts a blackened pot, his charcoal burner and a bag of charcoal.

Tucked under the trailer Wambua prepares his meal, silently. The world under his feet, the truck his home. At night he guards his treasure by sleeping in between the axles.

Red cushions, mirrors, beads and ringing bells. Bicycle taxis are on a quest for customers. Drivers are searching for their favourite bars in either Kenya or Uganda.

Many nationalities gather in Malaba. Somalis, Zambians, Ugandans, Congolese. Each has his own bar, his own group of girls. Somalis search for their own music, their own drug. And where they find *qat*, they won't find beer. And what's a Congolese to do in a local without beer, where *lingala* and *ndombolo* music have been replaced by Arabic tunes? Or where the girls don't understand French?

A procession of carnal desires starts, with girls wrapped in tight skirts and revealing stretch pants. 'Let me be your girlfriend, tonight...' Mystery and the subtle techniques of seduction have been thrown to the dogs. A direct approach rules the streets of Malaba. 'I want to fuck – who will fuck me tonight?' It is too early in the evening for truckers to be this desperate. Food first, then beer. A soccer game on satellite TV in the canteen. Then a woman. A matter of priorities.

The game of love on the East African trucker route is like Russian roulette. The trade route is a hotbed of HIV/AIDS. Advertisements along the road demand attention: 'Protect it with Protector. So Strong. So Soft.'

Few give a hoot about the slogan, Arap Petrol suggests. In the Borderpost Bar, he empties his fourth pint of beer in twenty minutes. Driving makes one thirsty. His 'Malaba girlfriend' sits next to him, not saying a word, her eyes lowered. 'Using a condom while making love is for most of my colleagues like sucking on a sweetie with the wrapper on. Idiots. My luggage consists of clean Y-fronts and condoms. Many condoms. You have to be careful here. It is a matter of life and death. Stay away from the women, you hear me?'

Arap Petrol – he got his nickname because of his Arab background and his product – does not believe in a combination of love and trucking. He has his girlfriends, everywhere. And he has one woman who birthed his kids. 'Someone needs to wash my socks, and I need a mother for my children. When you're a trucker, you need to be able to be lonely and not go mad. You have to be able to love yourself. That way, you don't need someone else to love you.'

He looks at his playmate, and asks her if she'd like another coke. She smiles at him. 'Fries maybe?' A nod.

'When I leave for Uganda tomorrow, she'll cry herself a river because I am going. In the afternoon she'll receive another one of her boyfriends. That's how she makes ends meet.' He wouldn't call it prostitution. A hooker sleeps with each and every one who is willing to pay for the service. 'What prostitute would wash your socks, have sex with you, and ask how your first-born is doing? She'll even know his name. I am not the only man in her life, I know. I can't afford to be her only man. She is not the one-and-only in my life, and she knows. I am a trucker, I transport fuel. But I have two highly explosive cargos I need to discharge.' His girlfriend taps him playfully on his thigh.

The lovebirds cuddle the night away in Borderpost, where a bottle of beer only costs a few pennies and the speakers were blown a long time ago. Fabien will not be found enjoying Malabo's nightlife this evening. He sleeps guilelessly.

With his left hand, Kennedy plays with a handful of paintbrushes. In his right hand he keeps a pot of white paint. His eyes scan the parking lot for trucks with missing obligatory signs. 'Tool box', 'Transit Goods', 'Battery'. Or a fuel tank without a specification of its size, which is always greater than the measurement the artist is asked to paint. Why tempt fate when smuggling fuel is hard as it is?

The area just before the offices of Customs & Excise is like an anthill. Everyone carries something, moves something or sells something. Kennedy is just one of many. His fellow salesmen sell cloyingly sweet tea, or dry pancakes wrapped in old newspapers. Thermos flasks, washing powder, blankets, shoes – everything is for sale. Drivers offer their diesel when customs officials suspect them of carrying too much for their destination. 'When you do away with three hundred litres, you'll still make it to Kampala.' Young boys in shorts run around with funnels and jerry cans, to buy any excess and sell it for a minute profit.

Others bring in water. With lightning speed they wash the dust off the trucks. No one gets to cross borders in a dirty truck.

Kennedy's eyes seem out of place in this universe of odd-jobbers. As if sweating and slaving away under the cruel sun is beneath him. Although tattered, he maintains an air of distinction. 'I am an artist,' Kennedy confesses. In Malaba the brush is his bread and the paint his butter. If he were able to follow his heart, he'd be painting art, abstract work. Some of his work is on permanent display at Gallery Matatu, one of the main centres of modern art in Kenya. Tourists in flip-flops and diplomats in suits buy their beloved African art here. In 1988 Kennedy even made it to Denmark, to exhibit his work. He has the newspaper clippings to prove it. It has been the highlight of his life so far. Now he paints elegant letters in white paint on perishable metal.

The sun burns relentlessly. It is midday. Fabien has been waiting for hours at Customs & Excise. Pushing, smiling, laying it on with a trowel, pleading and remaining silent. 'Too many stamps. Officials are a hungry breed.'

On the Ugandan side whirlwinds pick up dusty sand and carry it up high. Police officers, appearing as ghosts in the dusty fog, turn away from the wind to protect their faces from the sharp grains of airborne sand. The area becomes a mysterious place, full of abandoned trucks. Only the tank boys stay, as they always do; in all weathers. In the dusty fog they repair brakes and engines, and they change tyres. The sounds of a sledgehammer blowing on a twisted axle echo between the trucks - a desperate attempt to bend stubborn steel.

Just outside the fence of Customs, Freddy, a Congolese driver, tries to talk his way out of an awkward situation. No, he can't foot the bill for his drinks. A lovely lady wanted some change as sort of a down payment on services to be rendered, but she stole all his cash. The freelance fuel sellers splutter. Yeah, they know the lady. It's one of her trademarks. No problem. 'We'll pay your bill today – tomorrow you give us some of your fuel.'

Ismail, a young Rwandan trucker, snuggles up to his girl in the nearest canteen. Hand in hand they walk to his cabin, kissing and laughing in clouds of dust. He has got his stamps; tomorrow he may leave.

Fabien also flashes a smile – his first. 'Tomorrow we'll leave, at sunrise.' However, there happens to be a 'but'. The traffic officers weren't too happy with his indicators. To have them repaired, Fabien needs a part from Nairobi. He disappears, looking for a phone. He needs to talk to his boss, and ask him to send the part with one of the express buses to Kampala.

Malaba, in the early hours of the morning. Freddy has come under attack. His boss has showed up, unexpectedly. The fuel sellers are waiting for their payment, after helping Freddy with his tab. He tries to calm them. 'You will all get your money. But not right now. How about next week? I can't just tap diesel from my tanks, under the watchful eyes of my employer. Come on guys, be flexible!'

A promise once broken is bad currency in no-man's land, where everyone knows everyone, and words spread easily. He will not get the assistance everyone so desperately needs here. Freddy's days seem to be numbered.

A branch, two metal sheets with seven-inch nails and a few fuel drums make up the roadblocks just outside Malaba, Uganda. Red letters painted on a grey background make the difference between the police post and a bandit's trap. An old man with a greyish beard plays with the steel points. Balancing like a Hindu guru on the nails, he wraps his arms through his legs, behind his back and past his head. He leans on one arm, says something and meditates.

One of the police officers is fed up. 'Bugger off, idiot.' The guru meditates, unperturbed. The officer grabs a pebble and throws it at the old man. 'Buzz off.' Disturbed from his trance, he walks away to continue his meditation on the roadside. A few minutes later he appears again – this time marching like a major. His pants have unravelled. Sticky hair. Bare feet, scarred from blisters, wounds and sores. He holds a baton under his arm, true to his present profession. The 'major' snubs the agents, lifts his middle finger and then takes to his heels, just when a bicycle taxi shouts Fabien's name.

'Your package has arrived on the bus from Nairobi. The mechanic is on the back of the other bicycle.'

Lush green and high trees have replaced the savannah. Flowers bloom in neat gardens. Green jungle. Good roads without potholes. Monkeys swinging in the trees, right beside the road. The source of the Nile, its wild waters channelled to give Uganda seemingly unlimited electricity.

I sense a strong difference in atmosphere once we have made our first couple of kilometres into Uganda. A certain grimness that leaves vague imprints on life in Kenya is missing in Uganda. After fifteen years of progress and development, the mood in Uganda is optimistic. Every year is better than the last one, unlike the situation in Kenya, where, thanks to years of misrule under President Daniel arap Moi, life gets worse every year.

But despite the positive trends in their country, Ugandan officers are as corrupt as their Kenyan counterparts. They fine truckers 75 eurocents for plastic covers that are not tied according to rules as the officers define them on any given day; two euros for incorrectly filled out insurance papers; 35 eurocents because the last few metres of the trailer ran through a red light or because the police officer has decided that the cargo is stacked too high.

Wambua: 'It infuriates me; this endless harassment for no reason whatsoever. Why don't they just hang a note around their necks, like professional beggars do? "Blind, orphan, widower and handicapped"? That way, you just throw out some cash through the window, and continue your journey. No loss of time, no worries – same amount of money. They pretend to be officers, guarding law and order. In the meantime, they just beg for money. They should get an honest job, like you and me. Nothing wrong with honest sweat. Aaaah, Africa... When will you come right?'

The convoy is heading for Kampala. Ismail with his load of match sticks; Freddy doesn't know his cargo, only the recipient: the Rwandan Army. The Zambians, Johnson and Johnson, drive a truck full of cosmetics. Arap Petrol cargoes his A1 jet fuel.

Everyone will have to wait in Kampala for a few days. Paperwork and stamps necessary to continue the journey to Goma (Congo), Kigali (Rwanda), Juba (Sudan) or Bujumbura (Burundi) are done here. This is a city where private guards patrol the streets and private property with shotguns; it is also a city where God's ugliest birds fly around, shit the streets, eat the rubbish and live on the roofs of office buildings. Marabous, big birds, with dirty pink necks and long beaks. This is also the town where Sylvia wants to kiss, provided I pay her, and the sounds of the disco drone till sunrise.

Wambua curses his job. Again he has to sleep under his damned truck. Climbers overgrow the old customs building. His colleagues hang their laundry to dry on mirrors, or are cooking a meal on charcoal fires. Chickens run around as far as their ropes allow them to. Oil leaks from a tanker in thick splashes. The hot sun makes it as fluid as water, spreading it out over the red soil.

Fabien is starting to worry. He has made it only to Kampala so far. Tomorrow he wants to speed things up a bit. Every day earlier than he is expected to arrive in Bujumbura will reward him 100 dollars extra – a little treasure. He yearns to see his wife and kids, who live in a tiny village north of Kigali.

Fabien wants to devour the miles.

Mirima Hills, the border post between Rwanda and Uganda, is a dump amidst the savannah. Outside the hamlet the treetops make a wide roof, consisting of thin leaves on ample branches. Hills everywhere. On the left are those of Tanzania, on the right those of Uganda, and ahead of us those of Rwanda. The first few of Rwanda's famous thousand hills.

The Ugandan border post was blown away late in 1978 by Tanzanian soldiers while marching on dictator Idi Amin. Next to the ruin of that border post are flagpoles with the Ugandan colours proudly fluttering on top. On the other side, Africa's most uninspiring flag flaps in the wind: Rwanda's tricolour, in its centre a dull 'R'.

In a restored office in the old building, a photographer has opened his shop. With a little sign he tries to sell himself: 'For passports and visa'. In his windowsill lie cut Polaroids and a pair of scissors. Outside the ruin, a toilet cleaner observes each visitor to his empire. If I want to relieve myself, I'll have to pay three times the normal fee, he tells me, because I did not pay the last time I was here. 'But I have never visited Mirima Hills ...' For him, all whites are the same.

'No, that's not it,' a young woman explains. 'You don't understand. He is a Tutsi. His entire family was murdered. He is a pain to everyone, but we just let him be.' The toilet is all he has left as a safe domain.

Mirima Hills is an amiable mess. Business and formalities take place in a relaxed atmosphere. People seem more interested in a good chat than in the boring nitty-gritty of work. Everyone converses. About nothing, about everything. About the one and only road, a dirt road, which turns into slush after a short shower. Or about the thirty-two cows which were recently arrested for illegally crossing the border. A serious crime, for which the area commissioner was called to investigate.

In the evening a Bollywood movie blasts its gunshots, its fights and its sugary sweet romance out over the entire village, through speakers no one can escape. A generator cuts through the silence of the night. Oil lamps shine. A slaughtered goat hangs by its legs in the evening sky, dripping the last of its dark red droplets.

Fabien is in need of carbon copy paper. Each driver is supposed to provide his own. Uganda will not waste its hard-earned tax money on carbon copy paper. A businessman saw the niche in the market, and now has a monopoly to provide carbon copy paper. His prices are extravagant.

It is the only reason why people settle in Mirima Hills: to make money, in any way they can. With so much paperwork needed, there are so many opportunities to provide services. There are moneychangers on the bridge in no-man's land. There are police officers who allow the money changers to operate on the bridge in no-man's land. There are shoe shiners, and there are butchers. The place even has a butler with a bow tie; he works in the three-star hotel, where the communal toilet is a drop latrine, and the most exquisite dish on the menu happens to be a fried egg.

Ismail is waiting here as well, cuddling a new girlfriend. 'They see me as a sugar daddy. I help them pay the school fees for their kids, they make me relax.'

Zak Abdallah waits. His truck is an old Mercedes. 'I am 65, I need a rest. My life goes zigzag – up and down. I am not getting ahead. I am still sleeping on the ground; I still have to cook my own meal.'

I have come across Zak many times before. He always wears a dark blue beret and a smile. However, today he is *not* smiling. 'I'm getting tired, but I cannot retire. No money. All I earn goes straight to my kids. I want them to have a better life than I had. I am so tired of roaming around. Every day I read the paper, I read everything that's happening in the world. I just don't get it any longer. The world is not what it used to be. I roam through a place I understand less, the more I travel.'

The old man is the epitome of disenchantment. He toils for a pittance, not enough to offer his son a better life than Zak lived himself. 'You'd think we would be one collective bunch; we're all on the same road for the same reason, heading for the same destination. Forget it. There are drivers and there are drivers. I spend my nights on a flimsy mattress under my truck, no matter what the weather. Others can afford to take a real shower, in a real room, and sleep in a real bed. No – I am sorry to say, but this is not a life. Not at my age.'

I see Fabien at breakfast. The mud outside has not left any marks on his bright clothing. Neither a spot on his cream-coloured shirt, nor a smear on his ironed white trousers. Yet he radiates unease. His fatherland is just a stone's throw away and he wants to see his wife and kids. But what else is bothering him? 'Too many prisoners.'

Fabien is a Hutu. Extremists from his ethnic group killed a million people during the genocide of 1994. Tutsis took revenge on his family, arrested them or chased them away. 'There are things one shouldn't talk about too often. They are so bad that no sentence or word can make up for it.'

Ismail, also Rwandan, managed to lay low during the mass killings. He is a Muslim, which makes him neither Hutu nor Tutsi. Muslims were neither the perpetrators, nor the victims. Ismail transported refugees as a driver for Médecins sans Frontières.

What created a trauma for Fabien, left Ismail untouched. He flirts with his girlfriend and sings praises to a trucker's freedom. 'I could be so stinking rich, were it not for the bureaucrats. They suffocate Africa with their rules, their stamps, and their corruption. Why am I here, with this girl? Because a few offices away some official is choking on my documents. I'd prefer nothing more than working and earning money for my wife who is about to deliver my first-born. But what do I do? I am wheedling this gorgeous babe here ...'

Arap Petrol has no desire to snuggle up to any of his 'girlfriends' today. He's in trouble. His tyres keep deflating for some weird reason. Sometimes with a puff and a sigh, sometimes hardly noticeably. He and his tank boy have fixed three tyres so far. Useless. On the Rwandan side – after his paperwork has gone through he suddenly hears a sighing sound. He was just making himself a nice cup of tea.

Arap gives the finger to no one in particular. 'Even when I'm not moving, things go wrong!' He decides to drive with one wheel less on one axle. He's just had it with his share of luck on this trip. Some assholes had already stolen most of his diesel, as well as his jack. Now his tires have gone. 'Just go to hell,' he says to nobody. The merciless sun ushers in another screaming hot day.

Ismail is a happy man. Having just arrived in Kigali news reaches him of his wife's delivery. A son, sure enough. 'Allahu akhbar.' He has no time to visit them. The ceremony during which his son will officially be named is only in a week. But first he needs to deliver his cargo in Congo. After that he might have two days.

The lodge close to the customs area is spotlessly clean. The owner, Consolata, has covered the mattresses with plastic. Sheets slide away, the sweat pouring from my body onto the plastic makes sleeping impossible. The comfort of her guests is secondary to Consolata's investment. 'I don't know how they do it, or who does it, but believe me: sometimes these mattresses are hardly recognisable as such. I have introduced fines, for damages beyond reason.'

The owner gives me too many details – I don't need to know more.

Waiting. This eternal waiting for papers to come through. Isaac Zabbhan has earned a master's degree in waiting. For the past month he has been bored to death on the tarmac of the customs area in Kigali. He ate his last food four days ago, and spent his last money two days earlier. All that he has left now is a skinny chicken in a basket. His boss forgot to give him money for duties, and numerous times he promised to sort it out. So Zabbhan waits. What else can he do?

In *The Shadow of the Sun* (2002) the Polish journalist Ryszard Kapuscinski wrote inimitably on the African art of waiting. Europeans become irritated, irascible and rude. Africans don't.

> *I have observed for hours on end crowds of people in this state of inanimate waiting, a kind of profound physiological sleep: They do not eat, they do not drink, they do not urinate; they react neither to the mercilessly scorching sun, not to the aggressive voracious flies that cover their eyelids and lips.*
>
> *What, in the meantime, is going on inside their heads?*
>
> *I do not know. Are they thinking? Dreaming? Reminiscing? Making plans? Meditating? Travelling the world beyond? It is difficult to say.*

Hills surround us. We climb, wind, descend, ascend, brake, twist and accelerate. 'This is when you need turbo,' Wambua crows. 'Turbo pushes you through everything and anything. Turbo is pure and unrivalled power. We'll have to do it with the explosions of gasoline only. Guys driving turbo are home by now.'

Zebras roam the countryside. A little later, banana trees grow as far as the eye can see. Fields and green hills where, in 1994, Hutu extremists killed an estimated one million people in a hundred days. Manually, purposefully, deliberately.

'It is peaceful now,' proclaims the Rwandan immigration chief at the post on the Burundi border.

It's after 6 p.m., and although he's still working, he points at the office on the other side of the border. 'I belief they've closed shop for the day, but try your luck.' The officer wants to go soon to get his beer at the bar in the only establishment on the Rwandan side.

'We have peace, but next door it's still a mess. They are slightly stressed over there.' Night falls when he stamps our passports.

With Fabien and Wambua, I cross the border – nothing more than a bridge over the river that washed countless bodies away into Lake Victoria all those years ago. Only a trace of moonlight breaks the pitch-dark. Coniferous trees stick high up into the air. Silhouettes of hills.

Burundi's border is indeed closed, the officials have left, and the barriers are down. We will have to sleep in no-man's land. No toilet, no bed, no shower. Only the chill of the night. 'Don't worry,' says Fabien. 'It is too cold for mosquitoes. We will try again tomorrow.'

Wambua expresses his philosophy: 'They close the border just to bother us. No other reason. It is in their nature. Officials. Don't take it personally. We still live in the 16th century.'

Music plays in Burundi on the other side. A song by Brenda Fassi, South Africa's most famous pop star who first conquered alcoholism and then Africa. People dance outside, lit by lanterns, in a *zone rouge* where active rebels roam and shoot. Africa celebrates life, while grenades explode many hills further down the road.

The final stretch. The *zone rouge* is an area where all the trees have been felled. Trees hide enemies. Every twenty kilometres a roadblock halts all traffic. Soldiers hunt for rebels, ready to sow death, doom and destruction. We progress slowly, until suddenly Lake Tanganyika becomes visible, beneath us in the lowlands.

The lake lies in the valley like a copper plate, the sun reflecting in the water – that cruel, copper ball in the firmament, too bright to observe with the naked eye. Men and women work the land, hand on plough, sweating and toiling in the hope that they will survive today, and tomorrow.

Post Script

This journey took place in February 1999. Since then a peace accord has been signed for Burundi; corruption in Kenya is declining according to a third of polled Kenyans; HIV infections are coming down in Uganda thanks to continued awareness campaigns; and Rwanda got a new flag, a new coat of arms and a new national anthem. Minibuses on the road are no longer called 'Kosovo' but 'Fallujah' after the city in Iraq – the most recent *hotspot* in the world. Brenda Fassi died; her body could not heal the effects of her former substance abuse.

NO MORE LONGING FOR OUZO IN KISANGANI

Evangelos Valavanis (71) has taken up residence in a small room in the home of his friend Taki Malamas in Kisangani. A mattress on the floor. A hernia makes it hard to walk, and he has been having attacks of malaria. From one window he looks out over the back of Malamas' house. Valavanis borrowed a chair and a mosquito net. Cherished objects. He sighs. 'A life of slogging ends here.'

Four years ago, Valavanis left his home in the rain forest of the Democratic Republic of Congo. In the mid-1970s, the former sailor had settled in the middle of the jungle, near the town of Buta. He owned a couple of acres of coffee, which made him a comfortable living. He also ran a few shops in Buta, where he sold necessities like soap. His business, however, had collapsed in the early 1990s. The road to Uganda had become so bad, trucks could no longer come by to collect his coffee beans. Transport companies struggled to make a profit, with trucks needing serious repairs after each expedition into Congo.

Shortly after the war started in Congo, Valavanis left his home and knocked – destitute and in despair – on the doors of the Catholic mission in Buta. They gave him a bike, and Valavanis found a man willing to cycle to Kisangani. The journey on the remains of what was once the main road from Cairo to Cape Town, took the cyclist two months with the sickly Greek on a cushion on the back. Valavanis paid him all the money he had left: the equivalent of ten euros.

On his behalf, Valavanis's friends now write letters to the Greek embassy to facilitate his return to Europe. They also pay for his hernia operation, his food and his drink.

Valavanis spends his days in a chair in Malamas' garden, while listening to the sports news on a cheap radio, waiting for a reply. The transistor, a belt, a pair of shoes and a few rags are his only possessions. 'I know a few sentences of English: *I am poor, I am hungry, I have no money.*' Valavanis holds his belly while he laughs, showing his last remaining teeth.

Then he turns serious again. 'I've got no one left. My brother must be somewhere in the States, but he doesn't respond to my letters.' He asked the International Red Cross to trace his brother, with no results. 'It's most likely he's dead.'

He wants to go back to Athens, where he was born. 'My friends tell me Athens has changed beyond recognition, and warn me I won't find my way around there. Still, I want to go back. What have I got in Congo? Nothing. I suffer too much. Let me die in Greece."

His mate Yani Giatros slaps Valavanis warmly on the shoulder, and promises to do his utmost to get him to Athens. Giatros himself does not entertain the thought himself. His roots have grown too deep into Congolese soil, into a life in Kisangani. This is where his wife lives, where he has a house and where he runs his business. 'This is home.'

'I could not go back to Greece – boredom would kill me. The beauty of Congo is that here everything is still possible. Europe is finished, nothing left to try or explore. Young people in Europe have become addicted to ease and convenience. What happened to a desire for adventure, a hunger for the unknown?'

Recently, his 26-year-old son came to town. They were talking of going into business together. After a few months the young man went back to Greece. 'He said life in Africa is too tough. Imagine that. My son...'

Home, friendship, family – they are extensions of each other. Where do you feel welcome, wanted, loved even? Who misses you when you're not around?

Since the Dutchman, Jan van Riebeeck, set foot on land in South Africa's Table Bay in 1652, millions of 'aliens' moved to Africa. They came from the Far East, the Middle East or Europe. They were fortune hunters and slaves, scum of the earth as well as missionaries, farmers, miners, bankers, aid workers, diplomats and journalists.

By the mid 1970s, around two thousand Greeks had settled in the east of Congo. They socialised in the Club Hellenique in Kisangani, a city of over six hundred thousand souls in the middle of Congo's vast rainforest. Of the two thousand, nine Greeks remain in October 2000. Who do they rely on, and what defines home for them?

Muscles like hawsers, chiselled torsos strong enough to swim effortlessly in the mighty Congo river, fishermen row their pirogues standing up through the stream, throwing out a net here, throwing out another one there.

The river is filled with wooden structures, with ropes holding tight the traps set out. Men yell, call and laugh. Dark brown mud sucks at the bare feet walking through it. Pigs move about through garbage. Electricity wires run along above the mud huts, without providing any power to those who live and work here.

Life in the hamlet on this island in the Congo River must look much like what Henry Stanley found on his expedition of 1877. The village drum is still made of wood, but nowadays rests on an old, dilapidated rim of a car wheel to enhance the timbre and resonance. The Stanley Falls, so named by Stanley himself, are – though impressive – in reality no more than a few rapids around big boulders. In his book, *Through the Dark Continent* (1878), Stanley writes about his adventures with the gifted pen of a tabloid hack, increasing his own heroism like a modern whisk expands milk into froth:

> *[L]ouder than the noise of the falls rose the piercing yells of the savage Mwana Ntaba from both sides of the great river. We now found ourselves confronted by the inevitable necessity of putting into practice the resolution which we had formed before setting out on the wild voyage – to conquer or die. What should we do? Shall we turn and face the fierce cannibals, who with hideous noise drown the solemn roar of the cataract, or shall we cry out "Mamby Kwa Mungu" – "Our fate is in the hands of God – and risk the cataract with its terror!*

In October 2000, instead of hearing 'the piercing yells of the savage', I hear muscular men breathing deeply, fighting the strength of the Congo, trying to catch a meal. The cataracts still roar, though.

About six hundred thousand people live in Kisangani, Congo's third largest city. Or should that be four hundred thousand? No one knows for sure. Statistics are hard to come by, for a city tucked away so far in the back of beyond. Such facts existed, once. But in Congo 'development' progresses, for lack of a better word, *asynchronistically*, a synonym for 'with its own dynamic' and a euphemism for 'backwards'.

In the 1950s, Stanleyville (as it was known then) was a showpiece of white colonial rule: a haven in the jungle, to be enjoyed by administrators and the business elite – wide avenues and neatly manicured parks with high palm trees. Most of the modern houses were designed in art deco style with its typical round shapes and unexpected forms.

White citizens would parade along the banks of the Congo. Just before sunset a plane would fly over and spray against mosquitoes. The wealthiest in town had a choice of six cinemas and three casinos. Sources of this wealth were originally coffee and latex extracted from the land through the brutal abuse of Congolese labour, later complemented by gold and diamonds.

The riches have evaporated, the glorious days are gone. Stanleyville is now Kisangani, a city of potholes, poverty and despair. Once the colonial rule with its racist structure of European 'citizens' and Congolese 'évolués' had come to an end at independence, many a settler left his former paradise. He took with him his investments, his experience and his international trade network. His departure was a blow to the economy. The decline was further hastened by decades of misrule under the leadership of Mobutu Sese Seko, toxic foreign mingling and the rise of almost surreal levels of official klep-tomania.

The war that broke out when armies of the neighbouring states of Uganda and Rwanda marched into Congo, first in 1996 and again in 1998, brought Kisangani to the brink of the abyss. And now the jungle is having a field day, grabbing back what humans have taken away. Moist, plants and neglect slowly turn buildings into ruins. Mortars and grenades achieved the same, in mere seconds. Nowadays, cars must waltz to navigate the potholes on the avenues.

A few inhabitants try to maintain an illusion of order. They clean up their gardens and cut grass. The most courageous of the city council work-ers try to keep the streetlights working. Even if only one light per street.

Congo has an incredible talent for wealth. Its soil is fertile, the rains are willing and the earth filled with highly-priced minerals. The sixty million Congolese are energetic and creative men and women of perseverance. And yet, most are dirt-poor. For the last one and a half centuries Congo's blessings have been its curse.

From the day a Belgian king dreamt of his own colony in the heart of Africa, Congo has been toyed with to squeeze as much wealth out of it as possible. The national elite played the game too, for their own benefit, critiquing as they went along the evil foreign powers who were out to enslave the nation, but at the same time aiding those same powers to rape their country and filling their own foreign bank accounts in the process. Former dictator Mobutu called this style of governing 'Bantuism'. 'That's how we do things in Africa,' he once said in an interview.

Despite many attempts, however, no one from within or without has been able to get Congo to kneel down and enslave it. The country is too huge, too complicated, too diverse, too inaccessible to be controlled. Yet, in a paradox typical of Congo, the country has nevertheless ended up on its knees; in a state of chaos where nothing functions as it does elsewhere.

And somehow, it still works.

Even at the end of the day, Kisangani's humid heat feels as if a wet towel is smashed in my face. Dark clouds move fast over the city. Thunder rolls. Lightning hits the forest, far away in the south.

Unperturbed by the weather, people move homewards. Some with briefcases in hand, others with bowls of fruit on their heads. Those who can afford it, hire a *tokela*, a cycle taxi.

It is the year 2000. Kisangani is held hostage in the fighting between two former allies: Rwanda and Uganda. Their presence in Congo has become messy, with officers, entire platoons and politicians all keen to put their hands in the cookie jar. Soldiers of formerly friendly powers are now fighting for control of Kisangani. Nothing can get into the city, nothing can get out.

Albert Kabongo is sure: somewhere on his desk he has this one fact sheet he wants to show. Sales figurs. Prices. 'Where is it, it must be here …' His chair is torn and worn. Apart from the state of his furniture, Kabongo's office looks like offices in Congo are supposed to look. He has a separate desk, a table for meetings where he can sit at the head and stare people in the face, while everyone else has to turn to him. On a small table near the window is a phone. Laughter. 'Hasn't been working for a long, long time now.'

Kabongo runs Primus, a beer brewery in Kisangani, owned by global beer giant Heineken. He tends to laugh out loud with long howls, his twinkling eyes hidden behind his glasses. 'To work in Kisangani is to perform acrobatics. Nothing functions. Yet, we produce beer.' Another round of laughter. Together with the textile factory and the soap producer, Primus is the last of the industrial Mohicans of Kisangani. 'Every day, I congratulate my technicians for keeping us on a roll.'

Kisangani's brewer and bottler has to fly his material into town. Roads no longer exist after decades of neglect and torrential rains, and the river crosses a front line, which makes it impossible to get anything ferried from the capital, Kinshasa. Trucks bring the malt to an airport in Bukavu, from where it is shipped to Goma. Planes fly it to Kisangani.

Belly laughter, a slap on the table. Kabongo is invincible. In a quagmire of impossibilities, he flounders so as not to drown.

Apart from dealing with troubles on the side of production, Kabongo also needs to creatively counter a steady decline in purchasing power. Luxuries cost a fortune. Sugar, for example, sells for two euros a kilo, one loaf of bread costs one euro. A bag of beans, tens of euros, is beyond the reach of most. A well-paid office clerk takes home 115 euros a month, at best.

'We continuously need to move our expenses around. As you might understand, this is not really a profitable business. We await better days.' Primus in Kisangani produced 25 000 hectolitres of beer in 1996, before the war came to town. In the first eight months of 2000, Primus produced 7 000 hectolitres. To stimulate production, Kabongo lowered the prices to bars and shops. Staff, however, demanded a salary increase because life had become too expensive.

Kabongo practises his talent for micro economic magic. 'This city has a potential market of a few hundred thousand beer consumers – too many to let go of too quickly. 'You have to stay alert, never lean back because of a perceived monopoly, or give up hope. One day, all will be fine.'

Along Fifteenth Avenue, where houses have suffered greatly during the 'Six Day War' of August 2000, music plays. *Lingala* – the rhythm of Congo. Walls are blackened, bullets have left their marks

A bottle of beer is opened in the shade of a tree.

One bottle. To share between two men and one woman.

Henry Stanley explored Congo more or less accidentally. The Scottish missionaries of David Livingstone had asked Stanley to continue Livingstone's works after his death. Assisted by three Europeans and three hundred Zanzibari, Stanley left the Spice Islands in the Indian Ocean and headed for Lake Victoria and Lake Tanganyika, to end up in the basin of the Congo river. He relied on the expertise of the infamous slave trader Tippu Tipp, Zanzibar's wealthiest merchant, who had made his fortune selling ivory and humans. Tipp's hunting grounds lay in Congo. Stanley made it through to the Atlantic Ocean.

The moment news reached Europe of Stanley's arrival on the West Coast of Africa, king Leopold of Belgium called for a meeting with Stanley. The Belgium monarch wanted a colony, despite resistance from his own politicians who feared the huge expenses of a colonial adventure.

Leopold sent Stanley off to Congo again, this time to collect information about the slave trade of Zanzibari hunters in Central Africa. The tide had turned in Europe; trading humans was no longer morally acceptable. If Stanley could write about atrocities committed in Congo, Leopold could surely find enough allies to help him 'free' Congo of the scourge of human trafficking. In 1885 the European powers of the day gave Leopold a blank cheque to do what the king felt he needed to do 'to combat slavery' in Congo.

Leopold ruled his 'Free State' with a fist of burning iron. Although his formal mission was to fight slavery and to uplift 'the natives', Leopold allowed his administrators complete freedom to kill, steal, mute, loot and rape; terror was the taxman's preferred way of doing business. For those willing to see, it quickly became clear that Leopold's drive to end Arab slave trafficking was the guise under which he could freely exploit the Congo. Leopold's 'Free State' was so laden with atrocities that his rule became the first target of a globally concerted effort to fight large-scale abuse of human rights.

Joseph Conrad's famous book, *Heart of Darkness* (1902), is a portrayal of the administrator 'Mr. Kurtz', tucked away in the jungle, whose fence consisted of poles with human heads. Conrad came to Africa in 1890, dreaming like so many others of grand deeds he, as a white man, would do. He describes how the eloquent words of Mr. Kurtz took him away on waves of enthusiasm and of purpose.

'He began with the argument that we whites, from the point of development we had arrived at, "must necessarily appear to them [the savages] in the nature of supernatural beings – we approach them with the might as of a deity," and so on, and so on. "By the simple exercise of our will we can exert a power for good practically unbounded," etc. etc. From that point he soared and took me with him.'

Confronted, however, with the gruesome terror of the realities in Leopold's 'Free State', Conrad left Africa, permanently weakened through tropical diseases from which he would never recover. He was morally as well as psychologically a broken man due to his confrontation with the 'mission of the white man' in its darkest days. In 1924, Conrad published an essay in *National Geographic* on his crashed dreams.

> *The subdued thundering mutter of the Stanley Falls hung in the heavy night air of the last navigable reach of the Upper Congo [...] and I said to myself with awe, 'This is the very spot of my boyish boast.' A great melancholy descended on me. Yes: this was the very spot. But there was no shadowy friend to stand by my side in the night of the enormous wilderness, no great haunting memory, but only the unholy recollection of a prosaic newspaper stunt and the distasteful knowledge of the vilest scramble for loot that ever disfigured the history of human conscience and geographical exploration. What an end to the idealised realities of a boy's daydreams!*

Not a great number of whites have stayed in Kisangani. Too many 'boyish daydreams' have been shot to smithereens. Those who share my skin colour are almost without exception aid workers. The Belgians who owned the city, handed her over to the 'evolués' – 'natives' who had received a Belgian education and so had 'evolved' from 'negro' to – well, to what?

What remains are their mansions, slowly turning into ruins. Their gardens no longer grow bougainvillaea or birds-of-paradise, but maize and cassava. Businessman Edouard Izi formulates his opinions on the departure of the Belgian settlers carefully, with a controlled rage. 'I don't blame the individual settler for leaving, for packing his suitcases and bags and crates, leaving us to our own devices. Maybe they thought, We have made enough money here; let them rot in their own shit. If only the Belgians would have done it like the whites in South Africa. It would really have set us on a course to a better life. Our settlers left too early, too easily.'

Against its own explicit desires, the Belgian government had, decades earlier, been forced to take control of the Congo. The king, who had made a mess of his colony, would otherwise have gone bankrupt.

At the start of 1960, the government of Belgium had no intention whatsoever of leaving Congo. Only a few years earlier, it had been said that Belgium needed a minimum of thirty years to provide a foundation for Congo's independence and 'political emancipation'.

The wave of independence sweeping over Africa, however, did not stop at Congo's borders. A nationalist, intellectual elite was able to generate support quickly amongst a population denied its basic human rights. Riots in 1959 warned the colonial administration that time was running out.

In a high-paced move, inspired by panic and a sense of insult over the 'ungratefulness' of the Congolese, Belgium threw independence at the new elite in an attempt to remain in control from abroad. Belgium was instrumental in the assassination of the charismatic, nationalist leader Patrice Lumumba, who had dared insult the Belgium monarch on independence day.

The murky role played by the Belgian government enraged many a Congolese against the settlers who stayed on. Most of them had not changed their opinion of a Congolese as, at best, an 'evolué' – a person somewhere between a 'native' and a 'civilised Christian', called to dance to the white man's tune.

After Mobutu Sese Seko took the reigns, assisted by foreign governments, the new head of state used the angry sentiments of his citizens to strengthen his own power base. From the 1970s, he set out on a course of *Zaïrisation*, forbidding foreign names, foreign fashion designs and foreign ways of thinking. He told both his people and his army to take from the Belgian settlers what he himself couldn't give them. After each flare-up of anti-Belgian sentiments, a new group of settlers left their beloved Congo. They no longer felt at home once black soldiers started kicking in *their* doors.

For as long as I can remember, I have had a vaguely uncomfortable feeling about white presence in Africa. That feeling is best compared to a small grain of sand in a shoe, causing blisters and, eventually, breaking the skin. Too many men have claimed to act in accordance with some kind of 'divine' mission, which put them on a pedestal, high above other mortals, while looting a country's wealth and destroying every potential for progress and liberty. Double standards create terrorists and freedom fighters, regardless of place or time.

Using double standards to measure the behaviour of people of different skin colours does not go down well. Most people will, at one time or another, get angry with those who claimed to be 'of higher moral order', and they will tear the self-proclaimed saints from their pedestals.

And yet, despite the deep-seated anger amongst many, I still come across

Congolese who, out of desperation and with an emotion I can only describe as self-disgust, sigh and lament, 'If only the whites had never left, we would not find ourselves in this predicament.'

For the settlers, Congo was not as much of a home as they had claimed it to be. They left with their tails between their legs, once abuse of power became too hot and too close. Like those white Zimbabweans who moved to neighbouring countries after Robert Mugabe took away their farms; or the Asian Ugandans, who were given marching orders in the early 1970s.

How many threats do you need to receive before the message arrives loud and clear that you are no longer wanted? That even though you are not personally responsible for atrocities committed, you are still being blamed. Someone needs to pay. And the moment whites or Asians have left, the focal point of hatred will shift – immediately.

Businessman Edouard Izi: 'We live with a very strong myth in Africa. It's the one of "African solidarity". In reality though, many amongst us wouldn't give anyone else the time of day. Look at Rwanda: one million people slaughtered in a hundred days. Fellow countrymen did that. Volunteers.'

I wonder, can a white person in Africa ever call himself an 'African'? I don't mean it the way the 'Afrikaners' did in South Africa – that hodge-podge of Europeans who gave themselves a label, so as to claim a collective historic right. I mean a white person who will stay when things get tough, even beyond the point of no return.

On the streets of Kisangani I only come across a few Greeks and a handful of Lebanese.

The smell of spiced coffee fills the office of Moussa Hassan. One of his assistants brings the small cups, while his maid offers tiny pizzas and small tins of cheese. Hassan opens a tin in an irate and impatient way.

'I accept it's so bloody expensive – what I find hard to digest, though, is that it's next to impossible to come by.' Cheese, coffee and pizzas make life in Kisangani liveable for Hassan.

The diamond trader contemplates leaving the city too. Of all the traders that once did business in this part of Congo, he's the last one left. He struck a clever deal with the leaders of the city, and so forced out his competitors. Hassan thought he had struck the deal of a lifetime – believed he had found the opportunity to make enough money, once and for all, to retire in his late thirties. He would have the exclusive right to buy and sell diamonds, for which he would pay the governing rebel movement a meagre hundred thousand dollars a month. Hassan had calculated a future turnover of three million dollars. However, his scheme failed when the flow of diamonds dried up. 'If business doesn't pick up soon, I quit. Why stay in a city where diamonds are no longer available, and you can't get any cheese?'

Those who offer their rough diamonds to Hassan come few and far between. The gems come wrapped in folded A4-paper, and sorted to size, quality and colour. Hassan scrutinises them under a magnifier, holding them one by one with a set of tweezers. And names his price. Good stones he might buy for 120 dollars per carat. His offer for industrial stones will never be more than seven dollars per carat.

Most of the traders I encounter while meeting Hassan, leave disappointed. They are not prepared to give their riches away for a song and a smile.

Better save it for a later day, explains Desiré Ebua. Ebua chairs an organisation of middlemen. They are the ones who buy the precious stones from the individual miners sweating away in deep pits. 'Hassan has himself to blame for the state of his business. He offers too little and so destroys the market.'

Even in times of war, few are willing to spend months on end in the jungle for more than peanuts. The war has brought militias and armies to the bush, and most of the soldiers have difficulty appreciating the hard work of ordinary men. Miners gathering enough stones to warrant a journey back into the city, risk robbery at the hands of military. Commanders in charge of areas where diamonds are mined have befriended dealers in the capitals of Rwanda, Uganda or the Central African Republic and steer the flow of diamonds towards their own mates, in exchange for kickbacks. Not much is left for Hassan.

The monopolist remains stoic in the midst of this tight squeeze. Life has been worse for him. He was born in Sierra Leone, a paradise for anyone 'addicted' to the sparkling gems. That's where he learnt the tricks of the trade.

'I just love those precious stones with all of my heart and all of my soul. If ever I would have to go back to Beirut because no country in Africa will have me anymore – if I really had to go there, I'd be a diamond cutter. They're in my blood, those damned stones.'

Diamonds and Africa run through Hassan's veins. This is the continent where he was born, this is where he learnt to wheel and deal, to make great numbers of friends while limiting the number of enemies. This is where life taught him to survive, if at times only by the skin of his teeth. Lebanese are to be found everywhere in West Africa; they are the middlemen, the traders, the builders. They buy and sell stuff no one else risks importing, or knows where to find for acceptable prices. A Bounty Bar or a Mars Bar near the front line? You can bet your life there's a Lebanese nearby.

The Lebanese stayed when the British, the French, the Belgians and the Portuguese left. The number of Lebanese worldwide is estimated to total around fifteen million, of whom only four million reside in Lebanon.

Hassan: 'The Phoenicians were our ancestors. Moving about and taking risks is what our genes dictate.'

Life in Africa in times of war can be risky, Hassan acknowledges. He lost a 24-year-old friend, who was mugged and killed for the fifteen thousand dollars he carried on him. 'Life becomes dirt-cheap.' Hassan shrugs his shoulders, and asks his staff to bring him a new tin of cheese.

His black employees obey his orders like the lackeys of a monarch. They kneel down. They whisper. One prepares a water pipe. Hassan will throw a wink at his fiancée with whom he has a child. She numbs her feelings by drowning herself in shows brought from far away by satellite TV.

Being a diamond merchant in Kisangani has proven to be a pitiful endeavour, especially compared to life in his beloved Freetown. 'Stones in Sierra Leone are amongst the best in the world – so much more appealing than the ones I'm offered here. Pure. Big.' But the civil war in Sierra Leone is too much for Hassan, hardened though he is.

'Rebels chop off legs and hands of innocent people. It ain't that bad here, yet. I know what destruction and decay is all about, and yes, Kisangani falls prey to both. Yet, this city still comes close to paradise when you compare it to other places. I will only leave the day the flow of diamonds from the jungle has dried up completely. Or the day I can no longer find cheese anywhere in town anymore. All I need to make a living are a pair of tweezers, a magnifier and a sensitive weighing scale.'

Taki Malamas and André Gerasimau fill the two ashtrays in no time. They smoke while drinking; they smoke while eating a sandwich. In the meantime, they muse endlessly in the Club Hellenique. The last of the Mohicans.

Wooden tables, shaky chairs. Posters of the motherland adorn the walls of the Club. Photos of rows and rows of olive bushes and white houses with blue window frames. A Greek flag hangs from a nail. Plastic vines finish off the work of interior decorators.

Nostalgia binds the men. To Greece, to the Club Hellenique and to each other. Beer helps them forget what they originally dreamt, all those years ago when they tried their luck in Congo. A desire for *ouzo* has vanished. Why dream the impossible? Malamas and Gerasimau have no plans to leave.

'No money,' Gerasimau laments.

'Married to a Congolese,' Malamas growls.

The two sports fields in front of the Club await better days. The goal posts look dangerous. The lights in the Greek church burn day and night. The portraits of Greek orthodox saints hang at sixes and sevens on the wall. Just before he left, the last clergyman dropped off the key for the padlock behind the bar of the Club.

Gerasimau: 'I go there, make my cross and say my prayers. What else is there to go for, without a priest?'

It was Greeks like Malamas and Gerasimau who took over the empty slots left behind by the Belgians. Plantation owners, tradesmen and those in transport were able to make a good living, for a while.

'Don't be fooled by what Belgians might say. It was us, the Greeks, who built this city,' Yani Giatros says jokingly on a tour through the city.

The slow but undeniable descent into chaos makes life tough, however. Twenty years ago, it took fifteen hours to travel the distance between Kisangani and the city of Isiolo in the north,

Malamas: 'That's only a faint memory. It'll probably take you two weeks now, if you get through at all. The rain forest has taken back what humans stole from her decades earlier. This way it's impossible to sell your coffee. By the time the truck reaches the border, your beans are rotten.'

According to businessman Giatros, life in the early 1970s was good. 'Then came the first nationalisations and Mobutu's lackeys went around staking their claims. In 1974, it became obligatory to dance every morning for half an hour to honour the president. Does it surprise you that many then left?'

Despite the present hardships, Giatros does not foresee himself packing any day soon. 'I will only leave once it really has become too dangerous.' He has a talent for making a buck anywhere, everywhere and at any time.

'You have to adjust to the logic of Congo, which is that there is no logic. A Dutchman would never survive here; you are way too logical – without logic, you crumble. Everything here has its own dynamics; play with it, as cleverly as you can.'

Post Script

Elections in July 2006 brought the war to an end. For the first time in over forty years, ordinary Congolese had a say in their future. During those elections, Taki Malamas, Yani Giatros and André Gerasimau still resided in Kisangani. None of them had any desire to leave. Kisangani is their home. Evangelos Valavanis, the man who travelled on the back of a cycle for two months through the jungle, now lives in Athens. His friends bought him a one-way ticket so that, when his time comes, he can die in his beloved city. 'He is still alive, as far as I know,' said Malamas.

Bikers perform stunts with their machines on a tarmac road just outside a camping area near Hartbeespoort, north of Johannesburg. Police vehicles drive up and down with their lights flashing, trying to maintain some kind of order. Someone shouts at them, 'Get lost, spoilsports!'

Burning rubber, bangs of backfiring engines, men with beer bottles, gorgeous women. Those are some of the keywords at the motorbike rally. A South African bikers' magazine organised the weekend.

'You hear the siren?' asks Rex Makhubela (50). 'Booze and bikes. Bound to go wrong. You'll hear more of those today.' Rex ('family names are for bosses only') is the leader of the Eagles from Soweto, the huge township close to Johannesburg. It says so on the back of his leather jacket, in big letters: President. On the front of his jacket, he wears a collection of badges from all the rallies he has visited over the years

The Eagles was the first black biker club in Africa. Almost everywhere on the continent, bikes are for couriers and losers only. Couriers use them to escape traffic jams and deliver their parcels quickly and smoothly. 'Real men' buy cars – big cars if they see themselves as 'very important'.

The motorbike conquered Soweto in the 1980s. Black men no longer rode boosted little scooters but brought in heavy machines of a thousand cc and more.

Rex only accepts a maximum of twenty-five members to his club. 'Otherwise it'll become a mess.' They are a close-knit group of black men who make enough money to buy an expensive motorbike and maintain it, as well as take it out on rallies. Soweto's youngsters love it: banging exhausts, shining chrome, tyres that shriek and smoke when you accelerate.

They drive Hondas, Harleys and Suzukis. Dressed in bandanas, bleached jeans, leather jackets and gloves. The Eagles seem to be the men my mother warned me against. In reality, they once posed for a Sowetan poster campaign against sexual and domestic violence: 'Real men don't beat.'

'We want to improve our image,' explains Rex when we meet again, a few months later. I am spending a few days in Soweto with the 24-year-old Thami Nkosi – born and raised in this huge settlement southwest of

Johannesburg – to get an idea of masculinity and male friendships in South Africa's biggest 'township'. There are numerous newspaper reports about guys killing their partners and the rape of girls. And some say AIDS is rampant here.

An estimated three to four million people live in Soweto. The township was established in the early 20th century to house cheap migrant labour for the gold mines around Johannesburg. This is where black South Africans wrote their history. It is here where Nobel laureates Nelson Mandela and Desmond Tutu lived, where the cadres of the African National Congress met and designed their sketch for a non-racial South Africa.

This is also the place where schoolchildren demonstrated on 16 July 1976 against the introduction of Afrikaans as the main language of education; they were shot at by the apartheid police force, and some were killed.

These days Soweto is the cradle of funky South African arts. Musicians, poets, painters and post-apartheid thinkers find their roots here.

By now the most important political battle has been won and many youngsters are no longer interested in the stories of resistance and heroism told by their parents. They are growing up in a new era, in an environment in which unemployment is their biggest enemy.

Thami is a member of 'Men as Partners', a group of young men trying to break the vicious cycles they see around them. While unemployment leads to problems like crime, violence and alcohol abuse, these problems in turn lead to further unemployment. In August 2005, Thami was invited to speak at a session of parliament about his work. He spoke passionately about love, friendship, personal responsibility and manhood.

'I had no role models that were of any use to me. My father was a womaniser and an alcoholic. He died of AIDS. I never really knew him because he left even before I was born. I only met him seventeen years later. He died shortly after. My uncles are the same. "Be tough," they tell me. "Stand up for yourself." Only if you make a living through crime and have two, three or four girlfriends do they consider you a man. I don't want to lead that kind of life. It leads to no good. I saw my mother suffering. Is this how I want to treat my girlfriend or, later, my wife? No thank you.'

AIDS, domestic violence, and sexual violence. Present-day family life in Soweto has its problems. Many relationships between men and women seem to be casual. The causes can be traced back to the days when gold mines began importing labourers from hundreds of miles away. They came by the thousands: men leaving their families behind because accommodation at the mines did not allow women. A few times a year a miner returned to his wife and children. Miners found girlfriends in the area where they lived and worked.

The lifestyle of these labourers created a new culture in which old traditions of responsibility and fatherhood no longer seemed valid. The men came to Johannesburg to earn money under extremely harsh circumstances, ripped away from family and customs.

'These days the young men are still circumcised in extensive rituals and procedures,' summarises social worker Zolile Cwahi, 'but no one can explain to the young men what it means to be a man any more. They slaughter the cow, but only a few remember that this was meant as an honouring of ancestors. No one can recall the original meaning of manhood; and no one seems to be able to offer a definition that suits modern times.'

Thami sits next to me. I look at him. With a sharp nod of his head, he acknowledges what Cwahi has been saying.

'What are traditions?' Cwahi asks. 'What is modern? It is all mixed. What is useful, what is not? You have to figure it all out on your own, find out what works for you and what doesn't. And in the meantime you have to make a living – either way. It's not easy to be young in Soweto. Or a man, for that matter.'

Cwahi describes how parents hardly talk to their children about urgent topics. On a daily basis he receives young people in his office, in need of clarification and answers their parents are unable to give them. Their most important issue: how to trust someone else in this thing called love? How do you know when someone is just playing games with you, and when someone is serious?

'They aren't used to honest and open conversations. Never in their lives have they spent time around a table discussing their issues, or asked older people for advice. Never will a parent tell his child, "Sit down kid, I need to talk to you about my life and what happened in it. I want you to learn from my mistakes." They fear losing their children's respect. So they keep silent, and let their children be uncertain about life.'

Cwahi sees how a new generation slowly reaches maturity. More and more young people are setting new rules, like Thami does. These youngsters are both men and women, most of whom have seen parents or uncles and aunts stumble and fall.

'They are,' Cwahi says, 'determined to make different choices.' They know about HIV/AIDS. They have tasted some of the temptations of a life of crime, drugs and booze. They still seek new role models – different from the American 'gangsta' rappers or the criminals in their neighbourhood, speeding off in stolen cars.

'The biggest favourite is the BMW 328i,' Thami says knowingly. 'It spins best when you pull the hand brake at full speed.'

Darkness sets in when Thami and I join Rex in his living room. Rex calls for his daughter – 'What's her name again? Oh yes, Gladys' – in the kitchen. 'Be a darling and switch on the light please.' Through the opened doorway I see his wife, his two sons and one of his two daughters. He does not introduce me to them – he is the man of the house after all. 'The horse that pulls the cart,' he says, 'the bull that leads the herd.'

We are talking about the reputation of his Eagles. 'People see the bikes; they see us all dressed up. They think we are out to pick a fight, or that we are criminals. Of course, those bikers do exist. We call them the 'ducktails'. They are the heavy guys; men flirting with death, crime and evil. We are different. If I don't stick to the law, I'll be arrested. I will then lose my job. Tell me, who will pay for my bike when I am unemployed? Who will provide for my family? How can I visit rallies? I am a biker, not a gangster.'

He laughs out loud – his logic is rock solid. Break the law, and you'll lose the love of your life.

Rex's living room is an example of what a home looks like for middle-class South Africa. On his coffee table lies a crocheted cloth. His television is tucked away in a cupboard of shiny veneer. Photos in soft focus of his wife and his children decorate the walls.

He makes money as a mechanic – taught himself the trade. He did go to school for a while, but his parents lacked the cash for further schooling. Rex had to work to keep his parental household going. He made one and a half rand in six weeks as a farm labourer.

'That is when I learned the meaning of "taking responsibility." No one will do it for you. Only I can make my life.'

The bikers of Soweto are a strange mix of ultimate machismo and extreme bourgeoisie. They cherish their homes, their furniture and their families. 'I am a real family man,' Rex can't stop saying with a self-satisfied grin.

At the same time they love their drinks, their freedom and their bikes. 'I need that bike to relax, to get away from it all. On my bike, I am my own king, master of my universe.' Again he calls into the kitchen. 'Why haven't you brought the tea yet? Our visitors have been here for over half an hour!'

His bike is his safety valve. That's how he lets off steam and forgets his worries at work or at home. 'Honour and pride sometimes make it difficult to talk, you see. I might just be too upset about something to talk it over. My sense of honour might be so disturbed that I know, now is the time to go for a ride, before bad gets to worse. Coming home after a ride, I have regained my senses. That's when I am ready to talk.'

Rex has come to an agreement with his wife, Anna (46), a teacher. She complained about the cost of his expensive hobby. Now he hands her a fixed amount of money from his salary, in a sealed and discrete envelope.

'She knows how much I make. Whenever twenty rand is missing from the envelope, she'll tap me on the shoulder.' What he makes by doing overtime, he gets to keep for himself and his bike.

Rex's major worry is how to keep his children on the straight and narrow. Temptation is all around. Crime and free, unprotected sex. He struggles with the challenges of youth.

'In days gone by, no one spoke about sex. But the world has changed. I cannot afford to stay silent. I know I should talk about sex, rape, AIDS. When my sons are old enough, I will – if I really have to. My wife will have to work on my daughters. Whenever she goes to church she hears: "Women, be careful." I don't go to church; I am too young to waste my time.'

Rex roars with laughter.

Thami takes me along, the next day, to meet some of his friends: Dibaba (23) and Jabu (27). He wants to show me how they spend their days. They still live with their parents, are both well educated and unemployed.

The TV is on, it is late morning. Often they kill time by pacing the streets, visiting friends or playing a game; or they work on plans for a grand future.

'To be very honest, most of the time I am bored to death,' Jabu says. Dibaba spends his time refining the business plans for a store in exclusive men's wear. 'Dunhill, Boss – that type of clothing. Clothes for the man who knows what he wants.'

'Who is that man, and what does he want?' I ask Dibaba.

He takes his time to formulate an answer. I glance around his home, and absorb what I see. It is a simple house, built with bricks, with a spacious kitchen and a comfortable lounge. Everything has its own place: the art on the wall, and the pictures of family members in the open cupboards.

The house is in a permanent state of construction, like so many other houses in Africa are hardly ever finished. Someone always has plans for an extension, or an upgrade – whenever money is available. Jabu and Dibaba's parents want to do something with the bedrooms. Just in case the family grows.

Dibaba has found his answer. 'That man takes responsibility for himself, he provides for his family. An African man is in charge, does what he has to do to feed those close to him.'

Jabu chips in immediately. 'When you live in Soweto, and you have no job or income, then you are not really a man. No matter how old you are, if you cannot take care of yourself you become a boy again. Being unemployed castrates you – you are no longer a man.'

This castration is felt worst in matters of the heart. Most women, both have noticed, are not the least bit interested in ambitions, talents or subtleties. 'Many talk of "love" the moment you have money in your pocket, the moment you can take them to fancy places or buy them expensive clothing. Most women aren't interested in *you*; they are interested in your money. It's tough to find a woman who is able to look beyond that.'

Dibaba found a girlfriend with a different outlook. She stays, even now, while he has no work. 'It is all about communication and observation.'

Both men explain how an unemployment-inspired castration seduces many to step into crime. Friends ogle you, show you their easily obtained wealth and challenge you to come on one of their raids. The *amakenza* are the men who have made it, even without a job. They steal cars, have numerous girls, obtain 'respect', and lead a comfortable life.

Jabu seems to have drowned in his soapie on television while Dibaba speaks. 'You point at something, grab it – no explanation, no complicated job interviews. You take care of yourself. But afterwards it starts to nibble at you, that is, if you have any conscience left. The guilt, the shame.'

Fast money, the brothers have learned, does not exist without demanding its price. As you choose your friends, you choose your future. Will you join those who drown their sorrow in a *shebeen*, or do you find friends who will stick around while you are walking a difficult road?

At the rally in Hartbeespoort, Rueben Matlapeng (35) checks the chicken legs and the sausage on the grill. The fragrance of fried meat fills the air. Two bikers pour themselves another brandy in metal cups and add coke. 'You haven't really drunk anything as long as the bottle isn't empty.'

Rex and his friends have chosen the farthest corner of the campsite to set up their tents. It's after two in the afternoon. Their bikes rest, beer bottles lie strewn all over the ground.

The only ones visiting the Eagles are black bikers from neighbouring countries. They're called 'independents': guys who haven't signed up with a club, because there simply aren't enough bike lovers around to form one.

White men stare at the black bikers. Blacks and bikes don't go together in their perception. Some black South Africans are climbing the ladder of economic success, and are able to gather wealth. They embrace what used to be the exclusive domain of whites – '*slegs vir blankes*'. So too in the world of bikers.

These days, black bikers are accepted at rallies. 'As long as it is before noon,' Rueben smiles. 'After that, everyone has been drinking too much, and everyone's dark nature comes out. It's not clever for us to visit the festival tent then.' He might accidentally bump into someone's girl, or look for too long at someone who might take offence.

'How did you get the bike?' whites will ask. A black man on a Harley; many whites still find it hard to see this as an honest combination. Andries Molise (29) bought his at the Harley shop where he works, in Johannesburg. Wide eyes. Andries doesn't just ride a Harley – he even gets to sell them.

The white bikers' area is permeated with the atmosphere of the old days when Afrikaners ruled this country. They fly their flags of a bygone era on the corners of their tents, and have their wives sew them onto their leather jackets.

The Eagles stick around their own tents and won't explore the rally grounds any further. 'I have no intention of being called a *kaffir*,' Andries laughs. 'That's asking for trouble. I used to respond. I'd say, "*Dankie, Baas*" but the fun of that has worn off. It's better to walk away from trouble.'

In the back of Rex's tent, Arnie and Line cuddle and try to sleep off yesterday's intoxication. Rueben pours himself another brandy 'n coke, while Rex eats his chicken.

Rueben pays tribute to the joys of riding a bike: 'The freedom of wind in your hair – you on the road – the power in that one hand that holds the throttle – the amazed stare of bystanders – your exhaust making a banging sound – the silence when you stop in the middle of nowhere and you switch off your engine. When I am not on my bike, I think about my bike. Goose-flesh is what I get.'

Rueben compares his lifestyle to that of his forefathers. Getting out there, sleeping in a tent, washing yourself in a small stream or in the rain, and seeing what's beyond the horizon. 'This used to be our way of life. Tents. A fire. Sleeping under the stars. Brotherhood. Talking long into the night. We do what our ancestors did.'

Rueben looks away, contemplates what he has just said and concludes, 'The only difference is: we have bikes!' He laughs at this insight and winks. 'Maybe I am just a boy who will never grow up.'

He drives a Honda, chopper style. At the ends of the grips he has tied long leather straps. As the afternoon progresses he will ride it in circles, dressed in the satin underwear of a girlfriend with a bandana wrapped around his head. A friend gets on behind him, and grabs Reuben by his imaginary tits.

The Eagles are good friends first and foremost. Class differences are irrelevant – these are men with a shared passion. Paychecks are minor details. Some have made it into the new elite of South Africa. They have good jobs, luxurious cars and expensive houses in gated communities where a barrier blocks unwanted people from accessing the area. Others still live in Soweto.

'We play about, compare bikes and try other people's machines out,' says Rueben. 'And we talk about stuff we would not easily talk about with outsiders.' Amongst the Eagles, he is the odd one out, being from the town of Rustenburg and all. He makes his living at a mining company, managing the storeroom.

'Men don't easily talk to each other about problems, let alone about love,' he says. 'Bikers, however, do. They talk condoms, kids and marriages. These are my friends – I can talk about home, my plans to get married or the company I want to start.' After a few drinks, they'll also talk about women, and how everything has changed.

Rueben and Rex have taken their seats in one of the tents, the cooler box full of drinks within easy reach. Rex pulls on the metal cord on his belt and finds his metal cup. Another brandy 'n coke. Outside, their friends laugh out loud.

Rueben: 'We often talk amongst ourselves about the changes we see taking place, changes in our relationships to our girlfriends or to our wives. Women have equal rights these days; that is what the law states. Fine, no worries there. Why should a woman have fewer rights than a man? But you know what? No one ever spoke about how to do things from now on, what is going to change, and what women expect *men* to do now. And that is where the problems arise. As a man you can say nothing anymore or ask anything. Women complain. Bitterly and loudly. About us, men. It wears me out. It seriously does.'

Rex looks out over the campsite, raises his metal mug and thanks his friend for wise words spoken.

A big poster hangs in the living room of biker Alfred Avhashoni Matamela's home in Soweto. It's his church group – Zion. 'Other Eagles call me the "Preacher". I like my nickname.' His house too is under construction. Corrugated iron plates form the roof, supported by strong rafters. Electrical wires are fed into plastic tubes hanging from the ceiling.

Alfred apologises for the mess. 'I already bought a plot of land to move to after my retirement – a place where I can grow potatoes in peace, and keep a few cows to help me through my old days.'

The tarmac in front of his house in the neighbourhood of Pimville in Soweto is decorated with big black circles. Here he practises stunts. Small boys applaud him, and try to whistle through their fingers.

'The bike is my ideal stress-buster. The moment I feel it come up, I go for a ride around the block. Having my exhaust make exploding sounds really relieves me. The sense of freedom – that is what it is all about. There are so many more ways of finding relief apart from going to a shebeen and getting drunk.'

Performing stunts on his bike is his favourite pastime. Once he passed a minibus on the highway, filled with bored passengers. In the lane next to theirs he jumped on his saddle and performed for them. 'Slowly their faces came alive again.'

Alfred combines his hobby with his strict sense of religion. For him there are no contradictions between the two. His leather jacket has many emblems, one of which reads, 'If Jesus were alive today, He would be a biker.' Others say, 'If u miss heaven, what in hell will you do?' and 'Can't cope? Jesus offers hope.' At rallies he is a lonely prophet, which is fine with him. He combines his passion with his mission.

No one recognises him at church on Sunday, dressed in his Sunday best. His neighbours know Alfred by his jackets and bandanas, not by the tie and suit in which he praises his source of inspiration.

In the past he had to do without a bike for five years in a row. His wife just hated the machine. Too dangerous, and too uncomfortable. Alfred had to buy a car, she demanded. He gave in. The restlessness set in, quickly. Something was missing.

'It became too much. I just had to have a bike again.' He suggested to his wife, 'What if you get your driver's license and you take the car, so I can ride a bike again?' During one of his rides he met the Eagles. They were doing their stunts, and he wanted to learn. They quickly became friends. 'They are part of my identity now, of who I am.'

The religious biker grew up without a father. He passed away when Alfred was still a toddler. His mother sent him to an uncle in Johannesburg to oversee his education. 'He taught me first and foremost to be respectful – that became the core of everything else.' Respect for his elders, his children and his wife.

His biological father had four wives, his uncle only had one. 'I do not want to live like my father lived. It just won't work anymore, with all those women and those kids. To offer them what they need in this world. Life is expensive; raising a child is expensive. I hear friends say, "It's our culture to have many wives and girlfriends." I think they just need excuses to live without discipline and restraint. They want it all; everything but a reprimand.'

Alfred had hoped his own son would be the successor whom he could give everything his father could never give him. 'I decided he was to get all my bike accessories. Helmet, regalia, jackets, bike.'

But it was not to be. A disease struck his son down. 'I am still praying for acceptance.'

The moon shines on the camp area of Hartbeespoort. The Eagles dance in the light of their headlights, next to tiny tents. In the main party tent of the rally the master of ceremonies announces the pageants for the evening: Miss Impala and Miss Body Beautiful. The Eagles decline. Too risky, at this hour, to mingle.

The gorgeous white women are eager to compete for the titles. Spurred on by hundreds of howling white men they show themselves in their most seductive poses. One candidate finds her boyfriend in the front row, and smiles erotically at him as best she can. He challenges her to show her breasts and bum: 'Yeah, baby!'

All day long the bikers admired bikes, they tinkered with keys and spanners, they opened throttles to maximise the RPMs and to hear their engines scream and whine. Now is the time for female beauty, soft skins and round curves. They want to see strings, tits and nipple piercings.

Early next morning a roaring engine wakes the Eagles.
'Time to wake up, lazy buggers!'
Andries grabs a beer for breakfast.
Rex toasts with a brandy.

The tropical shower pours down in a dark night. Loudspeakers drone with a heavy bass. A party. Liquor flows. Bodies move – a hormonal soup in the pressure cooker of a tropical night.

She seductively moves her hips, wraps her arms around his neck and grinds. He winks, fetches her drink, and grabs her waist. She throws her head back and waves her long blond curls.

People in their thirties, let loose in a post-conflict area somewhere in Africa. So feminine, so masculine. Stories mingle.

'I am ready to live a normal life, but you need to know I make many demands.'

'No, nothing is negotiable.'

'I want to leave.'

'Your scent excites me.'

'I want to linger.'

'Your scent repels me.'

'You are the perfect present, a gift from the gods, but I simply cannot do it. My fears reign; they are with too many.'

'I need a man who can take care of me like my father took care of me.'

'We don't make love, we make magic.'

'Men do not know how to tame me … I am looking for a sperm donor. Do you want a child too?'

Ever more ingredients are added to the soup. More vodka, more fishy stories. The clock ticks away. The rain stops. The rain starts again. Thick, spluttering drops. Is it love? Is it lust?

A taxi drives me back to my hotel. Torn wipers scrape the windscreen. The streets are empty and silent; generators have been turned off. It's too dark to see potholes. Somewhere in this city people dance: amorously, lovingly, lustily, lonely.

The tantric healer massages my feet and my hands. Her fingers rub hard over the skin on my head. The scent of incense fills my nostrils. I hear the wind bang against the window, bringing rain. Her touch brings back years-old memories. I was unaware they still lingered.

'Sexuality centres on the crucial question: "Who are you?",' a reverend in Botswana once said. 'Who are you as a person, what are your feelings, your dreams, and your hopes? Everything that makes you into you defines your sexuality. That's intense.'

The healer rubs and massages. She scans my body and remains silent. Although I am not naked, I feel more exposed than I care to remember, more vulnerable than during any of the wars I have reported on.

'Did you shout enough, after you found out about the affairs?' she wants to know. 'You have to roar like a lion; it helps you get rid of this old toxin.'

I wonder how something so pleasurable can also be this complicated?

The natural surroundings of a canyon in Hell's Gate national park in Kenya will forgive me, weeks later, for my yell. I warn my brother who is with me about the roar that is bubbling up inside me. Once I feel the high point of my scream, resonating in my solar plexus, I touch old emotions. The roar sets them free, so they can evaporate. While the echo of my yell rumbles in my ears, I prepare for a second one.

Until a voice from afar calls loudly. 'Is everything okay? Any problem down there?' I search above me on the cliffs and shout back, 'No problem, I'm fine. Thank you.'

Water from the hot springs steams as the stream falls down into the canyon. Dark green algae grow where the water hits sandstone. Again the voice.

'You sure? That cry of yours; it really sounded bad.' I trace the sound back to its origin and see, tens of metres above me, a Masai warrior on a ledge. A walking stick in his hand. His right foot placed up on his left thigh. A chequered bright red cloth wrapped around his shoulders. Immaculate English.

'What is the problem?'

I choose to swallow my remaining roar.

He watches carefully from his post as I climb up, sweating and sighing. Once we are within each other's reach, he looks me straight in the eye, and offers a hand. 'Daniel Olekesoto, pleased to meet you.'

———————

I have rarely seen public displays of affection in Africa. In between garbage and staring goats, uninvited eyes stare uncomfortably and sharp comments cut deep.

According to Sobonfu Somé in her book *The spirit of intimacy* (1997), relationships open when doors are closed, curtains are dropped and the fire smoulders. For the most, however, love is a practicality, a co-operation necessary to beget children and offer them a viable future as part of a bigger community.

According to an African saying, it takes a village to raise a child. Somé adds that it also takes a village to keep parents mentally healthy. The belief in the nuclear family as the cornerstone of society hardly exists in Africa. Circumstances do not allow 'going it alone'. Here everyone is responsible: everyone for everyone, and no one exclusively for themselves. Thinking of one's own direct blood relatives as the only safety net is a dangerous hindrance and seriously insufficient. What if a mother dies or a father disappears?

In Africa's large networks of the extended family, your aunt is also your mother, and an uncle is also your father. They may discipline you, and you may ask them for advice and assistance. They may command you to fetch their water, you may beg for a contribution for your school fees.

Women, Somé explains, maintain their own social webs and they enjoy their own privileges. And men, too, have their specific rhythms, their own tasks, and their own set of social obligations.

'Better' or 'other halves' are grandiloquent Western perceptions of love that are alien to Africa. Few fairy tales here dare to mention princesses woken up by noble princes, after which they live happily ever after. Even fairy tales need a minimum amount of credibility.

For Somé, sexuality is above all else a shared spiritual exercise of two people; an experience of the bond between an individual and his or her own instincts, deepest motives, hidden powers and spirit – as well as those of the partner.

Somé's words sound paradisiacal. Peaceful. Profound. Esoteric. Maybe love and intimacy work like that in hamlets far from modern life, where survival is only possible through the ties of kinship, friendship and shared economic interests.

However, this idealised, broad-based partnership is rapidly losing its appeal. The village as the centre of life has been evaporating for more than a century, and there is not a lot to replace it.

The nuclear family has shown itself to be way too fragile to bear the day-to-day pressures of African reality.

The smell of fried eggs and sausages fills the bedroom. My hipbones feel sore from a night on a thin mattress. When I open my eyes I see a picture on the nightstand. A young woman, probably a teenager, with her toddler daughter. They hold hands in the garden of a small house.

'Are you awake yet?' Innocent Jili calls me from his kitchen. 'Ready for coffee?'

Through the net curtains I see his friends sitting on the grass in the garden. Some talk, others remain silent. They look around, change positions or lie down. One of them cracks a joke that only makes the joker laugh. The others don't get it.

It's a Saturday. The young men are waiting for today's football game to start. They won't play today; they'll only watch.

'Waiting for better times,' is what they call their unemployed status. They fill their days playing football, doing chores, running errands, visiting friends and talking. Lots of talking.

After breakfast I greet Thula, Thando and Sifiso. Thula lies stretched out on the grass, dealing with a *babalas* (a hangover) after yesterday's pub-crawl in Ashdown, a township of Pietermaritzburg. He drank seven pints on a near empty stomach.

The crawl started innocently, in a little shop where the lady owner kept her cash register as well as her liquor behind grills. Thula and Thando played pool. In the second pub teenagers drank from bottles and danced seductively. The tougher characters from the neighbourhood spun their cars around the roundabout, hanging from windows with beer bottles in their hands.

The aged owner looked suspiciously at his customers, fearing for his bar furnishings, but he was still content enough to keep providing booze. As long as his customers paid and no one attempted to destroy the grills between him and them, he was not too worried.

Next stop on the crawl was the illegal shebeen, TwentyFour, where the kwaito star Zola barked his way into eardrums from huge speakers in a tiny room. Girls and boys danced. Girls seduced boys, boys seduced girls. Hands roamed freely over bodies that would disappear through a door in the back, to return fifteen minutes later, adorned with naughty smiles and sparkling eyes.

For Innocent Jili, Sifiso, Thando and Thula it was a normal Friday evening. A night during which the wheat is sifted from the chaff, the men from the woosies. There are only two types of men, one bar-hopper explained to me. Those who booze it up, flirt and fuck as if there is no AIDS-epidemic – known by their nickname *cruisers*. And those who do everything in measured ways, knowing when to stop.

'You simply switch off your brain,' Jili comments cynically about the cruisers. 'You pretend there is no tomorrow and live for today. And when tomorrow does come, you do what you did today all over again.' Booze and sex, *babalas* and STDs – many of the youths in Ashdown seem to be stuck in this vicious circle.

The young men in Jili's garden are conscious of the cycle, and look for ways to escape it, afraid of the consequences they know only too well. Even today, the neighbourhood has had to erect a tent just a few blocks away for yet another funeral. Another dead, another wake, another burial.

Friends, acquaintances and relatives arrive in small groups at the house where the white tent provides shelter today. Plastic garden seats, plastic tables. And a coffin. 'Every day we see people die because of AIDS,' Thula says.

'AIDS is about who is on top. It is about power, passion and orgasm. AIDS is about satisfying women sexually. As long as we dodge these issues, we are only talking about the side-effects and not the heart of the matter.'

Gethwana Makhaye is unusually direct. She is the head of the organisation Targeted Aids Interventions based in Pietermaritzburg, and doesn't like beating around the bush. A third of the sexually active population in KwaZulu-Natal is infected with HIV. 'Beating around the bush is a luxury no one can afford.'

Just like some of the other cultures in South Africa, the Zulu culture wrestles with some of the latest and most radical changes in which the old has lost its meaning and value, and no one yet knows what 'the new' is supposed to entail. Family structures have fallen apart. Unemployment, crime, AIDS and even the new liberal constitution undermine the foundations of a people. Large-scale unemployment (estimated to be around 40 per cent) especially deprives men of a sense of dignity. What society tells them to do – to provide – is not possible. And those men who *do* have jobs work far away from families and loved ones, often for weeks or even months on end. Migrant labour has had a devastating effect on the ways men and women relate.

Perceptions of sexuality and of male-female relationships are largely to blame for the scale of the epidemic, according to Makhaye. 'When I started working with AIDS ten years ago, we went out to teach the women to use condoms. We also taught them to dare to say "No" to their husbands.'

But decisions around the use of condoms, or the whens and ifs of sexual intercourse, are not made by women, Makhaye began to realise. Those decisions are mostly taken by men, most of whom regard using a rubber as unacceptable.

'If culture dictates women to obey their husbands or boyfriends, then it is not enough to only educate women. If power resides in men, then they need to be confronted and educated.'

To facilitate that change of course, Makhaye and her co-workers had to make a radical shift and abandon some of their own beliefs. 'Thinking that "all men are useless, all men are thick, all men are evil" doesn't work. It is essential to find the exceptions to the rule, and work with them. Men who do shed a tear when an eighteen-year-old daughter dies of AIDS are the vanguard of the kind of men we need to halt the epidemic.'

Makhaye targets younger men. She has given up trying to alter the ways of those older than twenty. 'Their opinions on sexuality, romance and power are too engrained to be able to change them. I am sorry to say, but the older generations are lost – all we can do is sow the seeds for a future recovery.'

Makhaye works with young football players, whom she sees as an alternative to the *omatlisa*, young guys with 'bling' and expensive cars, who pick up girls from schools and who seduce them with promises of cell phones in exchange for sex. 'Romance,' some of the girls believe. 'A quick and easy fuck,' is what the *omatlisa* want.

Young football-players like Thule, Thando, Jili and Sifiso are some of the idols of the neighbourhood. *Sekwanele Bafowethu* ('enough is enough') is their team. They are eager to make a statement, to show that being young and popular can also be defined in different, more constructive ways.

A generation has got lost. Structures erode rapidly. What do the Zulus have to fall back on?

Some outsiders regard the Zulu culture as one of the most conservative in South Africa when dealing with issues of sexuality. Others argue that Zulu culture was traditionally relatively liberal towards intimacy and even issues like homosexuality.

In his contribution to the book *Men Behaving Differently* (2005), anthropologist Mark Hunter describes how love, marriage and sexuality have developed over the past two centuries in KwaZulu-Natal. The starting point, he writes, is the kraal. He who was able to afford his own yard and his own cattle, could also gather wives. Wives provided labour and children, which allowed him to have even more cattle. Eventually a successful man would be honoured with the title *umnumzana*, man of huts, cattle, wives and children.

It was up to a young man to find a delicate balance between popularity, ridicule and envy. Popular men were called *isoka*, best translated as a ladies' man or Casanova. Too many girlfriends carried the label *isoka lamanyala*: dirty womaniser. Having no girlfriends turned a man into an *isishimane*, someone too afraid to talk to women. In the early stages of romance men and women did play around sexually, but had to limit themselves to so-called thigh sex to prevent the hymen from breaking – a broken hymen would lead to scandal, outrage and forced marriage.

When migratory labour split families in KwaZulu-Natal in the course of the 19th and 20th century, social manners changed drastically. Men left their yards to earn money in mines and on commercial farms often hundreds of miles away. Some women earned their own income as maids.

Migrants found new pleasures and romance with new girlfriends, and abandoned the old practice of thigh sex. They went all the way, with pregnancies and sexually transmitted diseases as some of the consequences. Men without regular income found it increasingly difficult to find women interested enough in them to take things further.

On the other hand, women who were left behind often found a 'lid' (a lover) without abandoning their 'pot' (husband). These days, a growing group of women, especially in the cities, find few reasons to get married; they stand on their own two feet and prefer to live a life without coercion or subservience to a man.

The heroic title *isoka* has lost its shine, especially due to the rapid spread of HIV. In this day and age an *isoka lamanyala* refers to a man with AIDS. And young men with many girlfriends are now labelled an *izinja*, a dog.

'Within Zulu culture it is not done to talk about sex,' says Innocent Jili. 'That makes it hard to find healthy ways of relating, when there is an epidemic raging in your neighbourhood. I want to live, and I want to have sex. Teach me how to combine those two.'

Abstinence is a major pillar in the story Makhaye tells her young football-players. Abstaining from penetration, that is. Not from foreplay, which can be hundred percent safe. 'Why enjoy a few seconds of something that could, in the long run, kill you?' Thando asks.

For these young Zulu men searching for a new set of rules pertaining to sexuality, mutual respect is the keyword. They want sex that leaves not just the guy, but the girl satisfied as well. 'I want to know how to pleasure my girl,' Thule states shyly while his eyes search the ground. Discussing sex and all the details teenage boys are eager to know, is hard. They cannot approach their parents – that would be disrespectful. Amongst friends the topic is usually limited to score keeping: how many have you bedded.

Even for the girls it comes as a bit of a shock when a man asks genuine questions and shows real interest. Not all of them can cope with that, say the young men.

'If a woman cannot deal with my genuine interest in her, than I lose my interest in her quite quickly. I want a relationship with depth, one than can weather the storms.' Thando looks around amongst his friends to see if they agree. A nod here, thumbs up somewhere else.

The young men explain how in the townships of Pietermaritzburg, life is regulated by few rules; respect and dignity are hard to come by. Self-preservation seems to be all that matters. But this has changed for them since they started working with Makhaye's organisation. The many long conversations about relationships, friendship, passion and sexuality have made a mark.

'We have become a band of brothers in which no topic is taboo,' Thando says. That brotherhood seeks to find a new balance between traditions, identity and modernity. 'I am proud of being a Zulu,' Thule states. 'Honour is crucial, and not just male honour. Also the honour of a woman.'

Thule explains how he finds partial inspiration in the life of Shaka Zulu, one of the most important icons of Zulu history, a warrior-king who, through his outstanding insights into strategy in the early 19th century, was able to unite the different Zulu clans.

Two women were crucial in Shaka's life. The first one was his mother, Nandi, who protected him and encouraged him to become the fearsome leader she had seen in his eyes at a very early age. The second woman was Pampata, a friend from his youth who spent her entire life by his side. He always asked these two women for advice and judged them to be his only true confidantes. So much did he feel indebted to them, that he once organised the slaughter of a neighbouring people to avenge what he perceived as an insult to his mother.

Little is known about Shaka's relationships with other women. Although reportedly he often walked around naked to show off his sizeable member, the stories of his sexual endeavours are few and far between. According to some, Shaka never was intimate with a woman. According to others he had an unwanted son killed.

The warrior-king invented radical solutions to keep women away from sex. He collected a great number of virgins whom he had guarded by the ugliest men his kingdom provided. Older women were ordered to safeguard the virgins' purity.

These days the virtue of young women once again dominates the agenda of the Zulu elite. They have reinstated a ritual to check on the virginity of girls, as a means of reigning in the AIDS epidemic. Young men, on the other hand, are free to play and explore.

With his shirt tucked halfway into the trousers of his school uniform, the sixteen-year-old boy runs across his father's yard on his way to the school bus. The moment he spots his dad, he stops, places one foot in front of the other, raises both his hands high up in the air and makes a royal bow to Jowet Mayisela.

'My children still know how to express respect for their parents and their elders', explains Mayisela (62). 'And if they forget, I'll hammer the message home.'

Mayisela is an *induna* (traditional leader) of the village Mafakathini, deep inside the hills of KwaZulu-Natal. Mayisela was appointed shortly after his predecessor had died. 'People voted for me because of the courage I showed during the conflicts of the last days of apartheid.'

A few cows graze amidst geese on Mayisela's yard. Goats graze a few metres away. Potatoes grow on an adjacent plot of land. Mayisela lives in the twilight zone between two eras. He grew up in the traditions of the Zulu and has to defend those as a traditional leader. He dresses in modern clothes, but has his spear and shield ready for those occasions when he needs them to fulfil his role as *induna*. But that role has come under pressure, just like many of Mayisela's convictions.

New values became entrenched in South Africa when, in 1996, the country embraced the most liberal constitution in the world and shook off the last of the reactionary feathers of apartheid. The 'new South Africa' tries to balance the norms and values of a liberal ideology, in a society that consists of numerous cultural and ethnic groups, some of which are still deeply traditional.

The 'new South Africa' tries to protect the poor and underprivileged with the means and machinations of modern times, while at the same time promoting individualism and materialism – aspects of liberal ideology that glorify the law of the jungle. While the constitution tries to safeguard the freedoms of each and every individual based on systems of belief and ideologies from the West, the country as a whole suffers daily from the excesses of that ideology: its radical and ruthless individualism.

The *induna* of Mafakathini still doesn't know what to make of it all, years after the new constitution was introduced. Structures and traditions that held sway for decades or even centuries are falling apart. The elders lack the authority or the means to discipline the young these days. 'We as elders are no longer allowed to discipline the young. Teenagers don't listen anymore, women don't listen anymore. You have to understand, for us, Zulu, a woman is like a child that needs the guidance of a man – you make decisions for her, you have to protect her from the outside world.'

The constitution, with its explicit clauses giving women and children inalienable rights, makes life for conservative people difficult. Mayisela can either conform to the new rules, or dismiss them.

'In our traditions we – the older men – have all the power. In the constitution we are powerless, and the children and women have their own rights. If I were to follow the constitution, I become powerless to do anything to steer my community. That is unacceptable. It is my duty and my task to do everything necessary to fight for the continuation of my group, my family, my clan, and my people.'

Jowet Mayisela leans forward in his rickety chair, outside in the chill morning air. 'How can I do away with my duty to keep everyone in line? Who will keep my sons on the straight and narrow, if I don't do that? Nobody. The traditional leader of Mafakathini must do it. After all, *I* am the man in my home. No one else.'

In the same village, slightly higher up the hill and later on the same day, people have gathered in a small building called 'House of the Ancestors'. The men are seated on the right and the women on the left. That is how it has been since time immemorial. A few women carry babies, tucked away in thick blankets, and have small milk bottles at the ready.

Outside two men are seated on wooden stools; they share a pot of *umqobothi*, homemade beer. They gaze into the valleys, onto far-away hills. A young man chops up wood for a fire that later in the day will be lit inside the House of the Ancestors to chase away the chill. This is the only suitable space for a serious meeting – big enough to house the group, while protected by the energies of their forefathers.

Mafakathini is situated on a high altitude and today the wind is especially cutting. The young man is one of the very few remaining in the village. Just like everywhere else in the province, most men have gone far away to seek a living. Fatherless families make up the majority here.

Only three of the twelve women gathered in the House of the Ancestors have a husband around. The others make do by themselves, either widowed, abandoned or liberated.

'So many accidents, so many illnesses, so much work,' one of them states. Funekile Phoswa (56) tends to a baby in her lap, one of her grandchildren. The father works far away, the mother lies sick in bed.

'We have to live without happiness. The man you found all those years ago, is only a shadow of what he once was. He drinks and sleeps till sunset. Young women rightfully ask themselves: 'I am still young – who will wake me in the middle of the night for some fun and games if my husband no longer seems interested, or doesn't care any longer?'

Her remark elicits loud laughter from the women.

Encouraged by the laughter, Phoswa continues. 'There are two types of men. The first type knows what to do to be a husband and a father. The second type has no clue whatsoever. The last kind of man you won't miss when he is no longer around.'

In the rural areas of KwaZulu-Natal men are absent in the tens of thousands, if not hundreds of thousands. Those who do still roam the hills of Mafakathini are mostly unemployed. Others have dropped out, or died because of AIDS. Sons, fathers, brothers, uncles.

With only a few men around, the young boys grow up without role models in their lives. Unemployment and the emancipation of women nibble at the perceptions men have of themselves. If he is no longer the main provider, what role then is left for him? A great number of men prefer not to wait for the answer and instead leave their families behind. The responsibility for pushing life forward has slowly become the sole responsibility of women.

Sbontile (54) sits in the biggest room of her shack, constructed from simple wooden slats and chipboard. The sun sets outside. For the last fifteen years her husband has lived and worked in Richmond, 140 kilometres away, in a forestry project. 'He keeps telling me he also has to work weekend shifts.' Her eyes show how bored she is with his excuse.

'Once a month he passes by. In the beginning I hated his long absence. I loved him, and wanted to be close to him. And nowadays? Something inside me has died. Gone.'

Sbontile has started to appreciate the liberties she enjoys as a women with a husband who is never around. Her freedoms feed envy amongst other women, whose husbands still come home often. She is able to make her own decisions while they have to await the final approval of their spouses. She tills the land. She selects the schools her children go to. As an independent woman, she can do what she feels is best. 'I do not need anyone's approval anymore. I am free. I am content.'

The following morning life starts at five. A solitary man carries his hand plough to his plot of land. Since the new government brought water to Mafakathini, the girls and women no longer need to spend hours every day collecting water. That task has been eradicated. However, the time that freed up has mostly gone to the last remaining men of Mafakathini. They have told their wives and daughters to take up hard physical work they themselves no longer want to do. On this early morning it is female power ploughing the land, sowing, weeding and collecting firewood.

'What makes a man a man, you want to know?' Jili has to think hard. I told him of my experiences in Mafakathini, just over a hundred kilometres away from Ashdown in Pietermaritzburg.

'Being a man means respecting yourself, knowing where you want to go and charting your course to get there. Taking responsibility for your own life, as well as for the people you are with. When you are a man you need to be able to lead. That means, knowing where to go, admitting your mistakes and adjusting your route.'

Jili and his friends are the odd men out in their neighbourhood. They have chosen a lifestyle others don't dare to follow. They take on responsibilities other men their age run away from as fast as they can. That attitude has created a reputation for the young football players that attracts young women, and lays the foundation for different kinds of relationships.

Thandeke Njilo for example, mother of a young daughter, fell in love with Thando. He adopted her girl, whose father had run a mile even before she was born. Thandeke thinks the world of her man.

'It is almost impossible to find a man like Thando,' she says while we walk through some of the hills around Ashdown. 'Liquor, drugs and sex is what life is all about for most men. Guys have no idea how to have respect for a woman. They think we exist to obey them, to be beaten, cheated on, raped or abused. To tell you the truth, we women can do very well without those kinds of men. Thando and his friends show alternatives. Trust me, every girl I know is intensely jealous of me because of the kind of man I have by my side.'

Makhaye's movement still has a long way to go. The football players of Ashdown are exceptions to the rule. They are out on a quest to find alternatives for the kind of masculinity that has no future. But these young men find themselves limited by many women's perceptions of femininity that are as destructive as male misogyny.

Men and women find themselves stuck in roles and ideas about relationships that keep both chained. Many 'disempowered' women thrive on what they can demand from the men who are interested in them. Many relationships seem to be nothing more than an exchange of services.

Sizwe Noah Mchunu, one of Makhaye's co-workers, drives a decent car. He has a steady job, a reasonable income and a solid reputation. He is in his mid-thirties and has all but given up on ever finding a partner.

'As long as women first want to know what car I drive and where I am parked before they ask me who I am and what I am made off, something is clearly going horribly wrong. As long as my chances with a woman are defined by the size of my car, something is bad to the core in the relationship between men and women. What about the rest of my relationship? I won't be able to survive a relationship in which I pay the bills in exchange for sex.'

Post Script

According to research published in June of 2009 by the Human Sciences Research Council (HSRC), South Africa's HIV prevalence rate stands at 11 per cent. That means that, since 2002, the prevalence has stabilised.

Which is good news.

Also positive is a stiff rise in condom use amongst people in the age group fifteen to twenty-four: from 57 per cent in 2002 to 87 per cent in 2008. Since 2005, HIV prevalence in this age group has come down countrywide with just over 1.5 per cent, from 10.3 per cent to 8.6 per cent. Knowledge about HIV amongst teenagers has doubled over the past three years.

However, when one looks at the different provinces, the various age groups and the difference between men and women, the overall picture does remain distressing. In KwaZulu-Natal, for example, HIV prevalence has shot up 10 per cent amongst people between 15 and 49, to a staggering 25.8 per cent.

They glance around nervously during our conversations, their eyes constantly roaming the surroundings. As soon as waiters come too close or hang around within earshot, they lower their voices or stay silent. Discretion is a suit of steel armour; it is lifesaving, literally. Secrecy, so that no one can harm those who experience the forbidden love between men.

At most, Philadelphia will raise one eyebrow or lift a little finger from the table when another member of The Family enters the establishment, often holding hands with a son or a daughter and with a spouse nearby.

'Many of The Family have come to today's wedding,' he whispers to Williams, his partner. 'Would the groom be one of us? Do you know him?'

The wedding ceremony in the garden of the Chinese hotel Fang Fang is in full swing. Edifying songs are followed by music from American western movies. A country-and-western duet is played; Willy Nelson and Dolly Parton declare their undying love for each other. Waitresses serve spring rolls. A marabou flies over my head, searching for building material for a nest in the middle of Uganda's capital, Kampala.

Guests are offered sodas and juice. The newly-wed, born-again couple will not allow wine, beer or liquor at their party. 'The devil lives inside every bottle,' explains an invitee. Children run around: girls in wide satin skirts and with ribbons in their hair. Boys are dressed in suits that will be too small in a month's time. The bride wears virginal white; her maids of honour are dressed in sober red. The groom is the only one in the crowd to wear a pinstripe suit and a top hat.

The wedding seems straight out of an old edition of the American Bride's Magazine. No trace of original Africa left. Not in the dress code or the choice of flowers. Not in the preference of the deejay. Not in the snacks offered on fake silver plates. Not in the atmosphere, which seems dejected and stiff.

The estrangement is made worse because of all the signs and signals of the coming Christmas. Baubles adorn the restaurant, shiny streamers hang in plastic Christmas trees. Santa Claus with reindeer, sleigh and snow while the mercury touches 30 degrees Celsius this afternoon.

'No, I do not know the groom,' Williams states after studying the wedding guests. With a wink to his love, Philadelphia, he adds: 'Must be an acquaintance of an acquaintance.'

Williams will at times throw jealous looks towards the newly-weds. His eyes tell it all. They are able to declare their love openly, make their vows under the watchful eyes of friends and relatives, and proudly wear a rose in a buttonhole on a wedding day.

Philadelphia laughs at his partner. 'Of the two of us, he is the romantic one. He enjoys it to the full when I come home with flowers or a romantic card. It leaves me completely cold, but if it makes him happy, I gladly do it.' Surreptitiously they squeeze each other's hands.

These two men appear to be opposites. Philadelphia is a medical doctor, Williams is an artist. Williams is soft natured and religious, Philadelphia is rational and eloquent. They have been together for over five years. Most couples in The Family won't last that long.

'Hit and run,' Williams says. 'A short period of lightning and sparks and back you go into your old life.' Most relationships cannot deal with the pressures from outside. 'But when you look around long and hard, you do find other men that have been living together for long. That's when you realise: "Hey – they too …?"'

Philadelphia: 'It is the public shame more than trouble between two people that creates problems.'

I will not ask the homosexual men I meet in Kampala for their real names. The consequences are grave, if their identities were to become known. They'll face a seething rage born of piety, carried by men of the Word. Using nicknames is crucial. Paul for the Catholic councillor (educated in pastoral work and theology) who himself is a celibate homosexual, Philadelphia for the medical doctor, Williams for his partner, Tall for the jurist and Jembo for the happy twenty-something.

Not one of them will invite me to his home. Too dangerous. The neighbours would want to know who the white man was, and what he came for. It would be impossible to give honest answers. Unanswered questions feed speculation, gossip and slander.

Life for a homosexual in Uganda is an existence with two faces, one of which has to be hidden completely from public view. No colleague may know, no friend, no relative. The stigma destroys, the judgement is deadly. We therefore meet in cafés, restaurants or on the streets of Kampala – places where others are too preoccupied to pay attention to us.

'I have told the CID to look for homosexuals, lock them up and charge them,' President Yoweri Museveni said at a conference on issues of African population growth, on 27 September 1999. 'The Bible spells it out clearly that God created Adam and Eve as wife and husband, but not men to marry men.'

Museveni's remarks were welcomed with great applause. Homophobia in Africa is as acceptable to the public as it is to the political elite. President Robert Mugabe of Zimbabwe once compared homosexuals with dogs and pigs. Sam Nujoma of Namibia suggested using special police units to track and 'eliminate' gays and lesbians.

Most African countries have laws explicitly forbidding sexual interactions between adults of the same sex. Lesbians have less trouble in their daily lives than gays do, although in many places men think they can 'cure' a lesbian by subjecting her to the 'treatment' of a gang rape. In Africa, the only country to legally establish the rights of gays and lesbians is South Africa, where homosexual couples have been allowed to get married since late 2006.

Any reference to human rights for homosexuals is usually brushed off. According to Museveni, the values that govern life in Europe and the United States have no place in Africa. Universal rights as laid down in the Charter of the UN 'are not universal for Africa', according to the Ugandan president, because the Charter was written when Europe still ruled the waves.

Some homophobes portray their struggle against homosexuality as a fight against cultural imperialism. For them, romantic love between men and between women is a threat to the African way of life. Many find inspiration for their conviction in the Christian faith – a religion deeply rooted in Greek and Roman history, both of which, ironically, gave homosexuality an important role to play in their cultures.

Historically, homosexuality was embraced as a fact of life by most African traditions. Amongst the Swahili in East Africa, homosexuals were the secret link between people engaged to be married; they brought messages back and forth between lovers. The only men a bride was allowed to receive shortly before her wedding were gays. They taught her the intricate details of domestic work and educated her fiancé in the tricks of sexuality through telling stories and performing dances. Statements such as 'homosexuality is non-African' are historically incorrect.

The aversion to homosexuality amongst many African Christians is so strong that the theme threatens to destroy the unity of the Anglican Church, one of the biggest Christian communities in the world. The inauguration in the United States of a known homosexual, Gene Robinson, as bishop has enraged Anglicans, especially in Nigeria and Uganda, which have a significant Anglican following. After the United Kingdom, Anglican communities in these countries form the second and third largest provinces of the Anglican Church internationally.

African bishops, led by the Nigerian archbishop Peter Akinola, demand the unconditional exclusion of everyone who refuses to condemn homosexuality. Akinola has found a strong ally in the Church of Uganda.

The attempts of the archbishop of Canterbury, Rowan Williams, in July 2006 to reach a workable resolution, were dismissed out of hand by Akinola: 'A cancerous lump in the body should be excised if it has defied every known cure.'

As usual, the dissident voice comes from Desmond Tutu, the retired archbishop of Cape Town and Nobel laureate. He has labelled homophobia a 'crime against humanity' and 'every bit as unjust' as apartheid.

'We struggled against apartheid in South Africa,' Tutu wrote in a publication by Amnesty International, 'supported by people the world over, because black people were being blamed and made to suffer for something we could do nothing about; our very skins. It is the same with sexual orientation. It is a given.'

Within the Anglican churches in Africa, Tutu is a lone voice. War mongering sets the tone.

The social scientist Sylvia Tamale, of Makerere University in Kampala, became the target of unbounded hatred shortly after a part of the Ugandan women's movement in 2003 had suggested classifying homosexuals as a 'marginalised group'. Tamale supported that call only to find herself – in her own words – 'caught in the eye of the homophobic storm, and [1] became a punching bag for the public to relieve its pent-up rage.'*

In a feminist monthly Tamale wrote the following: 'It is impossible to describe the depth of the ugliness, rage, revulsion, disgust and malevolence exhibited by the vocal homophobic public. The few voices in support of homosexual rights were drowned out by deafening homophobic outcries.

---

* Sylvia Tamale, 'Out of the Closet: Unveiling Sexuality Discourses in Uganda,' *Feminist Africa Issue*, no. 2, 2003.

Through radio, television, newspapers and the Internet, I endured the most virulent verbal attacks, including calls for the "lynching" and "crucifying" of Tamale. I had previously been aware of the intolerance towards and prejudice against homosexuals in Uganda. I must confess, however, that the degree and extent of this bias came as a nasty shock to me; such bigotry and injustice I had read about only in history books on slavery and apartheid.'

I find a key to understanding homophobia in Uganda in a reader's letter to a newspaper. James Ranula calls himself 'a law abiding and concerned citizen', and writes: 'Homosexuality is a habit like smoking, drinking alcohol and drug abuse et cetera – all highly addictive'.

The key word in Ranula's letter is 'habit'. By describing and fearing homosexuality as an addictive habit, it becomes possible to sketch how an ignorant person can be seduced into 'sin'. It is this fear that lies at the source of a great deal of homophobia. Homosexuality as a habit is seen as a danger, a virus that can spread. According to some moral crusaders, that virus needs to be contained and fought. 'I too could be seduced,' fears the homophobe, 'and if not me, then maybe my son or my daughter.'

Is love and lust amongst members of the same sex a matter of hormones? Is homosexuality hereditary? Does the brain of a homosexual indeed contain a neural link that causes homosexuality? Science doesn't yet know. However, that homosexual love, lust or attraction is not just a 'habit', is a scientific fact. Homosexuality is rooted deeply in the being of a homosexual.

Of the five gay men I met in Kampala, two discovered their sexual nature while attending the boarding school of their church. Once the lights were switched off, Jembo was pleasured by one of his fellow students. He had no clue who it was. For him it was enough to experience the play.

The Catholic councillor, Paul, was initiated into male love by Catholic friars.

Both of them are gay to their core – not because of a habit, but because they discovered an essential part of who they happen to be. The realisation about their orientation was a discovery, not an invention. Women simply did not raise those feelings in them.

'I was born a homosexual, and I have to deal with that – that is the way it is,' Jembo says. His eyes shoot from left to right on the terrace of Speke Hotel, in downtown Kampala. He stays silent when a waiter comes too close.

'Here in Uganda it is impossible to demystify homosexuality. We cannot stand up and explain what it means to be gay, or express how we feel and who or what we are. We lack that basic freedom, and so the myths about homosexuality are spread by those who have no idea what it really is. That is a fact of life here. If I were to deny my own sexuality, I would deny an essential part of how the Creator made me.'

Jemba and Tall speak of the gay culture of Kampala. It *is* possible to experience homosexuality in Kampala at secret parties and, very carefully, in public as well.

Life in villages on the countryside is too public to keep anything a secret. There, young men marry girls to obey the rules and norms of the community. Women in those marriages often do not get their fair share of sex, because their husbands are not interested. The men just bide their time, until they die.

To keep the outside world far from the bedroom, a homosexual has to invent many a white lie.

Tall: 'Not many relationships are able to withstand those made-up stories, told to friends and relatives.'

Sex and faith are in a tense relationship everywhere on earth. But in Uganda this relationship is particularly flammable. Take a culture that is historically deeply spiritual, add a European religion brought into the country with tremendous verve, mix this with traditional customs in a rapidly modernising society, and sprinkle a dash of the AIDS-virus into the mixture.

The result is confusion.

Generally in Africa, sex is outwardly considered as purely a means of procreation. But obviously sex has always been pleasant and enjoyable too. Even today, sex has many faces. A married man will have intercourse with his wife, within the confines of his marriage. However, that same man will often also have sex outside 'holy matrimony' – for fun and relaxation.

In the early 1990s, Uganda was far ahead of the pack in Africa in breaking through the barriers of taboos around love and sexuality. AIDS had reached epidemic proportions. Long before other governments dared to make the leap, Uganda advertised a message of abstinence, sexual fidelity and condom use. The public treatment of topics long seen as too sensitive to debate, helped Uganda successfully fight AIDS. The infection rate dropped from just above 20 per cent in the early 1990s to 6.7 per cent in 2005.

Even for Christians, sex became a topic to openly talk about. Reverend David Turyagumanawe published his book *Sexual fulfilment* in 1997, in which he describes how, as a young man, he was taught never to talk openly about his genital organs.

'We were told to call them the "shameful things". If you spoke the real names of these important sex organs you would risk being heavily punished. The psychological impact on children and adults through calling these important organs of the body "shameful" is and has been disastrous. [...] We need to move an extra mile beyond the role an aunt or uncle played in educating those to marry about sex. Even then, it seems that the aunts and uncles no longer practice this important role in our African culture. [...] Some people will say that Africans never decided to speak openly about sex because they respected it. If this respect perpetuates ignorance; then certainly it is not a culture and tradition to continue.'

Turyagumanawe takes the time to describe loving sexuality. His starting point is romance, intimacy and love – within a marriage: '[O]ur sexual relationships with our partners is the most beautiful thing that God created for couples to enjoy.'

The reverend states that sexuality is the play of two equal partners, in which women have the right to initiate acts and ideas to enrich the sexuality between her and her man. He describes in detail how a man can pleasure a woman by lovingly massaging her vulva. He even asked a student to make drawings of several sexual positions.

In the late 1980s and early 1990s Uganda took sex out of the dark alleys, the thorny bushes and the thin-walled bedrooms. 'To not be open about AIDS is just ignorant', president Museveni said in 1988. 'This is an epidemic. You can only stop it by talking about it – loudly, so that everybody is aware and scared, and they stop the kind of behaviour that encourages the spread of the disease.'*

Sex became a theme in both the church and the classroom, on the radio and in newspapers. The message was: Sex without risk does not exist.

That stark approach was successful in changing sexual behaviour. The age at which girls had sex for the first time went up. The number of sexual

---

* Yoweri Museveni as quoted by John Iliffe in *The African AIDS epidemic – a history*, 2006.

partners of both married and unmarried adults went down. The percentage of infected also declined. Museveni had pulled away a veil hanging over the intimate life of his subjects. But he had done so through a very strong, moralistic approach, that occasionally seemed at odds with his surroundings.

I hardly know a country in Africa where the gap between words and deeds (or maybe that should be the 'Word' and the deed) is as huge as it is in Uganda. The taboos mentioned by the Reverend Turyagumanawe in 1997 are still alive and kicking, ten years later.

Hugging and petting in public are still not acceptable, and invite lengthy debates in the Saturday supplements of newspapers. Only friends of the same sex are allowed to walk hand in hand. Newly-weds kissing each other after the wedding ceremony break laws of purity. And women will not hang their underwear to dry outside on a line – the man next door might get aroused. Despite two decades of debates about physical intimacy, the theme of homosexuality still remains unmentionable.

Slowly the gates that opened in the late 1980s to eradicate sexual ignorance to fight AIDS are closing again. Kampala is filled with posters advertising only abstinence – a campaign driven by First Lady Janet Museveni ('born again') and paid for by USAID, the international helping-hand of President George Bush ('born again'). The most important effect of this approach to sex and sexuality is that almost everything surrounding intimacy becomes, once again, a taboo.

'The core of their campaigns is simple: "Sex is bad!"' says medical doctor and homosexual, Philadelphia. 'They think information leads to debauchery. Slowly the lid is put back onto the pot. Nowadays, men get their information from porn movies or dirty magazines that are passed around underground. In those movies no one ever wears a condom, and directors leave out the moments when someone grabs a bottle of lubricant, or puts on a condom, because those acts break the "erotic" tension on screen.'

———————

When I contact prominent 'men of the Word' they speak to me in a very un-African way: insulting, demeaning, aggressive and arrogant. Neither pastor Martin Ssempa, leader of a born-again community, nor the Anglican archbishop, Aron Mwesigye, mince their words.

Ssempa especially seems to be filled with a passionate hatred. I read his letter in the *New Vision* of 3 June 2005 on the Ugandan Martyrs. In it

Ssempa fulminates against homosexuals, using a national saga. A hundred and twenty years earlier, Bugandan King Mwanga, had sent twenty-six young Anglicans and Catholics to the stake. They were some of his pages.

Mwanga treated them as his toys, although they had been entrusted into his care by their parents, for whom it was an honour to have children serving the monarch. However, inspired by missionaries, the pages no longer wished to bow to the king because that honour was reserved for God and the wooden statues of Jesus and his mother Mary. Mwanga felt he could not let his servants get away with mutiny, and he ordered their execution.

Ssempa portrays Mwanga as a child molester. He labels the executed pages as martyrs who refused 'to bend over'. Ssempa sees all homosexuals as child molesters, and therefore he knows no mercy for them.

'Why don't you include in your struggle, and with the same vengeance, the large scale rape of girls in your country by heterosexual men?' I ask him.

'We offer assistance to girls abducted by the Lord's Resistance Army, in the north of the country,' he replies.

'But how do you fight heterosexual rape of adult women in the rest of the country?'

He dodges the question. 'The defilement of girls is a worry for us.'

Ssempa has chosen his words intentionally. 'Defilement' in Uganda means sex with an under-age girl – voluntary or not. Even when a seventeen-year-old girl has consensual sex, it's still perceived as defilement. Her reputation would be shattered if someone found out.

Only a married woman is allowed to have sex, and only with her husband. If she is raped by her spouse, she has nowhere to go. Rape within the bonds of holy matrimony does not exist, according to Ugandan law. She gave her husband a lifelong right to sex the day she married him.

'Does their *rape* worry you, or only their deflowering?' I enquire. 'And why do you compare consensual sex between adults to child rape?'

Ssempa ignores my first question. 'Homosexuality is un-African; it is against nature, it is against the Bible. Even Mwanga wasn't originally gay. He was made a homosexual by the Islamic traders that came here.'

'Christianity is not Ugandan,' I object. 'European missionaries brought it to your country.'

Ssempa wraps up. 'If you had children, you'd know how bad it would be if anything were to happen to them.'

Archbishop Aron Mwesigye of the Anglican Church also gives me the full blast of religious indignation. He starts by yelling at me. 'You outsiders don't understand anything of life in Africa!' I have only just introduced myself.

'What do you mean, and who do you mean by "you"?' I ask him.

'Europeans. Outsiders. Foreigners. No one except us understands these things.'

'Well, then you seem to be the right person to try and explain it to me ...'

'For a book on men and masculinity in Africa? Do you really think you have the faintest clue about men in Africa? Only because you have spoken to some men here on the continent?'

I give it another try. 'If I am indeed so wrong about it, why don't you try to set the record straight?'

A diatribe is unleashed with only few new points. That gay love is un-African. That it is against nature, against the Bible, 'and the Bible does not allow compromises for the well-being of a few false prophets in the North.'

Eventually his anger subsides and Mwesigye is prepared to make an appointment. Before he commits himself, he wants to know a few things.

'Are you a Christian?'

'I was baptised in a Presbyterian Church in Lusaka.'

'Are you a homosexual?'

'I am heterosexual.'

'Do you sympathise with gays and lesbians?'

'I recognise their human rights,' I answer honestly.

'Wednesday at ten o'clock, my office.'

I wait for half an hour at the agreed location, the hill in Kampala where the Anglican Church of Uganda has its headquarters. No one has seen the archbishop today. I call him four times on his mobile. No answer.

Only hours later Mwesigye returns my calls. It will not be possible for me to meet him, he states. However, I can meet the representative for international affairs, Reverend Alison Barfoot, a white American woman with a doctorate from an American university, to talk about men and homosexuality in Africa.

'I might not be the right person to talk to,' Reverend Barfoot suggests politely and with a friendly smile. During our meeting on the veranda of the drab palace of the archbishop, she is mostly curious to listen. We speak about Christmas in Africa, about men and masculinity, and about the painful dilemma in the global Anglican Church concerning homosexuality.

After sunset, as I gather my belongings, Reverend Barfoot takes my arm. 'I will e-mail you a document that was written by the Anglican Church of Uganda in May this year after a series of meetings behind closed doors on the issue of homosexuality. Be aware, however, that not everything that was debated made it into this document.'

During the discussions, the chairperson asked all participants to think of words in their own languages that describe homosexuality. If a language has words for a certain phenomenon, that simple fact is proof in itself that the phenomenon exists. During the meetings clergymen from all corners of Uganda knew of words that imply homosexuality.

Barfoot: 'The conclusion, of course, is that homosexuality is not imported from the West or is just an aberration of present-day life. Homosexuality is also Ugandan, and it is also of the past. For political reasons this conclusion did not make it into the final version of the document.'

After my meeting with Barfoot I stroll through downtown Kampala. I walk past newspaper boys and men selling parking tickets. I meander past cars waiting for traffic lights, and avoid speeding mopeds. Odd-jobbers pass me by with plastic Christmas trees on their shoulders. For a dollar I could own one.

In the Uganda Bookshop I hear gospel music. All literature has made way for cards with season's greetings – bears wearing Christmas hats while playing in the snow. Next to the door, a light flickers on a Christmas tree.

At the end of the calendar year, Africa celebrates the change of season in Europe with rituals that go back thousands of years, to pagan ceremonies. Here, close to the equator, the solstice is hardly noticeable – the sun rises and sets at almost the same time every day, whether it is 4 May or 25 December.

Back in my hotel I read the document Barfoot has sent me. The clergy and theologians start the meeting by stating the blessings Christianity has brought to Uganda. They explain why homosexuality is unacceptable to them. Their point of departure is one sentence from the book of Leviticus (18:22): 'Thou shalt not lie with mankind as with womankind: it is abomination'.*

The theologians claim that a liberal interpretation of this one command would be like stabbing a dagger in the heart of Christianity. By accepting deviations from this 'law', the clergy assert with an air of drama, the entire Bible would become useless.

'For us in the Church of Uganda, the Bible is the cherished source of authority that is central to the faith, practice, and mission of our Christians. It is an absolute treasure that no one can take away. [...] If you take the Bible away from our bishops and clergy, they have nothing to offer the world. For all God's people, obedience to this Bible is the source of confidence, abundant life, and joy.'

Why, specifically, do the Anglican clergy and theologians of Uganda see the issue of homosexuality as contentious enough to split the Church? The Ugandan clergy prefer to take the Bible literally, word for every word, including Leviticus 18:22. They fear that interpreting the Word more figuratively might undermine its commanding power.

By clinging to a very narrow, literal interpretation of one verse in the Old Testament, the most outspoken clergy of Uganda unilaterally try to ban any theological debate about different interpretations of the Bible, as so many other clergy have tried before them. It is an eternal battle for the purest of purity that started even before Jesus was nailed to a cross. A battle that plagues every religion, every church, every form of organised spirituality where leaders fear losing control of their flock.

'For the Church in Uganda, to compromise God's call of obedience to the Scriptures would be the undoing of more than 125 years of Christianity through which African customs, belief, life, and society have been transformed for the better.'

---

* This is the translation in the King James Bible. According to scholars, the original Hebrew text is very difficult to translate and could mean a great deal of different things. The same book of Leviticus does allow enslaving members of the neighbouring state and condemns, apart from homosexuality, also the following: touching a woman when she menstruates as well as touching a pig, cutting of hair at the temples, approaching an altar when one's eyes are not perfect and wearing clothing that consists of two or more different fabrics. Eating shellfish is labelled as just as evil as a man lying with a man: an abomination. Breaking any of these other rules is, curiously enough, for the Church of Uganda a threat to neither the Bible nor the faith.

Christianity discontinued 'the most degrading form of gender inequality', namely polygamy. 'The biblical teaching of marriage between one man and one woman in a loving, lifelong relationship liberated not only women, but also the institution of marriage and family.

'The Bible's revelation of Father as Creator of all things, the Son as redeemer, and the Holy Spirit as the life-giving Spirit of God brought hope for deliverance from the fatalism that resulted from worshipping created things rather than the Creator.'

The document has a nasty sting to it, though, because of what it does *not* mention. The proclaimed 'liberation' of women through the eradication of polygamy was less of a blessing than the church wants people to believe. Encouraged by missionaries, huge numbers of men who wished to save themselves from eternal damnation, kicked out their 'excess' wives overnight. These women suddenly had no roofs over their heads, no access to land and no income. Many of them had to resort to prostitution in order to survive.

The result of overzealous missionaries trying to save too many souls too quickly was a sharp and sudden increase of venereal diseases early in the 20th century in large parts of Uganda.

Henry Stanley cleared the way for the missionaries when he visited King Mtesa I of the Baganda (Mwanga's father) in 1875. The explorer wrote about it in his book *Through the Dark Continent* (1878).

I have, indeed, undermined Islamism so much here that Mtesa has determined henceforth, until he is better informed, to observe the Christian Sabbath as well as the Muslim Sabbath, and the great captains have consented to this. He has further caused the Ten Commandments of Moses to be written on a board for his daily perusal – for Mtesa can read Arabic – as well as the Lord's Prayer and the golden commandment of our Saviour, Thou shalt love thy neighbour as thyself.' [...] But oh! That some pious, practical missionary would come here. What a field and harvest ripe for the sickle of civilisation! [...] Now, where is there in all the pagan world a more promising field for a mission than Uganda? [...] Here, gentlemen, is your opportunity – embrace it! [...] I assure you that you will have more converts to Christianity than all other missionaries united can number. [...] You need not fear to spend money upon such a mission, as Mtesa is sole ruler, and will repay its cost tenfold with ivory, coffee, otter skins of a very fine quality, or even in cattle, for the wealth of this country in all these products is immense.

Is it sheer coincidence, I wonder, that the bloodthirsty Lord's Resistance Army fought for decades to rule Uganda along the lines of the Ten Commandments, with Stanley as their original teacher? Is it also sheer coincidence that the one sect that killed over a thousand of its own people in 2000 was called the Movement for the Restoration of the Ten Commandments of God, named after the laws King Mtesa was ordered to learn?

Christianity did not just bring relief from old problems. The mystical vision of life that characterised traditional life was done away with. Everything that vaguely reminded people of superstition or idol worship was thrown onto the garbage heap of history to make place for insights, beliefs, symbolism and rituals from afar, which included pagan European ceremonies.

'The minds of the people began a gradual transformation, and everything African was considered inferior to anything imported.' Bernard Atuhaire wrote these words in his book *The Uganda Cult Tragedy* (2003), a study into the mass killings committed by the Christian sect in early 2000. Atuhaire goes back to the first years of Christianity in Uganda, to explain why the sect had been as successful as it was.

'First names became European or Arabic and society began to abandon those old ways which were not accommodated in the new era of transformation. It was the beginning of a "mental" colonisation, which has reigned ever since in the region. [...] Basically, everybody became a believer.'

However, it would be too simple to dismiss the excesses of Christianity in Uganda as merely the result of in imported religion. Missionaries achieved their successes because the 'new' faith could easily supersede the 'old' faiths, thanks to shared characteristics. The saints replaced the lesser gods, while the Creator replaced the main god of the indigenous spiritual stories. Even the prudish approach to sex and sexuality brought by the brothers to Uganda fitted seamlessly into existing taboos.

In his book *The African Aids Epidemic* (2006) the historian John Iliffe describes how the clergy first responded to the AIDS-epidemic with outspoken condemnation, 'especially where a harsh Protestantism was superimposed over traditional moralism.'

These days it is very difficult to pinpoint where the influences of traditions stop and where those of the imported faith begin. Especially because a great number of Christians condemn their own indegenous spiritual roots with a fiery passion, and add in the same breath how proud they are of their African identity.

———

Philadelphia ignores as best he can the angry clergy of Uganda, and their religion. Formerly a born-again Christian, Philadelphia wants nothing to do anymore with anything religious. 'I renounce a belief that orders believers to renounce me.'

His partner Williams listens to Philadelphia's words and shakes his head. He is soft spoken, his voice vibrates with melancholy. 'I am a Catholic. I have the right to stand in the light of God and be happy. He is my Creator no one has the right to repudiate me.'

Philadelphia ignored his own sexuality for years. From his eighteenth birthday he led his own born-again congregation. 'I desperately searched my faith for absolute truths which might liberate me from my own confusion.' His total lack of lust for and his indifference to women did not worry him. 'The Bible was the love of my life.'

Only after he had read the book *Papillon* by Henri Charriere (1969) on the French penal colony on Devil's Island did he start to sense something. He had reached his mid-twenties, and love, romance and sensuality started stirring in his life. 'So many men on that island ...?' He laughs.

Williams already knew at a very young age that he 'wasn't like the other boys' in his village. It took a move to Kampala for him to fully accept his homosexuality. He met a man who dared to flirt with him. Williams desperately wanted to give in, but felt limited by his faith. 'I told him, "Sorry, I can't – I am Catholic".' But the flirtation had lit a fire in him. Through friends he heard of a priest who could help him come to terms with his orientation and his sense of guilt.

Philadelphia listens to his boyfriend, patiently. Although he has seen first-hand the soothing effect Williams' belief has on his partner, he himself chooses to walk a different path. 'Everyone, homo or hetero, needs to create his or her own reality. Along the journey of life, you have to find peace with yourself. You have to learn to stand on your own two feet. You have to accept yourself for who you are.'

Accepting yourself for who you are is difficult in a society that places numerous demands on you. Relatives want to see offspring, a wife and a family. Ugandan newspapers openly call upon men to 'do the good thing', as Patricia Mantel wrote in a newspaper article, 'No excuse to be a bachelor,' in December 2005. In stern words she commanded the bachelors of Kampala to 'grow up' and 'marry quickly and start a family.'

Williams: 'A man's honour is still largely defined by his ability to take care of his ageing father and mother.' He suspects his parents are aware of his relationship with Philadelphia, but choose not to debate it. 'As it stands, I take better care of my parents than does my heterosexual brother. I am therefore seen as more of a man than he is. My parents ignore my private life, knowing that the truth will be too upsetting for everyone.'

Many a homosexual man in Uganda, however, is unable to resist the pressures placed on him, and consequently marry a woman. They have as much sex at home as it takes to have a child, and seek the realisation of their true sexual identity far away from home and hearth, during parties organised by The Family. The motto is always 'Bring a friend' so likeminded people can meet each other. Regular meeting spots are not an option. Cafés would be invaded by the police and nightclubs harassed by angry citizens.

'What those angry people do not realise,' says Williams, 'is that it is not God who condemns me. It is them. The message of God is a message of Love.'

'Only a few people in Uganda seem able to comprehend that message of the universality of God's love,' Philadelphia comments. In Uganda, the crucial story in Christian communities is the heroic saga of the Ugandan Martyrs, burnt at the stake for their mutiny against an indigenous monarch. 'The abuse of the Uganda Martyrs enhances their own agenda. Once you realise that, the saga loses most of its painful content.'

Everywhere in Kampala, one comes across schools, churches and institutions named after the Ugandan Martyrs, with faces of young men carved in stained-glass windows and woven into tapestries. Who were they?

The Catholic Church erected a shrine in Namugongo, outside Kampala, for the young men who perished at the stake. The round building is constructed with twenty-two pillars, one pillar for each of the Catholic pages who were executed by King Mwanga on 3 July 1886. Pilgrims come here annually – over a hundred thousand each year.

On a quiet afternoon I find women sitting on the grass, in the shade of the trees. A nun walks around with three friends and plays with the cross around her neck. A carpenter decorates the interior with Christmas regalia.

Ben Tenywa, the official guide, tells the story of the executions as it was told to him. He speaks of local kings receiving missionaries from all the different churches who expressed their wish to evangelise. They were hard-pressed to catch up with the Islamic preachers who had been working the territory for decades. But the rulers wanted more than just grace and divine forgiveness. Monarchs and chiefs need weapons to fight each other.

Therefore: only if the men of the cloth would bring modern weaponry were they welcome to spread the gospel.

To prevent the missionaries from getting too many followers amongst his subjects, king Mtesa and later king Mwanga gave them access only to their courts. There the king's word was most powerful, or so they believed, and therefore the missionaries could do little harm.

The evangelists were forced to focus their attention on the king's servants. The pages weeded the gardens, cleaned the palace, guarded the livestock and cooked the king's meals. Whenever the king so desired, they also slept with him.

One of the lessons taught to the newly converted Christians was never to bow to anyone but God, Jesus or Maria. They were also told of a king in heaven more powerful than the earthly Mwanga. Having been introduced to this much more mighty yet invisible monarch, some of the pages and personal advisers to the king refused to serve Mwanga. The king in turn feared being toppled by the competitor the missionaries kept talking about. Suspecting a coup, Mwanga ordered the brutal execution of the 'mutineers'.

For Ben Tenywa, the martyrs are a source of inspiration. 'They were young men who placed their faith before everything else. They were willing to die for the refusal to work on a Sunday.'

Tenywa gives details pastor Ssempa kept to himself, and sketches an image much broader than the pages' refusal 'to bend over'. 'Some books claim Mwanga was taught sodomy by the Arabs, but I doubt that. No one can be sure whether homosexuality existed before the Arabs or the

Christians came to Uganda. In those days, you had no idea what happened in the village closest to yours, or in the neighbour's bedroom. Sex and love found a home within the privacy of one's walls.'

Mwanga was removed from power in 1898 by the British, who deported him to the Seychelles. He converted there to Christianity and renamed himself Daniel, after the hero in the Old Testament who survived the lions' pit.

As I walk through the gardens of the shrine in Namugongo, I realise how the saga of the Ugandan Martyrs has become the most important story in Uganda's embrace of Christianity. It is a tale of the grace brought by a foreign religion versus brutalities of indigenous animism. A tale in which a local monarch punished his subordinates because he feared a coup, and who has been turned into a child-molester for dramatic effect.

The Ugandan clergy are bound by this narrative, a story their European predecessors jotted down at the end of the 19th century to glorify themselves and their mission. This myth and the church's totalitarian power over people's minds are in Uganda to stay – the most conservative of the clergy will make sure of that.

Men and women sit on wooden benches outside Father Paul's church. They are waiting for his advice, his blessing and his words of comfort. It could be about anything: worries about children, a job or spiritual needs. Father Paul shakes hands in a firm way. He has a friendly face.

In his tiny room a single bed is placed against a wall. Above it hangs an embroidered tribute to the Ugandan Martyrs. 'I honour them for their courage; not for what they have begun to mean to some people – a stick to beat the dog. Please, take a seat.'

When Williams needed support to come to terms with his own sexuality he came to see Paul, who became his mentor. Amongst his friends, Paul was known as a Catholic priest who had had first-hand experience of being gay. He does not threaten with damnation, but instead offers his ear and a blessing hand.

'It's not just that gays can't go anywhere without unleashing an unfair amount of anger; the political, cultural and spiritual elite also tell them that they are "not-African". Their identity is stripped away. "You do not belong here," is what they are being told.

'How can homosexuality be non-African? If history tells us of even one African king with a homosexual orientation, how then can homosexuality be non-African? If there were only one African gay or lesbian alive today, how could homosexuality be non-African?'

Paul is annoyed by the claim to an exclusive, genuine African-ness open only to heterosexuals. 'Most Ugandans are in a hurry to do away with their own roots and take on a Western lifestyle,' he observes. 'However, when talking about homosexuality, it is immediately condemned as "foreign" and everything foreign has to suddenly be resisted and dismissed. They say: "Homosexuality? We Africans don't do homosexuality".'

'This attitude in Africa is not restricted to homosexuality. 'Black magic' too is blamed on outsiders. It's always the tribe on the other side of the river who still practise black magic – even when people are aware of those things in their own community. For me, it is a sign of insecurity, a symptom of an identity crisis. Many people are struggling with this simple but huge issue of who they are. However, they find it next to impossible to live with that question because easy, sensible answers are not available.

Homosexuals can't walk away from the quest for identity, expounds Paul. Lust and butterflies continuously float in the 'wrong direction'. People around them condemn in strong words everything a homosexual feels inside. 'They hear that gays and lesbians are an anomaly. That they are an "abomination".'

Paul himself wrestled his way through these issues of identity when he himself grew up as a Catholic homosexual in the Uganda of the 1970s, a decade ruined by dictator Idi Amin. 'Everything around me collapsed and still I was fed this lethal, Catholic sense of sin.'

He fled to London and dived straight into a lifestyle beyond his wildest dreams. He made good money, did everything his darkest instincts inspired and enjoyed life to the full.

'It was hard to de-programme myself after having been raised to deny my own sexuality. I had the urge to destroy myself, to make up for denying who I was deep down. It was impossible to dream of curing my soul – to be made whole again.'

After a few years in London he had done it all; he had experimented with everything. But was this all there was to life? Feeling increasingly lonely in the metropolis, Paul realised that 'to have done it all' was not enough to fill the spiritual abyss he felt. He returned to Africa and joined a very active Catholic brotherhood in Nairobi.

'Those men did nothing else all day long but practise their compassion and love for human beings. They were driven by love.' He observed them and thought: 'I want what they have – a deep commitment to life, a power to surrender and enjoy existence.' Paul found new points of connection to his church. The dogmas of the Vatican ended up as bedside literature.

'They became a revelation to me. I realised the Church does not judge anybody's sexual orientation; she condemns the acts flowing from that orientation – a fundamental distinction. It is not the Church that hates homosexuals, but individuals who are unable to cope with their own sexuality or that of others.'

Now Paul felt he had something he could build on. Now, within the embrace of his own church, he could also embrace his own sexuality. Now he could start mapping a road for the future. He decided to dedicate his life to the Church to enable his own spiritual journey. A vow of celibacy became crucial.

'I do not believe in a judging, punishing God. Such a god seems to me to be a pagan god. I believe in a God who liberates humanity and manifests Himself. That is the basis from which I approach homosexuality – in a loving way. Homosexuals are harshly judged by people who choose to hide their anger and preconceptions behind an angry god. How is any individual supposed to respect himself, when he gets an angry god thrown at him? Self-respect and self-acceptance are essential for a human being to be healthy.

'Why judge another man purely because he's a sinner? Since when has God renounced sinners? A gay person loves another human being. Since when has "loving another person" become a sin in the eyes of God? I tell every homosexual who comes to see me that the God who created him loves him for who he is – warts and all. I say, "Do away with what others think, if only for a while, and tell me: what does sin mean to you, personally?"

DO IT YOURSELF

The eyes of Isaac Tsheko (76) move from left to right, and from top to bottom. In disbelief he stares at a poster in front of him on a wobbly, rusted table in his garden. He studies the drawing and the text intently, resting his head in the palm of one hand.

The poster shows a living room in a middle-class home. A man is seated on a couch opposite a cabinet with a television set. Tsheko's eyes wonder again to the man who, while dreaming of himself with a woman, has his hands inside his pants. Beneath the drawing the words: 'Masturbation – do it yourself.'

Tsheko shakes his head in disbelief and shock, turns towards his garden, listens to a rooster crowing and returns to the drawing. He looks lost; he is lost. 'What do they mean, "Do it yourself"?'

For the first time in my long years as a reporter in Africa I feel deeply uncomfortable. 'Don't I have any boundaries left?' I wonder. 'Do I honestly think I can ask anything I like?' Opposite me sits a man with grey hair. He carries an air of wisdom, serenity. He has offered me a warm welcome and his time.

My own audacity shames me. I shift restlessly in my chair. I wonder how my father would react if a man from Africa came knocking on his door to ask *him* about his sexual past. I swallow my shame and my pride. I tell myself: Hang in, Aernout. You did not come to Botswana to have your own sensitivities blow up in your face.

Is it true that Africa doesn't masturbate, as some want us to believe? Is 'solo sex' indeed so unheard of? Is there any validity to sweeping statements that African men perceive their seed to be so sacrosanct that it cannot be dispersed into nothingness – or even worse, collected in latex to be thrown in the dustbin? How come oral sex has no place in African sexual fantasy, if that really is the case?

I find many of the generalised statements about 'sex in Africa' hard to believe. On the one side stand those who still describe African sexuality as 'wild', 'primitive' or 'instinctive'. On the other side are those who state that physical intimacy in Africa is devoid of the things that add to the experience of sensuality and sexuality everywhere else, like mutual masturbation, fellatio or cunnilingus.

If Arabia can write *The Thousand and One Nights*, and Asian sexuality has for centuries been inspired by the *Kama Sutra*, why on earth would Africa lack its own mature, adult and playful approach to eroticism?

In the most respectful way I can muster, I explain to Tsheko why I wanted him to look at the poster. A *kwaito* song streams out of the house through his living room window. The demanding rhythm of the bass and the angry voice of the singer seem to irritate Tsheko. He throws angry glances towards the window, as if he can telepathically force his grandchildren to turn down the volume. The bells of a donkey cart roaming the sandy road divert his attention back to the poster.

Tsheko's body language tells me he'd prefer to be packing his *bakkie*. Some of the old and used planks have already been loaded up in his pick-up truck. He has tied them down to the chassis with a strong piece of rope. 'I need to build a new shack on my cattle post some hundred kilometres away. My hut started leaking a few months ago. Better repair it now, before time takes it away from me.'

The cattlepost is where he breeds and feeds his many cows to prepare them for the butcher. It's also where he grew up, and where his memories lie spread out, received by the earth. Today he wants to go there, to inhale those stories and images of old. One deep breath at a time.

Drought is also urging Tsheko to go visit his cattle. The last rains fell more than three months ago. They need extra fodder. 'Three years ago, the drought took sixty of my animals. Can't let that happen again.'

Tsheko's garden shows signs of the drought. The brown earth is like dust, easily picked up by a breeze, or by one's feet. The leaves on the one tree growing in his garden are brown. Tsheko: 'It's called a *mosala osi*, which means "the lonely one".'

Again he looks at the poster, and tries to find the words that best convey his thoughts. Tsheko describes what love looked like when *he* was young, over half a century ago, and how the times have changed. When he was a teenager and cared for the cattle, nature was his teacher. 'My family was poor; we had no money for luxuries like education.' At a young age, his father sent him to the cattle post to tend to the goats, just like his father's father had ordered him.

During his life, Tsheko witnessed the birth of a new world in the land of his ancestors, Botswana. He experienced the metamorphoses himself and broke with existing traditions. He told his father that tending to cattle would not satisfy him, and he left for South Africa to become a bricklayer. He sent the money he made back home so that his brother could get an education.

'We looked at the civilisation brought by the missionaries and the British administrators in the days this country was still known as the British protectorate of Bechuanaland. We saw it, and we wanted it. We wanted to move away from the harshness of existence, towards a tiny bit more comfort, a tiny bit less suffering. So, for the last couple of decades we have been copying a civilisation from afar. And we've done so successfully. Today life is better, easier. You can now do more or less what your heart desires in Botswana. However, we have paid a very high price for this civilisation.'

Tsheko jumps up as if stung by a bee, as if the words he just spoke have alarmed him. He walks towards his shed, grabs an axe and adds it to the cargo in his *bakkie*. He paces through his garden absentmindedly. His feet kick up dust and the wind lays it back down a few yards away. Then he settles in his chair again.

'I met my wife, Emily, in South Africa. The first time I saw her, I simply knew: With her I want to grow old. She is the one for me. I didn't just want to be an aquaintance; I wanted to make her a part of my life.'

He asked around if the young woman was 'available'. Then the couple began to flirt with each other and secretly strolled around together. 'We spoke for hours on end and cuddled. After three years, we got married.' His parents paid the *lobola*.

Tsheko rubs his hands together and stares at the window behind which a new rap song is pulsing. 'Everything has changed. No one is ashamed of anything anymore. Men and women kiss each other in public, they come and sit on each other's lap in my living room. No, honestly, I just don't understand it anymore.'

What disturbs him most of all, more than the public displays of today's romance, is its new character. 'It has turned into something so materialistic. Young men have no chance whatsoever when cash is tight. A girl leaves as easily as she arrived if a guy can't take her to fancy bars or restaurants, or if he doesn't buy her expensive clothing. Romance has suddenly been depleted, consumed, finished. Is *that* love? When you have to pay for someone's time and attention? I wonder… I wonder if young people are able to do something without expecting money in return. I tell my grandchildren, "Practise patience." But they have no clue what I'm preaching to them about.

'It's the same thing with sex. Quick, fast, rapid. Now! It all has to happen now! That brings nothing but trouble. Look at all those broken families. Look at AIDS. As a young man, I practised thigh sex. What youngster has ever heard of the term, let alone acted it out?'

No one taught Tsheko about sex. His parents had soberly forbidden him to sleep with girls, with the simple warning that 'that's how you make babies' and the threat of a serious wallop.

There was no temptation because girls never came near the cattle post. The young men he was surrounded by knew as little about sex as he did. A roll in the hay was on no one's agenda. They tended cattle – that was all life was about.

Again Tsheko scans the poster. 'What this man is doing is not of my culture. Whoever told you that our word for this is *ponya ponya* knows something I don't.'

The young man who had brought the poster to Tsheko's table in the garden is Ronald Ntebela (24), one of his nephews. Ntebela works for the Youth Health Organisation of Botswana (YOHO) in the capital Gaborone. He leads a crusade to add the 'D' to the ABC of their AIDS campaign: 'A' for 'Abstinence', 'B' for 'Be faithful' and 'C' for 'Condomise'. The 'D' would stand for 'Do it yourself'. YOHO claims masturbation goes back a long way in the Tswana culture, and believes it could offer a tool for the fight against the spread of the HI virus.

Ntebela brought me to Mochudi, the region where he was born, because this is where his extended family lives: aunts, uncles, nieces, nephews and cousins in many degrees of kinship. Isaac Tsheko is an uncle. Even for campaign leader Ntebela, chatting to strangers about sex is one bridge too far. That's why he suggested we drive here to chat about *ponya ponya* with his relative. And now, when his uncle declares never to have heard of the term, Ntebela has vanished.

Tsheko breaks the awkward silence between us. 'If I were a young man wanting sex, I'd go for condoms. This *ponya ponya* business seems pointless.'

Tsheko gets up, a faint smile on his lips. He really needs to go. His cattle are waiting.

'Until we meet again.'

A firm handshake.

Over a third of the adult population of Botswana is infected with HIV. Life expectancy has dropped to 42 years to AIDS. Campaigns to tackle the spread of the virus seem to have little effect. YOHO therefore chose to launch a full-frontal attack on sexual habits, and dared to do what no other organisation in Africa has done: actively campaign for masturbation as a substitute for penetration.

'We need alternatives to intercourse as a way of tackling the epidemic,' says Dikitso Letshwiti (23). The 'Do it yourself' campaign originated with him.

'It is estimated that 93 per cent of our people have more than one partner. It's therefore necessary to teach people ways to enjoy their sexuality without risking their lives. Human beings are sexual creatures, but most people lack the skills to negotiate sexuality, eroticism and even romance.'

When it comes to physical intimacy, Letshwiti believes, fear dominates Botswanan society. 'Our culture is filled with taboos and frightens us about sex. The talent to deal with intimacy in a mature yet playful way, without losing sight of its serious aspects – that talent is hard to come by.'

Modern-day Botswana is stuck in perceptions of love and definitions of masculinity and femininity that make Letshwiti feel trapped. 'Imagine my girlfriend and I had a child. Do I have the right to change its diapers? I can already picture the looks on my friends' faces if they saw me with a dirty nappy in my hand. They'll make fun of me. Still, that is how I'd want to relate to my child. I want to be a caring dad. For most of my friends, that's worth a good belly laugh.'

Letshwiti has a world to conquer. His way of thinking has only a few admirers in Botswana. People come in droves to see the plays he performs country-wide. The radio shows YOHO participates in are hugely popular. The young generation wants to learn about love, romance, sexuality and friendship. But the changes come at a snail's pace, hindered by the many taboos surrounding sexuality.

Botswana's relatively new morality of conservative Christianity sees sexuality as an energy to be tempered, chained and caged. At the same time, modernity brings values which offer and demand instant gratification, and creates a society in which desires call incessantly for fulfilment. Sex between 'lovers' has become a consumer product to be paid for by dinners, jewellery, cell phones and expensive jeans.

'We call it "Going to the market to get a chick",' says Ntebela as we drive through Gaborone with his mate Bernard Waheng (22). 'A "chick" is any girl who only cares about the superficial stuff in life: "bling" or a phone with a weird bleeping ring tone.'

The two men whistle and turn around whenever a beauty passes by, exclaiming, 'Aiaiai – that can't be true!' or, 'How could He make them this stunning?' Ntebela and Waheng appreciate female beauty and the promises they read in its curves. Tight jeans, tighter shirts. The young men call their staring and commenting 'window shopping'.

Waheng once dated a young woman so beautiful, he could hardly breathe. For a very short while. 'She met an American and off she went. That's reality. What can you do? Girls … They want a guy with money and a car. Simple. Without money you can't play. Mothers raise their daughters this way. "Find a man to take care of you," that's what they tell 'em.'

As we drive to the university, the radio plays a song: *Ga-o monna wa*. It doesn't matter what you do to provide – steal, work, cheat – anything goes. 'You're not a man if you can't provide.'

Waheng continues, 'A man is lucky, I think, if he manages to find a woman with more depth, who can see through the facade. Those women are rare. Most look at your wallet and leave. Those women make you grow hard skin on your soul and offer the HI virus to guys who love to gamble.'

The university grounds are full of freshmen roaming around with uncertain steps and loads of pumped-up bravery. Three health workers mingle with them, posters tightly squeezed under their arms and 'Condomates' in hand. 'Now is the time to hammer in the message of safe sex. You might not believe it, but despite the raging epidemic, many still believe they're invincible.'

YOHO's poster comes in handy, the activist says. 'A bit of shock therapy hasn't yet hurt anyone. These youngsters come straight from Ignorance Square. Masturbation? As far as I'm concerned, any weapon is legitimate in the war against the virus.' Off they go to a workshop, a seminar and 'information dissemination' at the university clinic. 'Let no-one tell you in a few days' time, "I don't know…"!'

On the grass next to the student bar, freshmen sit in the midst of empty bottles and cans. Lovely eyes desperately seeking contact.

———————

'You heard that? "Shock therapy." I like that,' Ntebela grins. He was involved in the design of the poster for the 'Do it yourself' campaign. Both church and traditional leaders were up in arms. The state-owned media reported carefully at first, not knowing what to do with a call for the youth of the nation to masturbate more and penetrate less. YOHO has stirred society.

Phiri Boitumelo (59) was one of the first to march off to the offices of YOHO. As an employee of the Department of Culture, she was in shock and felt the need to sort out the 'boys and girls' of YOHO. Ntebela got a lashing.

During her tea break at the Department, Boitumela feels awkward repeating what she told Ntebela. The ultra-modern building is located along one of the busiest streets of the capital. Hawkers strut their stuff outside. The tempting smell of roasted meat enters the building in waves.

'My problem with this campaign,' says Boitumelo, 'is that whenever a person has an itch and they keep scratching the itch, they'll get a wound. It's the same with this masturbation. It would be better to ask God to take the itch away.'

She can't remember ever having had 'the itch'. 'When I was a girl, I was young in uncomplicated ways. I tended the goats. And I shared blankets with the big boys in the *kraal*. The worst they'd do was to fart and to laugh about those farts. Innocence and ignorance were my blessings. Things are not like that anymore. Used condoms litter the streets. No one has a sense of values and dignity left.'

No, Boitumelo doesn't beat around the bush. She does *not* like the way life has evolved. The bombardment of media messages irritates her. People have to produce, or so the ads say. Everyone has to be a success, or so people are told. Radio and TV demand of boys to have many girlfriends, and girls are told to 'score' boys.

'And everyone needs to have sex. Anyone watching television or opening a magazine can't help but get an itch. Sex has become the new initiation. Sex – as if there are no consequences, as if it doesn't lead to pregnancies, as if there are no diseases.'

Boitumelo has lost her cool. Talking about relationships and intimacy has opened up an old wound. She takes a deep breath, sighs and continues in a soft voice. She speaks of the man who could not contain his urges, who made her pregnant and started meandering from bedroom to bedroom, mattress to mattress.

'I threw him out. What a worthless character. I couldn't do anything else but throw him out. Taking care of my kids became *my* sole responsibility.'

'The itch, the itch, the itch' – Boitumelo repeats the word like a mantra. She shakes her head.

For her it's nothing more than an utterly ridiculous aberration, typical of the modern era. Life in Botswana has changed dramatically since independence in 1968. Shortly after Great Britain had left, diamonds were found. The mines have since provided the state with enough funds to finance public education and health care. However, labour migration to the mines rips families apart.

'Modernisation' barged into Botswana, and brought roads, hospitals, shiny office buildings and expensive cars.

It also brought new perceptions on love and sex.

Boitumelo: 'I don't believe in this masturbation. It'll only worsen the itch.'

Ronald Ntebela remains firm despite the denials of the elderly men and women he introduced me to. 'Masturbation is *not* alien. How could we have words for it, if the Tswana have never done it? *Ponya ponya, or goija* – "eat yourself". Those words come from the elders.'

Shame prevents people from talking, Ntebela assumes. 'Many people, old and young alike, are filled with shame. Sex is weird, dirty, strange – not something to speak about.'

To make his point, Ntebela wants me to meet a young rapper, Baker Pheko (24) and his girlfriend, Tlamelo Mogapaesi (21). Pheko published a CD with *kwaito* songs about the risks of drugs, the misery of unemployment and the sweetness of romance.

With a piercing in his chin and large shiny stones in his earlobes, Baker appears to be a man of the world – the world of 'bling' and 'chicks'. But he is nothing of the sort. He and his girlfriend of six years both wear a 'promise ring' to announce their engagement, and maybe even their wedding. He gave her the ring just before he left for Johannesburg to study sound engineering.

Baker sits opposite Tlamelo in her parental home. Crocheted cloths grace the armrests of the chairs and the couch. Flip flops may be placed inside, near the doors, while shoes have to wait outside. Drawings of Jesus decorate the walls.

Originally, she had many reservations when he spoke of his musical ambitions. She envisioned a life of floozies and booze. He had to prove his worth to her. 'I'm not interested in a "player". All musicians I know live care-free lives. Baker showed he can listen to me, to what I need.'

One of the tests he had to pass concerned his lust. Could Baker contain it or not?

'If he dreamt of another woman or played with himself, that would be adultery in my book. It's all quite straightforward. I grew up without these desires, without lust. I only want sex with one person, with Baker, when the time is right. No masturbation for me. Irresponsible behaviour is like volunteering for death row.'

So far, Baker has been listening silently. He nods, confirms with an 'ahum', agrees with a wink.

And I find it all impossible to believe: two young, healthy people. Hip. Modern. Self-assured. With no interest whatsoever in sex.

A while after Tlamelo has finished speaking, she looks at Baker as if to give him permission to speak. He says, 'As soon as I feel desire and she's not around, I call her. It's enough to hear her voice. The sexual tension disappears immediately, by itself.'

The moment we have time to ourselves in the studio in the backyard where Baker wants to play a few of his tunes, I ask him again, softly, 'Really? Never? Not once?'

He looks at me. A slightly arrogant, cynical smile.

'Nope. Never. I couldn't be bothered.'

Botswana is Africa's living proof that development on the continent is possible, and can benefit the population at large and not just a privileged, well-connected elite. It's Africa's only 'welfare state', with affordable education and healthcare for all, paid for by the export of diamonds.

Only a few are willing to criticise the governments for its suffocating red tape, and the decrees forcing modernisation down the throats of the local Bushmen. For most people things seem to be going well.

Yet, the society of Botswana fragments and crumbles. Families collapse even before they have time to settle down.

'Man caught in woman's underwear,' reports the front page of one of the tabloids. His fiancée found him in her own bed, wearing a pair of knickers that belonged to the woman next door. He had been too drunk to notice the difference. The fiancée found his Y-fronts in her neighbour's bedroom.

'My fiancé has been raped,' claimed the distraught woman and she laid a charge against her neighbour. 'That woman is sneakily trying to undermine my daughter's wedding,' said the future mother-in-law.

And he?

He only wanted his Y-fronts back.

A filthy teddy bear lies on the dark brown soil in front of the home of Monica Letebele[*] (49). The bear belongs to her grandson. A chicken is tied with a rope to a steel pole, but it seems to forget that simple fact every few minutes. Monica observes the chicken's struggle.

'That's how I feel. You find yourself tied to a guy and you slip and slide all the time. The moment my man dies, that will be that. Enough. No more men in my life.'

Three children mosey around the grounds: grandchildren, her daughter's brood. The boy, Vuyi, builds himself a car with Coca Cola cans. 'It's hard to survive with all these children of men who have mastered the art of disappearance.'

'Men,' she complains, 'have lost track of everything: their self-esteem, their responsibility, their purpose. They refuse to be held accountable for anything. Life has become one big party.'

The men in her life refuse to work; that's a chore they've left to her.

'I come back from work, and what do I find? I see him pumping his load into another woman. Aiaiaia – what can you do? Their minds are filled with promiscuity, their penises with HIV. Masturbation... If only, my friend, if only...'

Monica's man loves girls, and he loves to beat her. Twice she has filed a complaint of physical abuse but the police officers neglected to act. As a result she now remains silent, no matter what. 'A matter of respect for my family name.'

She did write a letter though, and put it in an envelope. 'If ever anything

---

[*] 'Monica Letebele' chose to keep her real name to herself.

violent happens to me,' she wrote, 'and I'm no longer around to point fingers, then trust that it is him. Regardless.'

It boggles her mind why he stays. She gives him nothing. They bicker and fight day in, day out. 'I threw him out three times, but after a week or so he always comes back. Nothing stops him from coming back.'

She takes me for a stroll through her neighbourhood. Most of the houses are inhabited by relatives: cousins, nieces, aunts, uncles. She walks and points. There in that house remain three out of nine adults. In the home behind it, six out of seven have died.

'AIDS and liquor – a deadly combination.'

Monica feels powerless. Her dreams only involve her grandchildren. 'I have hopes for them that they will do things differently. How? I have no clue. I honestly, really have no idea.'

———————

Hundreds of thousands of tourists visit Botswana every year, mostly to enjoy the stunning natural landscape. They return home with suitcases full of warm memories. Journalists sojourn in the country and report positively on its progress and development.

Still, I have a hard time coming to terms with the paradox of the people's kindness on the one hand, and, on the other, the stories they tell me of betrayal, increasing sexual abuse and even murder amongst loved ones. The mania of the day are 'passion killings', in which a man first kills his ex and then himself.

'Liberate your heart to live and love fully by letting go of the pain from your past.' The saying comes from Nana Adupipin Boaduo, and hangs on the wall near the receptionist of the University of Botswana. 'These words keep me going,' says the woman with a smile, once she sees me writing down the adage. 'I'll show you the way to Radithlokwa.'

Log Radithlokwa is a lecturer in sociology and writes columns for a quality newspaper. He fears no topic. A recurring theme in his writing is love and sex in Botswana. One of his most recent pieces deals with passion killings, an almost weekly phenomenon.

Radithlokwa opens our discussion quickly and forcefully. 'Our problem is: we have never really suffered in Botswana. No natural disasters, no struggle for independence. All the good stuff just landed in our laps. It's a curse, that's what I tell you.'

Botswana's progress has happened *to* Botswana. 'The gifts nature has given us prevent us from growing, changing and adjusting; from facing the problems we need to face, and drastically changing course. We can easily continue till kingdom come, because there is enough to keep us afloat.'

Botswana's core problem, Radithlokwa believes, is an invisible implosion of everything that was supposed to keep society together. A collapse that is hardly visible on the outside, like a cancer.

The extremely rapid modernisation of Botswana's society, financed through diamonds, has altered the way people interact.

'The extended family used to be the safety net. Now the state has taken over that role. But the state differs in one crucial aspect from the extended family: your uncle, your chief, your father and even your aunts held you accountable for your deeds and your actions. The state does nothing of the sort, unless you commit a crime. You can basically do whatever you want. This incredible liberty has not been anchored in a new morality yet.'

Money plays a core role in Botswana's contemporary society. According to Radithlokwa, 'personal growth' has been defined for parents and children alike as buying a new car, building a new house, making calls on the latest model cell phone.

'Home has been reduced to a geographical location where everyone gathers at the end of the day, because they all happen to have a bed there. Words of wisdom? Correcting a straying minor? A father sitting his son down to chat about life, love, fatherhood and responsibility? Whenever I look into my students' eyes, I see emptiness and loneliness.'

Passion killings are the extreme consequences of those two experiences. With hardly anything better to offer (or desired on the receiving end), men pay their 'girlfriends' for attention, romance and sex. The girls in turn expect those 'payments': rings, airtime and cocktails.

'Women offer themselves as a product to the man who then sees her as his property. If she chooses to date a man with more gifts or money to offer, her ex feels ripped off.'

His self-image, bought by drowning her in goods, lies shattered in the gutter. In the gutter, next to his broken self-image, lies his image of the world.

No one ever told him about affection, about love. No one ever explained that respect cannot be bought. He sold his honour the moment he started paying her bills in exchange for sex. His anger at the destruction of his 'bought' sense of honour can't be cooled, except through her death and his suicide.

Radithlokwa breathes a sigh. 'I have no idea how to get out of this mess. We are in the midst of an existential crisis – amongst men and amongst women – a crisis of the relationships they have with themselves and with each other. A crisis in the way they experience life. No one dares to talk about it; it's all too complicated, too sensitive. Worst of all: the crisis isn't serious enough to shake enough people out of their nightmare, yet, because too many people are stuck in the same situation. The nightmare has become the norm.'

We leave his office and Radithlokwa walks me to my car. He asks me whether he may speak candidly. I tell him, 'Feel free, anything goes.'

Radithlokwa thinks for a moment and then says, 'With all due respect to your story and its focus on self-help as an alternative to intercourse, the debate around masturbation is *not* the most crucial one in Botswana right now. Of course, masturbation can assist in containing the AIDS epidemic. However, what would really make a difference, I think, is a fundamental and deep change in the way we interact with each other. With ourselves. With life.'

On my way back to my hotel to pack my stuff and head back home, Ntebela calls me. He is hosting a radio show tonight, and would like the broadcast to deal with love and materialism. 'Wanna be my guest?'

I struggle. What on earth can I add to a show aimed at teenagers in Gaborone, on love, romance and intimacy? I'm a Dutchman in his thirties, a bachelor.

Ntebela pleads. 'We need to put these topics on the agenda. Help me achieve that.'

When I arrive in the studio in a fancy shopping mall, I find the other guests waiting. Two teenage girls: the one is fourteen, the other sixteen. Expensive clothes, fashionable hairdos, sexy cell phones. The moment the microphone is switched on, they share their insights, without a hint of self-doubt. They say that love is limitless and eternal, that love needs expression through Levi jeans and Gucci sunglasses, bracelets and cell phones with built-in cameras.

I am dumbfounded. Ntebela gestures to me to join in. I take a deep breath, trying to massage my irritation away from my vocal cords. 'You feel loved because your boyfriend bought you a pair of jeans? That's exchanging a product for a service, like going to the market and bartering to bring a chicken home. Every language has a word for that, and it ain't "love".'

A grin on Ntebela's face.

The girls do a quick reality check in each other's eyes and continue their story, undisturbed. They blabber about their sisters' boyfriends who prove their undying love by taking their 'special ones' anywhere the girls want to go.

About how hilariously funny masturbation is, and, no, they have never touched themselves. Of course not.

Ever.

They save themselves. For the love of their lives: the man who will give them his all.

Once they're done dreaming, the DJ plays a song.

I look at the girls and see their eyes twinkle.

TO PROCREATE, PROVIDE, AND PROTECT

'What does it mean to be a man today?'

The question still reverberates in the air. I hear the stories of other men, absorb them.

'The codes of old have disappeared,' a friend tells me. 'The Bushmen of Southern Africa honoured their code, the Samurai of Japan knew theirs by heart, the Knights Templar were engulfed in their own ciphers – none of that is valid anymore. If you want to make sense of things today you need to write your own code.'

Where do I start?

Flames lick the sky. Long swipes. A sweet smell in the air.

It is dark. My senses have abandoned me. It could be ten o'clock at night or five in the morning. Somewhere along the line I lost track of time.

A night close to Africa's southernmost point.

The flickering light of man-sized flames shines on dozens of bodies, dancing to the rhythm of drums. Huge drums, a hypnotic beat. I too dance. The rhythm seduces and liberates. The flames warm my torso on this cold winter's night in the southern hemisphere.

'Real' men don't dance around fires. Or do they?

'Real' men have it all: women, ambitions, children, a home, bank accounts and cars.

'Real' men don't doubt.

'Real' men play poker.

'Real' men plant their seed and watch their progeny mature from a safe distance.

'Real' men are a myth.

———————

An Ethiopian philosopher once summarised what, in his culture, is seen as the purpose of life. 'For us life revolves around the continuation of the species, of our genetic pool. You as an individual mean nothing at all. If you have to die to secure the survival of the group, than you will die. If you must bleed, you will bleed. If you must shine for the good of the collective, then you will shine.'

In other African countries I find the same line of thinking, worded differently for sure, but essentially identical. The individual means nothing, the group is everything. The collective helps you to survive, so you do what you need to do to help the group survive.

According to the way a person fulfils this core role, he earns bonus points: respect, a public display of admiration for the quality of his existence. 'Respect' builds the durability of his memorial as it is left behind in the minds and spirits of those around him.

A person becomes an ancestor through the respect people give him after he has lived through all the stages of life. In this perception of life a man has three core tasks to fulfil. He procreates so that his name and his genes will continue. He provides his dependants with food, education, clothing and housing. And, finally, he protects them against enemies, dangers and setbacks.

If a man fulfils these three roles in a more or less satisfactory way, he will have obeyed his biological and sociological directives, and can therefore be seen as a 'real man'.

However, his remembrance will blur, even during his lifetime, if he fails to accomplish any or all of them.

Three tree-trunks form a triangle, above the well. Years of sunshine has turned them to grey, the bark gone. The wood has been polished by thousands of foot soles pushing against the trunks while hands and arms pulled the water up. Ropes have left grooves up to fifteen centimetres deep in the wood.

The water carrier of Gabi knows his routine. He places one leg against the log, slings his other leg around the rope hanging into the well and kicks backward while his hands pull. Each kick brings the homemade rubber bucket higher. Sweat pours down his face.

Leg, right hand, left hand.

The rope dances in the air.

A cart next to the well carrying four big, green jerry cans awaits the water. The water carrier empties the rubber bucket carefully through a funnel, determined not to lose one precious drop.

At the well, he is the only man. Fetching water is a task for women and children.

'That is why a man has a wife and children,' comments village elder Danfalkeu Batouré. 'A man's only business near a water well is when being there is indeed his business.'

In the village of Gabi the rules and directives of life are clear.

Batouré lies stretched out on a mat under the central tree, in front of the village chief's residence. Other men have brought their own mats. Sandals have been placed neatly on the dusty soil.

In a side street a boy is trying to tame a young bull; the two young energies gallop for control. A woman, sickle in hand, has found herself a seat on the back of a cart filled with freshly harvested sorghum.

Batouré has formed a transitional authority with some of the other elders of Gabi to replace the chief, who died a few months ago. 'We are deciding who can fill this very important post.'

All of the elders, Batouré included, are dressed in *tunicas* – long robes made from pure cotton and always decorated with chic embroidery – which give them a distinguished appearance.

'The candidate,' says Batouré, 'has to respect the village and each of the inhabitants; he needs to serve everyone's interest in equal ways, always speak truthfully and radiate a natural authority.'

Gabi is situated in the south of Niger, close to the border with Nigeria. No more than a few hundred households – a hamlet of Haussa farmers and peasants. They scrape the earth for a living in-between the unforgiving Sahara desert in the north and the fertile, humid rainforest along the Gulf of Guinea in the south.

The Haussa are a pious people. They embraced Islam wholeheartedly when this religion spread out over West Africa. 'Everyone fears Allah,' sings Batouré. 'And that is how it should be.'

A breeze picks up the dust and throws it high up in the air. I have trouble breathing. My throat is not accustomed to this kind of dry heat. My water runs out quickly. I am fully aware of my vulnerability here on the edge of the globe's largest desert. These surroundings don't allow for too many errors. For those living in Niger, the Almighty's wrath is tangible.

Niger is listed as one of the top five poorest countries in the world, and clings to its position almost stubbornly. Most inhabitants feed themselves with what they grow, and sell whatever is left over. Those who don't farm, trade: cell phone airtime, frozen yoghurt, purified or unpurified drinking water, dried meat.

Apart from the farmers on the banks of the Niger River, agriculturalists depend on what the rain brings. And that is seldom enough. 'We cannot do anything,' complained President Mamadou Tandja in 2005, when yet again the rains had failed. 'It is up to Allah whether it rains or not.'

Aid organisations sounded the alarm bell and warned that people might die, a claim that, curiously enough, angered the president. He told the BBC World Service: 'Have you seen people begging on the streets? You have seen us. Do our bodies show any signs of hunger? Do not listen to ramblings that do not make sense.'

The BBC broadcast images of starving children with tubes up their noses, fragile arms and legs, and mourning women beside the corpses of babies and toddlers.

Mothers could no longer feed their kids; fathers left their villages in a desperate search for extra income. They had taken with them the last of the household savings as well as the keys to the granary padlocks. That's how the rules and directives prescribe life: men control the cash and carry they keys. All the cash. All the keys.

Months earlier, the United Nations had asked for funds to feed 2.5 million people, a quarter of Niger's total population, but had received next to nothing. Hunger in the Sahel was no longer a *sexy* enough cause. West African musicians therefore organised their own concerts to raise money. A few ministers even gave away a third of their salaries.

Gabi mourns the loss of life too. Batouré: 'So Allah desires, so it happens.' He estimates the village and its direct surroundings counted a hundred and fifty dead. On the fields around Gabi, sorghum awaits more rain; harvesting will take place soon, with some farmers having started already. In the shade of trees, women grind their sorghum. For the next few months, Niger seems out of the danger zone.

In the long run, however, Niger's problems are far from over. The population will double in the next twenty years. On average, a woman gives birth to 7.9 children. Most men are polygamous, and conceive twenty children or more. Despite a high mortality rate amongst young children, half of Niger's present population is fifteen or younger. Of them, only 38 per cent goes to school. Jobs are not available for them, while the pressure on fertile land increases.

For most men, having a respectable throng of children is still the ideal. Even immediately after yet another food security crisis. Regardless of the barren land.

'Yes, we've been told about that so-called explosion. We are aware of the statistics,' confirms Batouré. He himself conceived over fifty children, and jokingly admits he lost count. As time passed by, more than thirty of them died. 'What can you do? If Allah so desires, He will bless you with many children. In the Qur'an He promises to feed them. If they die, that too is His wish.'

Hunger is not simply a result of poor rains. Most often, food shortages are exacerbated by human actions. Food stocks grow and fall due to policy decisions and the workings and failings of the market. A failing market hurts many, but will always profit a few. Maintaining those failings is in their interest, an interest they will defend to the end, and if needs be, through corruption and violence.

Ordinary people pay the price for these failings; people like the men under the tree in Gabi, the water carrier of the village and the woman on the back of the cart.

The drought of 2005 was like any other drought that preceded it, or those that will surely follow, bringing death and disease in its wake. The livestock are affected; large groups of people need to sell their last possessions to buy a single bag of flour.

Once the drought is over, and the hunger has passed, those who survive start from scratch, praising the Almighty for pulling them through.

But apart from being powerless victims of invisible market forces, they too have a say in their lives. Each and every one makes choices, and either pays the price for them or reaps the rewards – or both. Even people in Niger can choose how to respond to their surroundings, can lay the groundwork for their own future, and influence the size of their own families.

Ramadan has wound down the normal pace of life in the Sahel. The streets of Maradi have mostly been abandoned, with a few men napping on mats in the shade of trees, walls or buildings. Teashops have closed their doors during the day. At the end of the afternoon, chefs come out of their homes to start cutting the meat and vegetables for their *brochettes*, but wait until after sunset to light their charcoal.

'Fasting is a period of contemplation and moderation,' Abou Abdou explains. 'Every temptation of the flesh is cast aside. I will suffer, I am hungry. For me this is a spiritual cleansing, a loss of all that is bad. It allows me to strengthen my ties with Allah.'

Abou Abdou approached me while I sat on a wooden bench near his mosque. My notebook had drawn his attention. 'What is it you're scribbling down?' And then he excused himself. 'I'm on my way to the mosque. Don't leave. Let's chat.'

After his evening prayers Abdou joined me. 'Acquiring knowledge is a great good. Wisdom, insight, perspective.' Abdou himself is a teacher at a secondary school. He studied psychology in Abidjan, the commercial centre of Ivory Coast. Abdou loved his studies.

'Fascinating stuff. But hey, who in Niger would like to hire a psychologist? People are afraid I'll mess with their heads. Ah, ignorance! I had to settle for a position as teacher. And you? Tell me what your mission is here.'

I explain as best I can my reasons for being in Maradi. 'What exactly is polygamy, and why do men aspire to have so many children? What role does religion play? How do the living conditions in Niger affect the choices people make?'

Abdou listens intently and sips his strong coffee, ordered shortly after sunset. 'Hmmm – interesting.' He keeps repeating those words. 'Very interesting. You are on a quest for something that touches at the heart of our culture, our belief system and men's priorities.'

I expect an exposé on the Qur'an, the history of the Haussa, and the importance of spirituality and religion, but instead find myself needing to adjust my antennae as soon as Abdou starts speaking. He mixes words like Freud, sex, lust and urges with Mohammed, belief and liberal society.

'If you want to understand our lifestyle, which includes veils and polygamy, a ban on alcohol and free sex, it might be helpful to go back to Freud and Carl Jung. My studies of works of Freud and Jung have increased my insights into Islam. Even Jung states that reason can only go so far in explaining things, and that spirituality is necessary to reach a state of psychological equilibrium. For Freud, every human act could be reduced to a need for sex.'

Abdou orders a new coffee and offers me one. He continues: 'I see truth in what Freud said. Sex as the main motive behind our thinking and behaviour. The urge to succeed, the need to impress. I see a straight line from Freud to Islam, and the place given to sex as a driving force in life. To prevent us from descending to the level of animals, which is what you see happening in liberal societies, our religion helps us curtail this strong energy of sexuality.'

I gaze into the cook's fire on the sidewalk. He prepares the coffee and snacks that his son will drop off at customers in the neighbourhood. A few houses away, a man swings a charcoal burner around, trying to ignite the embers. The orange glow leaves circles in the night. Abdou's words echo in my mind. Man is a sexual animal, and to tame the beast you give it what it needs, but you do so in moderation. He explains polygamy as a way of channelling male sexual energy.

Abdou: 'Man is insatiable. He will always want more than he has. His first wife is beautiful, the second comes from a wealthy family, the third is pious and the fourth is the chief's daughter.'

His words stir my response: 'But Abdou, what about *female* sexual energy? It doesn't appear in your story at all. I'd say it's not wise, to put it mildly, to deny that energy. What do you do with a woman's desires? You can't just forbid it… Jung also said: "Where love reigns, there is no will to power; and where the will to power is paramount, love is lacking."'

Abdou looks at me. A vague grin plays on his lips, one that combines arrogance and pride with a hint of pity for me and the values I was raised with. He ends our evening chat abruptly. 'That question is typical of your culture. Were we to bump into each other more often over the next few days, we would have more of these moments. My culture is different from yours.'

'I am aware of that, Abdou – that is why I am here. I'd like to understand some of the crucial forces in your culture. By comparing yours to mine and mine to yours we might eventually understand each other, and – who knows – maybe even learn from one another…'

Abdou scans me sharply as he thinks over both my question and my answer. He adds surreptitiously, leaning over: 'Maybe men fear the female sexual energy? Her beauty? Her attraction? That's why he keeps her at home, forbids her to leave his place. That is also why most men will not receive you, a stranger from afar, in their homes.'

As I walk back to my hotel, I think over our conversation. I have a sense I understand what he said, but something bothers me. Using Freud to explain the laws regarding polygamy as laid down by Mohammed? The global village, I think, certainly has some increasingly interesting potpourri.

The Qur'an allows a man to be married to four women concurrently, provided he can feed, house and clothe them and their progeny, and only if he treats all equally. The fourth chapter of the Qur'an also allows certain kinds of family planning, if a family grows larger than can be provided for.

Polygamy is found all over Africa, and is practised by Muslims, Christians and animists alike. In countries where the practice is forbidden, men choose to entertain concubines or girlfriends. However, all over Africa more and more women refuse to share their men with other women, while increasing numbers of men can no longer afford several women with children.

In days gone by, a large family was a sign of wealth and prestige. In rural areas men needed the extra labour to work the land. Having many children also meant 'being remembered after one's death'.

Men in the trading centre of Maradi are slowly making a shift away from polygamy. In particular, well-educated young men are aware of the risks of having to feed fifteen bellies or more. Mohammed Kilima (32), an electrician, and Zakari (25), an accountant, settle for three to four children. 'That should do,' says Zakari.

Zakari still lives with his parents, while the apple of his eye resides in the capital, Niamey. 'The distance feeds the desire; with every passing day it grows.'

Kilima lives in town with his wife, Asamaou (28), and their son, Almustafa. The men are inveterate romantics – Zakari, who is engaged, even more than the married man, Kilima.

Zakari mumbles. 'Far from my eyes; close to my heart.' His eyes glaze over in a syrupy stare. The wedding date is set for sometime next year. Zakari chooses to work hard, so he has enough savings at his disposal. Only the best of the best for his woman. Until then, he writes her love letters and dreams of her.

Zakari finds inspiration for his poems in the works of Socrates, Nietzsche and Saint John of the Cross. 'I love reading the *Pensées de Socrate*,' he says while he drives us through town in his delivery van. Another verse. '*L'amour est à l'âme de celui qui aime ce qui l'âme est au corps qui l'anime.*[*] That is true love for you.'

Back in South Africa I will find the quote in the essay *Réflexions ou sentences et maximes morales* of François de La Rochefoucauld, a 17th century thinker who inspired Nietzsche. Zakari quotes this German philosopher regularly. The accountant loves the sayings of sages from all corners of the globe, whose wisdoms he recites as if they were songs.

Zakari and his beloved see each other every few weeks. They chat and so strengthen their connection. Hugging, kissing and caressing are not allowed, yet. 'When I close my eyes I see her. I dream of her sheer negligé, her stockings and the soft skin beneath.'

For now, these dreams satisfy Zakari. 'With visions like that, I feel I'm the happiest man alive.' His friend Kilima nods with appreciation. Himself a married man now, he fondly remembers his days of romance and courting.

Kilima invites me to come to his home, much to my surprise after Abdou convinced me no one would offer me that honour. He also introduces me to his wife, Asamaou. Their living room is decorated with long, flowing pieces of cloth. They watch James Bond's *The world is not enough* with gorgeous

---

[*]   For him who loves, love is for the soul what the soul is for the body it animates.

'Bond girls' in charming gala dresses. Following the movie comes an Argentinean *telenovela*, with lots of lethal stares, square jawlines, cliff-hangers, and a permanent state of war between all.

'Have you noticed,' Kilima says, 'that no one in these programmes is ever really happy? What kind of life is that?'

Asamaou turns her gaze to the floor the moment Kilima starts talking of the poems he wrote her while they were still courting. Reciting any of them now would be inappropriate. 'Romance does not belong out in the open.' Asamou clearly feels ill at ease. She grabs her veil and heads for the garden. In her absence Kilima recalls the days he had to fight for her attention.

'When everything is still unknown, when desire burns because you are not allowed to heed it – in those days, love was different from what it is now. The moment you share a space together a certain tension fades away. Periods of struggle and conflict arise, followed by spells of co-existence and peace. Desire grows during those patches, a longing back to the unknown, the thrill of the chase, the hunt, the romance. A longing for someone else.'

In a world filled with bans and prohibitions, temptation seduces. Nothing is as flammable as a lingering desire for new discoveries, new conquests. Kilima has a tough choice to make. Look around, or stick around?

Kilima and Zakari seem to be exceptions in their hunger for love and romance. They don't just want to be adored and served, they also love to adore and serve – or so they say.

Most other men Zakari introduces me to are less interested in fleeting emotions and burning passions. The last of his friends, Amadou Salifou (39), is also the most outspoken.

'I have two women for no other reason than that I can. The prophet writes that it is good. The moment my business picks up, I will take a third wife, and even a fourth. I have eleven children now, and one of my wives is pregnant. I want as many children as Allah gives me. I am not worried about anything. Allah will provide. That is how it is written. That is how it will be. Insh'Allah.'

———————

Socrates, Nietzsche, Freud, *telenovelas*, and James Bond – along the dusty roads of Maradi people find inspiration anywhere. Each, however, will always return to the sources they all share: the prophet, the Qur'an, and above all else, Allah.

Yusuf Adamou (29) pours water from a plastic tea kettle. First he washes his head, his ears, his mouth and his nose; after that his feet, and finally his hands. Men await his evening prayer in their mosque, the sun has just set.

'Allahu akhbar.' Adamou's flock kneels in the direction of Mecca. I feel too much of an observer and take a few steps back into the road, which houses praying men, moving mopeds and playing children.

No conversation passes without continuous references to the rules and laws of the faith. Africa is a deeply religious continent – Muslims no more or less than Christians or animists. The pious experience of faith in the south of Niger, however, seems to merge with what some have called *miserabilisme*: a deep-seated conviction that life will never get any better. Life is supposed to be miserable, and there's nothing anyone can do about it.

That is, in a way, how the president explained the food shortages. That's how men explain their choices. That's how hawkers account for the mess around their stalls. Things are as they are, needing neither explanation nor solution.

For a great deal of religious Africans, God's largesse increases with one's own self-declared impotence, or so it appears. The more insignificant man professes to be, the more significant they think they make God. The more powerful people make God, the more they *think* they are praising the Almighty. The more God is made out to be a stern judge, the less likely it is that a person will escape his fate.

God sets the number of children. God chooses who gets to live, who becomes ill and who dies of malnutrition. Rains and storms; an official stamp; security on the road: it is all given to God, and God alone. The fear of God leaves little space for negotiations, for experiments or risk-taking.

Maradi in Niger does not have a monopoly on this perception of the relationship between man and God. Existence in Africa very often inspires images of divinity that inspire shock and awe, a surrender to fate and a deep belief that nothing is what it seems.

As the West African philosopher Hampâté Bâ wrote:

This you must remember: the fact that a thing cannot be seen, handled or perceived does not absolutely prove it does not exist.'

While waiting for Imam Amadou, I recall the meetings I had in the afternoon with four older men in the popular *quartier* of Maradawa. Their faces had been purposefully carved with many deep cuts, in ceremonies of initiation, decades ago. They were dressed in colourful *tunicas*. Goats shuffled along, now and then getting up on their hind legs to nibble at leaves. Children toyed and tussled.

We spoke of fatherhood and they asked me for my marital status and whether I have children. 'I made other choices,' I answered. 'Marriage and kids haven't happened in my life. Not yet.'

'I have heard of that,' *haji* Mohamar Sani (65) said in a refreshingly neutral way. 'Life in Europe is too expensive to raise kids.' He himself is the proud husband of three wives, and the proud father of twenty surviving children.

Mohamadou Omoro (77) asked me, compassionately: 'Who will remember you after your death? A child is like a picture of you. When you die, others will see your image in the face of your child. A child is also your gift to humanity. You have breathed life into a new generation. Were I to die tomorrow, my picture will have been taken.' He drew a cotton cloth tight around his face and resumed playing with his prayer chain.

'Europeans choose material objectives; you demand that a person makes his own fate; your choices affect life now, here on earth, to achieve gratification now. We don't. We in Africa prefer the spiritual life, faith; we tend to the well-being of our spirit. For us, life after death is more important than life before death.'

Mohamar Sani emphasised this point by recalling his pilgrimage in the early 1960s. On foot he and his dad had crossed the Sahara from Maradi to go to Mecca. It took them four years. They hardly spoke along the way. 'We don't learn through endless chatter; we learn through observation. I scrutinised my father's every deed, and now live as he lived.'

Father and son survived by begging and by calling upon other people's hospitality. Having arrived at the shores of the Red Sea, the duo only had money for one man to cross. Mohamar had to stay behind. He returned to Khartoum and begged until, eventuality, he had enough to follow his father onto Mecca. 'On my pilgrimage I proved able to suffer without complaint. For us, that is a sign of courage and masculinity. To endure suffering as Allah lays it on you.'

At a respectable distance stood his 23-year-old son, Abdul Razak, observing his father speak in the quartier Maradawa, as his father observed his grandfather all those decades ago.

When Imam Yusuf Adamou taps me on my shoulder, my awareness pops back into the present. He has just finished evening prayer, and can spare me a few minutes before his dinner is served.

'My day consists of praising Allah, and acknowledging Mohammed as his prophet. Everything I do serves that, even the meal I am about to eat.'

Adamou takes hold of a plank and reaches for his pen carved out of wood. He dips the pen in some ink, slaps it gently against the side of the plank and starts writing on the prayer board.

As his hand moves elegantly over the wood, he says, 'You wanted to know more about polygamy, and about children, you said. Having more than one wife, and having many children are what brings paradise within reach of a man. Would he only have one wife, it would be more difficult for him to remain faithful.

'The amount of love a man can give is enormous; the moment he feels that love, he can't but ask the object of his desire for her hand in marriage. In a subtle way of course. First he'll have to find out, through the services of relatives or friends, if she's available. Has she menstruated already? Has she not yet been promised to another family?'

A new dip in ink, a new gentle smack against the board.

'Having many children is like handing presents to Islam. A way of strengthening our faith, so one day Islam will conquer the world and dominate the other faiths.'

—————

Under the central tree of Gabi more men join the impromptu gathering. Teacher and psychologist Abou Abdou tells the newcomers what the meeting is about. I have asked him to be my translator. The *lingua franca* here is Haussa; those who speak French left the village ages ago and took up jobs in towns and cities.

We spend quite some time under the tree; village elder Danfalkeu Batouré is reluctant to chat about men and manhood. But as our audience grows, Batouré seems more willing to use the occasion to lecture the village, while talking to me.

'Being a man means, first and foremost, being polite to your parents and your elders,' teaches Batouré. 'Secondly, it means you take care of your family.'

Most of those who join late, stay on the right hand side of the tree. Some join the men on the mats on the ground. I notice how clothing defines who sits where. The men on the mats all wear *tunicas*, whereas the men on the other side of the tree wear torn T-shirts, faded trousers and worn shoes. I ask Abdou about the distinction.

'They are the village's power and strength,' explains Ousman Danbaba (45), pointing at the men on the other side of the tree. Batouré leans back against the tree, and closes his eyes. 'They do the hard work, they fight a fire, till the land. They are dynamic. European clothes work better for them than any *tunica* would.'

It dawns on me that the men in the *tunicas* are the guardians of the village traditions and customs as well as of the laws of the Prophet. The men in the torn T-shirts are the rank and file. They carry most of the burden of old habits that no longer fit seamlessly into their lives. Their eyes light up when I ask the dignitaries for the purposes and goals of old customs in an era of new challenges.

'You need children to take care of you when you grow old, to be remembered after your death,' Dandaba says.

I retort, 'I understand why having a child is crucial. But why fifteen, or thirty?'

Batouré opens his eyes. 'If you only have a handful of children, and they die, what then have you got left? You cannot run that risk!'

In Niger, one in four children dies before celebrating its fifth birthday. Batouré himself had to conceive fifty children, to see only twenty of them reach maturity.

'I appreciate that a man of your generation could not take that risk when you were still young,' I carefully say. 'You seem to me a man with many years of life experience.'

For the first time in over an hour, Batouré shares a smile.

'I am 130 years old; life holds no surprises for me anymore. I drink my juice, eat my meal.'

'With your standing and position, you must be aware that these days far fewer children perish than previously. Medical care is one of the reasons Niger's population is growing as rapidly as it is. Don't you think that, being blessed with the ability to cure and heal, we have a responsibility also to protect those who survive against a life of poverty and misery?'

As if stung by a bee, Batouré's kindness instantly evaporates. 'Death does not wait. You can't fend off death. Death is all powerful. It is Allah who decides, not medicine. Everything belongs to Allah.'

Silence sets in under the tree. Batouré's voice sounded angry and threatening. After a while, a man from the other side of the tree carefully and serenely draws the attention with a modest cough. He introduces himself as Isaka Mai Ada, 43, married to one wife, with five children.

'It is true that our past taught us that a man needs many children to work the land. But what now? The fields are no longer fertile. The land I own can't feed a family of fifteen.' Other young men nod in agreement. Ada continues, 'Most of us are aware we will have a problem in the future; we know we have little to offer each child if the family keeps growing. But that doesn't mean we suddenly stop having children. We don't know of the methods you know of. How can I prevent my wife from becoming pregnant again?'

The 'rank and file' men stare at me curiously. The men wearing *tunicas* also await my answer, some with more than just a hint of disgust in their eyes. In broad sketches I paint two of the most realistic options in a place like Gabi: *coitus interruptus* and periodic abstinence. Condoms and the pill seem to me too liberal for Gabi, not to mention abortion.

When I've finished my sentence, I wait for Abdou to translate.

Nothing. He remains silent.

I look at him and gesture for him to take his turn. He stammers, speaks one short sentence where I needed many more. Questions from the men in torn shirts are no longer passed on, and Abdou gets into a debate with the dignitaries. Then turns to me.

'Batouré thinks it's a disgrace for a man of your age to be childless. You will have to fetch your own water, work your own land, scrub your own pots. Those are chores for men who have lost the plot. Weak men. Boys'

Stuck.

We have reached total deadlock.

I feel the verbal slap on the hands that Batouré just gave me.

The first men take their cues and leave their mats under the tree on the village square. Batouré plays with his string of beads. It's noon, the sun is at its highest and hottest point of the day. It's time for prayer.

Batouré bids me farewell. 'The next time you pass by, I'll give you my unmarried daughter. A man your age needs children. Trust me. I have lived long enough to know what I'm talking about.'

COFFEE IS A GENTLEMAN

Standing in the back of a pick-up truck, the men wear black suits, white shirts and black ties. Each man holds with one hand onto whatever he can, clamping on for dear life, while in the other hand he carries a brass instrument. They trumpet an infectious tune, while centrifugal forces pull them left as the car drives around the central traffic circle of Moshi. They all sway the other way when the driver turns left, away from the roundabout.

A white sedan decorated with purple and blue balloons follows the mobile ensemble. The bride is hardly visible behind what looks like an exploding wedding gown.

The Sunday is the only day everyone can make it to a wedding. Other newly-married couples will make their round of honour at the central circle today, each with their own brass section, on their way to their own ceremony

Once the newly-weds leave the round-about, Moshi becomes dead quiet again. The streets of this town in northern Tanzania are spick-and-span. Lawns are cut short.

Of the four faces of the clock tower in the middle of the round-about, only the one on the east shows the right time. The only living souls visible are the two guards near an ATM, automatic rifles in their laps.

The smell of roasted coffee permeates the town.

Strong coffee. Real coffee.

No café in Moshi will pour its customers instant coffee. This is one of those rare places in Africa where the black liquid comes from real beans – real coffee with a genuine aroma and a delectable, bitter aftertaste.

Far away, the last of the glaciers of Kilimanjaro reflect sunlight; it's estimated that they'll be gone by 2050. It was there, on top of Africa's highest mountain where, in 1961, a new flag was raised to honour Tanganyika's freedom – *Uhuru* in Swahili. Tanganyika was named after the lake on the border of Congo, but the country was renamed Tanzania when Zanzibar joined the union in 1964.

The slopes of Kilimanjaro have been home to commercial coffee bushes for over a century. Men of the Chagga ethnic group have been tending these beans, which once fetched good prices. In 1997, a kilo of coffee beans was worth close to two euros; five years later the value had dropped to a quarter of that price. These days, because of the rising costs of chemicals and fertiliser, a farmer hardly earns anything.

To make ends meet, the male coffee growers rely increasingly on what their wives can add to the household kitty. Men are no longer the sole providers, which also means they have lost their sole right to make decisions. Their pedestal has caved in, and there's nothing they can do about it.

'I feel inferior. Incapable. Unworthy. I can't come close to providing my children with what my father gave me: a future.' His T-shirt is ripped; he walks around in flip-flops and short trousers with holes.

Rogerthe Tarimu (62) is one of the biggest coffee farmers of Lyamungo, at an altitude of two thousand metres. Rogerthe's father built the sizable farmhouse in the 1950s with the profits he made from coffee. After his father's death, Rogerthe took possession of the property. He lives on the left side, while his cows reside in a barn on the right. Tools are stored in a shed.

One of his sons washes a pick-up truck, another nourishes seedlings by carefully watering them. Tarimu removed a large section of his coffee plantation. 'I want to experiment with new types. People say they are more resistant against some of the diseases that plague us here.'

Investing in coffee despite the problems with the prices? 'I have to try at least. Maybe the prices will go up again. This year was better than last year, and last year was better than the year before.'

He does have a Plan B, though. Just growing coffee has become too much of a gamble. The market has become too wobbly. Tarimu has shifted his attention to bananas, vegetables and his cows. At least he can eat those himself should the value of coffee plunge again.

Statistics from the coffee growers' co-operation of Moshi (KNCU) show that not only have the prices of coffee come down, but production has also come close to collapse. In 1984, all the farmers connected to KNCU produced nearly 20 000 metric tons of beans. Twenty years later those figures have dropped to a mere 3 400 tons. For most coffee growers, the profits from growing coffee are too small to warrant investments in new plants, fertiliser or pesticides.

Fewer Chagga grow less coffee and receive less for what they produce. Tarimu: 'Coffee has become a frustrating business; there's nothing I can do about those global prices. You can only endure them.'

He and his colleagues search for ways to raise production. Their biggest problem is a lack of land.

Tarimu's father left him 5.5 hectares of land. Most of his peers make do with a fifth of that. Their fathers had to divide the land amongst more sons. Tarimu was lucky; he was his father's only son. His sisters, being women, were not entitled to inherit; they had to rely on what their own husbands were given by *their* fathers.

Tarimu has no option but to divide his plots amongst all of his sons. The Chagga rules are clear. The youngest will inherit the most because it is he who has to take care of his parents when they're old. Everything else will be handed out equally to the others, even if that means that none of them has a plot big enough to provide for their new families.

Would it not be better to hand it all to just one son? In his lifetime, Tarimu has seen how once profitable farms have been cut to sizes that offer no real prospects for development or growth.

'There will come a time when what is left cannot be divided any further. For now, I know that each of my sons will be able to survive. That's what really counts. You have to understand, there is no alternative. It's my duty to divide my plots honestly amongst my sons. How they'll manage is their responsibility, and depends on the choices they'll make.'

None of the growers can go higher up the mountain. The nature reserve there is off-limits. Tourists pay many dollars a day for the right to meander along the slopes of the mountain, and so provide a solid flow of cash to the state coffers. Going down the mountain is no option either. Coffee likes moderate temperatures and besides, the Masai still roam around there with their cattle.

Selling the land to try a new life somewhere else is no option. 'Trust me, every arable square inch of Tanzania is in use,' says Tarimu. And even if land were available somewhere else, a Chagga still would not easily be allowed to sell his slice of the earth.

For the Chagga, land is a gift from the ancestors. Selling it is like spitting in the face of an ancestor. Only if the entire family approved, could a sale be made, provided that the graves of relatives remain property of the family. That land may never change hands.

With a fixed amount of land, a growing population and declining prices for coffee, the Chagga find themselves in a downward spiral. Twenty, thirty years ago, that seemed impossible. The sons and daughters of coffee growers were privileged; they enjoyed the best education coffee could buy. Many of them moved to the towns and cities to find jobs in offices. They made their professional career far away from Kilimanjaro.

The most successful amongst them hired labourers to tend to the coffee, as an extra source of income. The land they owned was enough to feed goats and chickens for the later years of retirement, while enjoying the savings of previous nine-to-five jobs.

This, however, is no longer realistic. A wave of liberalisation in the 1990s demanded by the many international donors of Tanzania, closed down several factories and offices. Jobs are hard to come by these days, whether in villages, towns or cities.

The Chagga had to fall back onto their mountain, their coffee, chickens, bananas, and their livestock.

'Highly frustrating.'

Tarimu leans forward and grabs a ginger cookie from a bag I have brought. He opens a soda. His friend, *haji* Marua Lema (46), a certified accountant as well as experienced coffee grower, nods and adds, 'Coffee used to be a gentleman. Gone are those days.'

'Coffee gave us access to education,' Lema muses. 'It bought us nice homes. The profits of coffee turned us into somebody. No one could tell us what to do; we had money, we were free men, we were farmers. Now we have descended to being peasants again. Imagine this: I can't finish fixing up my own home anymore. No money for the windows, for the electrical wiring, for the final walls inside. It won't happen. I need a million shillings [800 euro]. My bank account is as good as empty.'

Some of the coffee growers can't deal with their slide into poverty, say Lema and Tarimu. First they'll start ignoring their plants, and after a season or two they can't be bothered plucking the beans.

Tarimu: 'Would you, for a few lousy bucks?'

After the frustration come disappointment and anger. They can no longer pay school fees. Lema: 'What man are you, if you can't do for your children what your dad was able to do for you?'

A few of them waste their last income on booze or marihuana: a short-term blank in which problems seem to disappear. Tarimu: 'Then he wakes up the next day, and realises his problems have only started, because he slept with a prostitute who is infected with HIV.'

—————

Tarimu and Lema have expanded on their present lives and told stories of their youth. What is missing amidst the coffee bushes and the banana palms are stories of the days before 'coffee was a gentleman'.

Who were the Chagga, before beans brought purchasing power? Access to the roots of the Chagga seems to be cut off. I decide to go back to Moshi for a day to find answers there.

Even in the regional capital, however, no one can tell me anything about the Chagga heritage. Heading for the Kilimanjaro Regional Library is a bit of a desperate move. The African libraries I have visited in the past were mostly a sorry bunch of books donated by either evangelical organisations out to spread the Word, or by book addicts far away in the West with a sore conscience about dumping their old loves.

But the moment I enter the library of Moshi, yet another of my preconceptions is blown to pieces. No 'sorry bunch of books' here; on the contrary, shelf after shelf contains a wealth of printed beauty. Art books on the Tate Gallery, expensive photography books on West African masks, accessible works by psychologists writing about identity and the anger of a marriage having lost its spark.

The rich collection of books draws in large numbers of young men and women, no older than twenty-five. They browse through encyclopaedias, dictionaries or mathematical works. They study biology or Tanzania's system of law. Some type figures into calculators. All seem to suck up knowledge, with a vengeance.

But books on the Chagga?

Nowhere.

Not one book on one shelf.

I ask librarian John Joseph for assistance. 'We do have the books you're looking for, but no one ever reads them anymore. People here tend not to look backwards, they prefer to look ahead. I moved all of those books to the storeroom years ago. Let me see. Grab a newspaper and a seat. I'll be with you shortly.'

After a few minutes, Joseph lays down a stack of eight books. 'It's not a lot and it's all dated but maybe it will be useful. Be careful though, some may fall apart.'

An old travel guide from the 1950s, a history booklet published in 1965, an anthropological study from 1977, and a publication on coffee. I take a sip from a cup of coffee and start perusing.

'Until recently, nearly all the writing about our country was done by foreign travellers,' writes P.H.C. Clarke in *A short history of Tanganyika* (1965). 'They wrote down what they saw, but they did not see everything nor did they go everywhere. About those places and things they could not write. [...] [W]hile you are reading this book, try to think of the many things that are not written about, the things only known to the African people to whom they happened. Try to use the reports [...] not as the whole history [...] but [let them] help you towards a true picture of it.'

Clarke's book teaches me that the mountain now known as Kilimanjaro appears already in writings from 40 AD. A Greek merchant mentions in the *Periplus Maris Eruthraei* a mountain with a snow-covered top, somewhere in the east of Africa. It took twenty-five days to sail from the end of the Red Sea to the town of Rhapta, from where it took another fourteen days of walking to reach the mountain.

Many of those who set out in the 19th century to find the snow-covered mountain were German missionaries, who mingled their eagerness to evangelise with a desire to explore. The biggest geographical mystery in the mid-1800s was the location of the source of the Nile. Maybe the snow fed the mighty river?

Johannes Rebmann, Johann Ludwig Krapf and Jakob Erhardt were some of the explorers/evangelists who opened up what we now know as Tanzania for European settlers. Before they headed into Africa, they visited the slave and ivory traders of Zanzibar for whom East Africa held few secrets. These traders mainly used three routes, two of which led to very sizeable lakes. The third ended near a huge mountain with snow.

The first European to catch a glimpse of Kilimanjaro was Rebmann, reportedly a peaceful man who once defended himself from lions with an umbrella. He was also the first explorer to contact the Chagga. When Rebmann wrote to Europe confirming the existence of a snow-covered mountain, his information was originally received with laughter.

But when Jakob Erhardt in 1856 sketched a map of Africa based on

Rebmann's experiences and the information gleaned from Arab traders and African travellers containing two snow-covered mountains and a huge lake, geographers in Europe got all excited. Could that lake be the source of the Nile? Or maybe the snow on those two mountains?

The first recorded ascent of Kilimanjaro* was undertaken by a German baron, Karl Klaus Von Decken. He managed to reach about 1 200 metres below the top in 1861. The first successful attempt to master 'Kili' took place in 1889, when Hans Meyer reached Kibo, one of the three summits. By then, the Germans had taken control of *Deutsch-Ostafrika*, which included Tanganyika and present-day Burundi and Rwanda.

Sometime after the mid-1850s the courts and parliaments of Europe became convinced that having territories overseas was essential to a portfolio of grandeur and global influence. With Latin America having shrugged off the yoke of colonialism, and most parts of Asia already taken, every powerful eye in Europe now stared at Africa.

The historian Clarke wrote, 'They thought that colonies were necessary for a powerful country, just as some people think that a big motorcar is necessary for an important man.'

The Chagga resisted the settlers, missionaries and administrators at first. Having refined their military skills against marauding Masai, the Chagga had long been able to defend themselves. Chief Horombo had united most of the Chagga clans under his rule. He had constructed a fort, defended by walls two metres high and 100 metres long. One of his successors was Meli, who managed to defeat a German force. Meli was hanged after German commanders finally defeated him in 1891.

Germany had dramatically underestimated the budget for maintaining colonies. Berlin had to pump a fortune into its East African 'provinces' to build roads, railways and farms. Without local taxes, the colony would quickly have collapsed.

The Chagga around Kilimanjaro had watched the Germans plant coffee, and saw the income the crops generated. Even before Europeans arrived on their doorstep, the Chagga had been quick to embrace new technologies and techniques if they thought them beneficial. The Chagga, for example, used tools that originated in the coastal area, and designed their own technological and social structures for irrigation.

---

*   The origin of the name Kilimanjaro is the Chagga-word *kilimakiaro*, meaning 'the mountain that is hard to climb'.

The Chagga made the move to coffee easily and rapidly. The first seedlings were planted before 1900 in the shade of banana palms. Within a few decades, nearly all Chagga had turned to growing coffee, much to the dismay of European settlers who feared the competition for markets and labour. But the colonial authorities applauded the commercial spirit of the Chagga – they desperately needed the taxes.

While the Chagga men grew coffee, earned money and paid their colonial taxes, the women were put in charge of the bananas, their staple food and the raw material for the local beer, as well as the cows and the chickens. Men no longer wanted to waste their time with those 'inferior' sources of income.

By the end of the 1940s, the Chagga had grown into the wealthiest people in the region. Collectively, they developed into the biggest meat consumers of East Africa. Six thousand metric tons of meat ended up on the plates of the coffee growers every year: 44 000 heads of cattle and 25 000 goats and sheep. Most of it was bought from the Masai, who still pastured in the lowlands.

And the best was yet to come. Consumers in the West couldn't get enough of their coffee. The newly independent nation under the leadership of Julius Nyerere thrived on self-confidence, hope and enthusiasm.

In the 1960s and early 1970s Tanzania was on a roll. The Chagga were doing well. Fathers sent their sons and daughters to the best universities in Nairobi and Kampala, since Dar es-Salaam was too close for the gentlemen who grew coffee. Reputations were at stake; children needed degrees: medical degrees, technical degrees, agricultural degrees.

'The ambitious Chagga became addicted to education, to rising in status through training,' write anthropologists Sally Falk Moore and Paul Puritt in *The Chagga and Meru of Tanzania* (1977).

Seated in the library of Moshi, I look around.

A new generation of Chagga losing themselves in books, making notes, studying for diplomas.

One can hear a pin drop.

'Coffee is a gentleman,' Lema said. But the gentleman has become a sorry pauper. Incomes have shrivelled up and plots are too tiny to make any sizeable production possible. For the most desperate of the coffee growers, the soil at the foot of the mountain holds an alternative to agriculture.

There, in the blistering, unforgiving heat of the midday sun, men dig by the thousands inside Mother Earth. They're searching for the precious tanzanite, a deep, dark blue gem found only near Kilimanjaro. A good stone weighing only one gram brings in a whopping 400 dollars. And where there is one, there has to be more. The miner with luck and determination on his side can make a fortune. But most miners spend years grovelling in gravel for nothing.

The road to the miners' village leads through a landscape reminiscent of a teenager with acne. Dirt and sand is piled next to big holes. Hope and hopelessness are tucked neatly together on a few square metres.

Human beings seem like minuscule ants digging for dear life. Sweat makes trails through fine dust on black skins. Trained muscles take out hundreds of tons of sand annually on a meticulous quest for precious minerals.

Nearer to the main road, the tanzanite buyers sit on plastic chairs under a bush, protected from the sun. Their tiny, highly sensitive weighing scales measure cargoes in tens of grams. What is found here, in the acne landscape, hardly weighs more than 0.3 grams.

The most lucrative veins containing tanzanite are tapped by Tanzanite One, owned by a South African mining company. Those veins that can't be exploited commercially are the domain of small entrepreneurs who will allow anyone to come and sweat for a meal and a roof. Those sweating on the sandy plains hunt for stones light enough to have been swept down by the rains.

Douglas Alois (32) works the middle layer. The concession he calls home is owned by a businessman from Dar es-Salaam. Douglas just finished the night shift, and hangs about in Mererani, a busy nothing in the middle of nowhere. It is not a market place, yet it is. It is not a hamlet, yet it is.

The soil of Mererani contains gems. Gems attract miners. Miners attract a mishmash of service providers. A tailor keeps his sewing machine going with his foot. A woman hawks bananas.

The miners are easy to recognise: their clothes are grey with dust and so too their hair and faces. Only their eyes stick out of the grey – bright whites containing brown irises.

The only ones spared a life of greyness in Mererani are the Masai who stand out brightly, clothed in red fabrics and their hair coloured with ochre.

'In Mererani, they are the ones who buy the stones to sell to middlemen,' Douglas points out. 'They're a necessary evil, if you ask me. They make lots of money over our backs, but many miners are too desperate for cash, or feel they are too near a vein to leave the pit and sell the stones themselves.'

The miners live a life of voluntary slavery. Douglas sleeps in a shed he shares with sixteen mates – no mattresses. For the last four years he's been eating maize porridge and beans. 'We eat what the owner provides us with. No tea, no sugar, no fresh vegetables, no meat.'

Once they hit a vein, they will share the profits with the owner, who hires his son and brother to oversee the work. Until then, they slog away.

A board of checkers lies on a tree trunk under a lean-to. Someone painted the fields white and green a long time ago. Blue and red crown caps make up the checkers. 'Meet our entertainment system,' Douglas jokes. Abdi (32) and Boutros (32) kill time playing the game.

Boutros: 'This is our life here, digging and checkers. Once a week, on Sundays, we all walk to Zaïre, a place nearby, for a wash, a scrub and a few jokes.' Located next to mines, Zaïre of course has all the characteristics of a village near mines and miners: hookers, smugglers and gangsters. Boutros chuckles, 'And don't forget the shower.'

The young men were drawn to Mererani by stories of grand successes and rumours of sudden wealth. Once here, most find it impossible to escape the web of hope that keeps Mererani alive. No one has money for a ticket out. 'Once inside, you're stuck,' Douglas says.

He left his job as a waiter in a tourist hotel near Arusha. 'Haven't seen my family since. Haven't tasted meat again. I will keep digging till I find what I came for.' He is aware that it might take a long time, and it might just as well never happen.

The soil of Mererani seems to have given away most of her wealth. Experts say Tanzanite One has veins that will last until sometime around 2020, after which the world will no longer be able to find new blue stones.

Yet, Douglas and his men are convinced they'll hit the jackpot.

Boutros is the only one who struck blue once. After many years of hard labour for no money, he suddenly made a fortune in a few weeks. He claims it was over eighty million shillings (just over sixty thousand euro). He handed half of it to a friend, a wealthy businessman, for safe-keeping. With the other half he had three simple houses constructed. The friend, however, kept the cash. Boutros sold two of the houses to pay for a lawyer but lost the case due to corruption. Now he's back at the mines.

Mererani seems to cast a magic spell. Men come and can't leave. Those who do find tanzanite in big enough quantities to start a new life often come back quickly. 'You wear your fingers to the bone year after year. And then you find what you came for. Loaded with cash you go back home, and to make up for all your years of suffering, you go wild. Women, booze and drugs.'

Most of the miners have not the faintest idea what investing means, nor banking. The dreams that keep them going as they slave away – a shop, a farm, a factory – turn out to be too grandiose the moment they win at Mererani.

Douglas is sure he won't make mistakes. 'I know about life out there. The day we hit tanzanite is the day I start investing. I'll get away from this hellhole and never, ever return. Next month, next year – everything will be different.'

Laughter.

Faith.

Doubt is not an option.

––––––––––

My path lit by a full moon, I amble along the tracks past coffee fields and palm trees. A truck ploughs its way on a muddy road, its headlights shining deep into the fields. Lights are visible through closed curtains, behind glass windows, in homes built with bricks and cement. The money from coffee brought electricity and running water to this place, far from cities and highways.

My bed for the night is placed in the middle of a round hut with a thatched roof. A shower, a clean toilet, a spacious bed with crispy clean sheets. Someone placed a branch of a bougainvillaea on my pillow. My hut is constructed amongst coffee plants – a village experiment to bring tourists as close as possible to the coffee growers.

Most of the thousands of tourists ascending Kilimanjaro every year usually just fly in, climb up, take a picture and go back home. Hardly any of them ever speak to a Chagga. The village council hopes that perhaps there are enough visitors amongst those thousands who would like to spend a few nights in a coffee plantation to complement the village's income.

Silence flows into my room through an open window with the chill of the evening. A lonesome cricket makes its presence known.

I grab my notes from the library and search for the entries I made on the traditional Chagga way of life. A century ago the German scientist,

Bruno Gutmann, roamed these same slopes where I now find myself. In their 1977 book, *The Chagga and Meru of Tanzania*, Falk Moore and Puritt refer to the Gutmann's observations and compare their own findings with his. During Gutmann's days the Chagga had just started planting coffee. He had encountered a people with a very clearly defined cosmology, philosophy and a very strong sense of spirituality.

'Those things Europeans classify as the natural and the supernatural were one in Chagga cosmology. There was nothing in the world without a supernatural effect or element, nor anything that was not accessible to the malign or benign acts of spirits. [...] Coaxing was achieved through the performance of ritual acts which attempted to control and appease the spirits.'

According to Chagga cosmology, a delicate balance between masculine and feminine forces lies at the core of existence – not unlike Daoism with its famous *yin* and *yang*. Life is created through a wholesome interplay of these energies, whereas an unbalanced interaction leads to death and destruction.

'Hence there was a symbolic and ritual preoccupation with food and sex, with eating and fertility as the basic means of preventing death, both immediate and eternal, and perpetuating life.'

Continuity provided the basis for existence, and achieving continuity was therefore everyone's responsibility. Every person, however, needed to take note of the ever-changing nature of things. None of the forces at play were classified as either 'good' or 'evil', as in the Western way of thinking.

'The cyclic renewal [...] had to be actively continued by keeping everything about the life of man in its orderly place. The basic orders celebrated in Chagga ideology were separation, combination and sequence. [...] Since the combination of masculine and feminine could be dangerous, the partial segregation of things masculine and feminine was a safety measure.'

The Europeans who came to Africa one and a half centuries ago brought with them a fundamentally different cosmology, at the centre of which one finds a struggle between 'good' and 'evil', man and nature. Of course they also claimed to be the only ones who knew where the boundaries are drawn.

These days, a sizeable chunk of the European population has turned its back on their own classical cosmology, which has lost its appeal. Large numbers have given up the quest for a spiritual alternative that could satisfy a deeply felt hunger for certainty, and instead find solace in consumption and entertainment. Other groups find their way towards worldviews and wisdom of the kind that Europeans trampled upon here in Africa, over a century ago.

I continue browsing through my notes and read again about the necessity of procreation and the seriousness of barrenness or infertility, which is punished by leaving the dead far away in the forest to be devoured by animals.

'To die without offspring,' observed Gutmann, 'either because of youth or because of sterility was to interrupt the vital cycle, to break off the continuous ancestor-descendent chain, to make an end where there should have been perpetuity.'

I read about many rules and customs designed to ingrain definitions of masculinity and femininity, and to separate the two. A man and woman, for example, are not to be sexually active for three years after she gives birth to a child. He is allowed to have sex with other women, provided they are either widowed or barren. She is not allowed to grow or sell bananas, which, due to their shape, are the exclusive domain of men. Men and woman are not allowed to befriend each other platonically, to prevent doubts from spreading about his masculinity. A husband and wife each have their separate huts, and he may call her to his if and when he desires her.

Most of these customs and beliefs were no longer valid by the 1970s when Falk Moore and Puritt studied the Chagga. 'Colonial rule, Christianity, coffee and education radically altered many Chagga customs and conditions. [...] Step by step involvement in a cash economy has carried political and cultural consequences which cumulatively were not planned by anyone.'

I close my notebook and wonder. If the rapid development and economic growth amongst the Chagga so completely severed them from their cosmology, what would happen if the engine of development came to a standstill?

Earlier in the day I was told about a stiff increase in domestic violence on the slopes of the mountain. The women of Lyamungo complain endlessly when they chat about their men. Men apparently drink too much, loaf about and aren't worth their salt.

Reminicere Nkya pushed her foot even harder on the pedal powering her sewing machine when I asked her for her thoughts. 'Men in Africa don't work – simple as that. They all dream about sitting in an office, commanding others what to do while their women plough the land. Some go as far as to take their wives' savings straight to the nearest bar. Let me tell you, it wasn't like this when I grew up. My father worked himself to death wanting our future to be better than his. Those men are extinct. The only reason we stick with our men today is for our children, and nothing else.'

Her husband, Eliakim Sauli Nkya, didn't flinch a muscle as he heard his wife's litany. He let it all come down like a tropical shower in the rainy season. Later, when we went for a walk to admire his beans, he conceded to most of it.

'Everything has changed, and that isn't easy. We had the coffee and therefore the money. We had the money, so we were the ones to make the decisions, after listening to everyone else. The roles were clearly defined. The women sold the bananas, the milk and the eggs. That was their business and whatever they earned was theirs. These days we have to put all our money on the table and negotiate what to spend it on. You must understand: that leads to trouble.'

I do understand the tension many of the Chagga experience. A culture that was once adamant about the distinction between masculine and feminine and emphasised the boundaries between the two, now has Eliakim and Reminicere negotiating how to spend the few bucks made by selling a basket of eggs. And it is all because of something utterly beyond their control: the price of a cup of coffee in a café in New York, Rome or Singapore.

Progress is a much gentler environment for change than regress. A workable distribution of the fruits of one's labour is what's at stake during periods of progress. In times of regress, when the world markets refuse to pay decent prices for coffee beans, it is the image staring back at you in the mirror that's at stake.

Many men on the slopes of Kilimanjaro find that image too hard to look in the eye. Nkya: 'They simply can't come to terms with the fact that they are no longer the lord of the manor.'

I have trouble falling asleep.

The next morning at eight a.m., Lema knocks on my door. 'Come on, let me show you the beauty of Lyamungo.' He proudly guides me to one of the irrigation channels through which crisp clear water flows, straight from the glacier. As we pass the homes of coffee growers, Lema points out the neatness of his village. The pathways are cut straight with a shovel, communal grassy fields are mowed. Hedges are tidily clipped. Bougainvillaea blossoms in deep, bright colours. Hibiscus grows proudly in some gardens.

Some of the homes are big and graced with huge verandas. A few have facades painted in red or blue with white or cream window frames. I express my admiration. I have hardly ever visited a village in Africa that is this tidy.

He repeats what he said earlier. 'Coffee is a gentleman, and through coffee we too were gentlemen for a long time.' Lema gasps, 'Those days are gone. Finished. So far we've managed to keep watering the flowers. What good would it bring if they wilted?'

Lema turns away to continue our walk in silence. He greets people to the left, salutes people to the right. A few minutes into our stroll he turns towards me. 'We will breathe new life into this coffee of ours. A life of frustration and despair is no life at all. As long as people continue to drink coffee, shouldn't we be able to make a living growing these wonderful beans?'

WAITING FOR THE KOLA NUT

Abdullahi opened up his wooden tea shack in December 2004, and named it 'God time is the Best'. A tiny *toko*, tucked away in a side street in the Liberian town of Harper. Behind his tea shack lies a ruined building, shot to rubble very early in the civil war that raged for fourteen years.

He has three shelves on which packets of cigarettes, cans of cola and batteries lie waiting for customers. On the lowest of the shelves Abdullahi keeps his coffee, tea and sugar. His helper kneels down just outside the shack near a fire on which he fries eggs and boils water.

A tense atmosphere. Abdullahi is having an argument with a customer. 'Those days are over,' he says in a stern but self-assured tone. 'You have to treat me with respect and dignity.'

The customer raises his voice, unaccustomed to being objected to. 'If I ask you for a tissue to dry my hands, then that is what you do, instead of giving me this dirty rag here.' The angry customer points at the spotless white towel Abdullahi has offered him.

'Those tissues aren't yours; they belong to another customer who left them here. I can't give away what doesn't belong to me.'

The patron does not take no for an answer.

'That's not how things go. When I ask you something, you comply.'

Hastily, a kitten runs out of the wooden shack.

'No, the days of you commanding everyone in town are over. We now have peace and democracy. I am human; I have rights. You need to honour my rights. I will no longer stand your barking at me.'

The client throws small change on the counter and stomps away, cursing and growling. Abdullahi stares at him, shaking like a leaf. There goes one of the former gang leaders who, during the war, always knew how to cleverly align himself with the most powerful militias and thereby scrape together his wealth.

'This is how things always go,' Abdullahi grumbles, grabbing the towel from the counter and hanging it on a nail in the wall. 'He used to be one of the bullies here in Harper. He still thinks he owns the world and the world owes him. He comes a few times a week, orders, and leaves without paying.

Big mouth. I have had it with him. I'm trying to make an honest living. His days are over.'

An estimated 20 000 people live in Harper on the coast of the Atlantic Ocean. This is where the first Americo-Liberians came ashore early in the 19th century. The newcomers were former slaves who, inspired and supported by religious groups in the United States, returned to Africa.

A weather-beaten statue high on a hillside near the shore commemorates their arrival: ships landing and men shaking hands. But the arrival of the former slaves was hardly as peaceful as the image suggests.

The Americo-Liberians founded their own republic in 1847 with a constitution and a flag inspired by that of America. They gave their nation a motto that ignored the existence of those whose land they had peacefully invaded. 'The love of liberty brought us here.' As if there had been no people already inhabiting the land.

The former slaves quickly became the new elite and formed a ruling class that thrived on the backs of those it governed. In the middle of the 20th century, president William Tubman set out to bridge the gap between the two groups. Under his presidency, Liberia experienced rapid growth with an economic expansion second only to that of Japan.

When Tubman died in 1971, Liberia had the biggest merchant fleet and the highest developed rubber industry in the world. It ranked third on the list of iron ore exporters. The capital Monrovia daily received flights from all over Europe, and it became home to Africa's first Intercontinental Hotel. Every investor worldwide knew there was money to be made in Liberia.

Until the global market for raw materials imploded.

When that happened, Liberia had next to nothing to fall back on. During the economic progress of the 1960s and early 1970s, the government squandered its money. Funds flowing into the state coffers were used to build white elephants. Hardly anything was invested to lay a foundation for the future. No roads were constructed, no schools, no clinics, no hospitals. No teachers were trained, no nurses, no doctors.

The ruins in downtown Harper tell tales of wealth and progress. President Tubman was born in this town in 1895. He became president in 1944 while leading the True Whig party, the political organisation that governed the country for decades, and he was closely associated to the Liberian branch of the Freemasons. Tubman's name is written in huge characters on one of the walls of the now partly destroyed temple of the lodge on the highest hilltop of Harper.

Children play with marbles on a dust road. Women do their laundry. The only fancy cars that pass by are those covered with United Nations emblems. The tropical beach is deserted; human turds lie in the sand.

Water no longer flows through the city's plumbing which was installed when the future still looked bright. Those that can afford it have their electricity provided by generators. Everyone else palavers at night with nothing more than kerosene lamps or candles.

I stroll from one villa to the next. Grit cracks under the soles of my shoes. Clothes dry in between pillars that once held up a roof. A view of the ocean. Palatial mansions, sometimes with fifteen rooms or more. Galleries. Large lounges. Roofs have now vanished, like the wooden floors, the door posts and the windows.

The inhabitants of the town negotiate with the jungle. The bush slowly but surely takes back what was once hers. Tree roots break open foundations and walls. Creepers work their way up along bricks and through holes and cracks.

Some people have built sheds in the gardens of villas, others cook beneath broken stairways leading into thin air. Every building tells a story of comfort, ease and luxury. And every ruin speaks of years of destructive rage.

Liberia's violence came in waves. First there was the coup d'état of 1980 in which soldiers ruthlessly overthrew the True Whig party. With public executions the military finished off the rule of the Americo-Liberians. Samuel Doe was pushed forward as the new head of state, hardly thirty and close to illiterate. The new regime claimed to act on behalf of the original peoples of Liberia, but relied heavily on the Americo-Liberians to keep the machinery of the state going.

Doe promised his subjects impossible riches while he and the members of his regime looted the state coffers. Drunk with power, the new rulers started fighting amongst themselves. The cruelty with which Doe went about his business boggles the mind. Old comrades and fighting buddies became sworn enemies. Each searched and found enough supporters in his own ethnic group to go to war. Ethnic tensions steadily escalated into a fully fledged civil war.

By the end of 1989, Doe had only enemies left. Each of them had his own private army. Doe's rule ended in an orgy of violence with him at its heart. Prince Johnson, a born-again Christian and infamous warlord, tortured Doe to death while filming the proceedings.

'The man won't talk!' Johnson shouted. 'Bring me his ear!' He forced Doe to eat it. Then torturers cut off Doe's genitals which they themselves consumed.

After Doe's death the warlords and their militias went berserk. Warriors dressed themselves up in women's clothes, with wigs and painted nails. Horrendous stories trickled out: gruesome massacres committed by drugged child soldiers, cannibalism, black magic and the shameless self-enrichment of the gangs' leaders.

Violence spread throughout the country like wildfire. During the years of fighting, every Liberian had to leave his homestead at least once. In a population of just over three million, a quarter of a million people lost their lives. No property was safe from the raging hordes: cars, plastic tubs, stereos, and spoons. And the villas of Harper.

After 'elections' in 1997 the violence subsided for a while. Warlord Charles Taylor had won on a campaign that can best be summarised by the slogan 'Choose me, or choose war.'

Just like Doe before him, Taylor used his days in office to enrich a small select group. And, like Doe, Taylor made many enemies doing so. New 'rebels' rose up. Only once they were knocking on the gates of Monrovia was president Taylor willing to take up an offer of asylum from Nigeria, on 11 August 2003.

A peace force of the United Nations supervised the disarmament of over a hundred thousand fighters, of whom ten thousand were still children. They each received 300 dollars in exchange for their weapons and, hopefully, peace.

Ellen Johnson-Sirleaf won elections in November 2005 and so became the first elected female president in Africa. 'After 158 years of men in power, it's time for a woman to show Liberia what she can do,' she said in a meeting we had in her garden.

Her opponent was the famous football player George Weah. He enjoyed a passionate following of mostly young men comprising many former fighters. Weah was their idol; he had used his talent to make a name for himself and earn a fortune. They hoped to reach fame and glory themselves, quickly. They were impatient, demanding education, jobs and most of all a new perspective. Now.

The youngest generation of Liberia is the only one in the world less educated than its parents. These youngsters witnessed death and destruction on a scale that very few of their peers elsewhere have seen. Thousands were personally involved in bloodbaths, destroying infrastructure and fellow citizens. Only with a weapon in hand could they dare to dream of a say in their own future.

Young people in Liberia, writes Stephen Ellis in his masterpiece *The Mask of Anarchy* (2001), 'believe that they can acquire the good things in life through aggressiveness but, above all, by a good fortune which has its origin in the invisible world. They seek to acquire what Liberians call "power,", not power in the conventional political sense, but the ability to prosper, from which all else will follow.'

Every post around the temple of the Freemason's Lodge is decorated with a compass and a square. The name of the temple is written on one of the walls, in large characters: 'Morning Star – Masonic Lodge No.6.'

White and red marble plates still decorate the walls and the floor of the temple. In the darkest days of the war, marble had no value whatsoever, and no one was willing to carry the weight.

Near the entry, a small Bible dries in the sun. The breeze plays with it, rustling the pages. The image pulls me up the stairs, into the temple.

Four young men observe me inquisitively. They are seated on rickety chairs shaded by tall pillars. From a radio comes the excited voice of a presenter. The wind carries his words away.

This is the first Freemason's temple I have ever entered. The term Freemasonry evokes a sense of mystery for me. It conveys images of Templars and King Solomon, of secret brotherhoods and a profound spiritual knowledge. The word also scares the living daylights out of fundamentalist Christians who imagine this secretive alliance is in partnership with the devil.

Few can talk authoritatively about the role the Freemasons have played in Liberia's history. Many rumours do the rounds about human sacrifices and Satanism. There is little solid proof. What is certain is that, before 1980, many a politician or wealthy businessman in Liberia played a leading role in the Lodge.

Freemasonry came to Liberia with the former American slaves. Its rituals, customs and wisdom quickly merged with those of the existing religions in the new motherland. It is because of the quality of this merger that the international Freemasons cut ties with the chapter in Liberia – or so it is said.

Being inside the Morning Star temple of Harper is unsettling. The building is stained dark by salty sea air. There is debris everywhere, a layer of water on the floor.

'This is the room where they used to sacrifice humans. Everyone wore black.' The voice gives me a fright. The man behind me seems to be in his early thirties.

'Whenever there was a service here, security was tight – all the roads were cordoned off so no one could come near. No one was to see what happened inside.' The man passes me, walks inside and introduces himself as Nehemiah Hills.

'That's all over. I'm in charge here now. I guard the mast on top of the building for a cell phone company.'

Liberia is full of stories of human sacrifice, ritual killings, cannibalism and black magic. No Liberian seems immune to tales of gods, spirits and people trying to outsmart each other.

In 1928, the anthropologists James L. Sibley and D. Westermann noted in their book, *Liberia – old and new*, in the vernacular typical of their day: 'To him, men (living as well as dead), demons, animals, plants and inanimate objects are essentially of the same kind. They lead their existence on equal conditions, and are equally able to influence man for good or for evil. The native has towards them all the same feelings of awe and respect and fights against them with the same means.'

Over seventy years later, Stephen Ellis adds as subtitle to his book, *The Mask of Anarchy*: 'The destruction of Liberia and the religious dimensions of an African civil war.' During the war, every leader of every gang tried to instil obedience in his fighters and fear in those of others by claiming special ties to the unseen world. His invincibility was guaranteed by what couldn't be seen.

'The power, the strength – you don't know what is true and what is not,' says Nehemiah Hills. 'You don't know of everything that happens. What you don't see, you don't know. That doesn't mean it's not here. The fact that you can't see it, hear it, feel it or smell it, doesn't mean it doesn't exist.'

Nehemiah leads the way up the stairs. The decorations on the walls are different on each floor. Glass bricks have been shot out; windows have been removed.

'The work of fighters,' Nehemiah says. 'I was one of them.'

On the top floor Nehemiah points at the buildings in Harper: the UN offices, a demolished church, the harbour. He sighs, 'The destruction hurts when you see it, doesn't it?

'I fought with Charles Taylor in the beginning of the war, when my eyes were still closed.' His family had been murdered by the opposing force. What was he to do? There were no jobs, no education. The only way to earn a living was by getting a gun. 'Easy. Go to the market and wave your gun in women's faces. Ahhh, Liberia – so many victims ...'

He did not last long as a warrior ('I was still a boy') and fled to neighbouring Ivory Coast. In a refugee camp he met a woman and got her pregnant. 'That was my sole responsibility. *I* did that, no one else. From that day onwards I was no longer a boy. I had become a man.'

He was never able to finish school. Each time he paid his school fees, the war flared up again and tuition was postponed indefinitely. Getting this job was, for him, like winning the lottery. He guards the tower, chats with his friends, plays cards and hands over his salary at home.

'Many of my friends are my former enemies. We fought against each other, or we fought with each other. During the war no one could be trusted. If I found or stole something during a battle, my comrade in arms could just as well kill me for it. Now we visit each other; we share our food. No one ever asked anyone else for forgiveness. I forgave them; they forgave me. We know. Some things shouldn't be spoken about too much.'

He takes a deep breath and gazes out over the ocean. As I look at him, memories pop up of interviews I did with Nehemiah's fellow fighters in Liberia, Sierra Leone and as far away as Uganda, Congo and Mozambique. Tales of terror and horror blended with surreal images of extreme human experience.

Mothers shot as they held their babies tightly against their chests. One bullet, two lives.

Or the bet between two young teenagers, armed to the teeth, on the gender of the foetus inside the belly of the pregnant woman approaching them on the jungle path – and how they resolved to find the answer.

Being forced to drink the blood of her four brothers and then to eat their penises.

Nehemiah stands up and walks all the way down to the entrance, to his Bible drying in the sun. His favourite verses come from Psalm 23.

> 'Yea, though I walk through the valley of the shadow of death, I will fear no evil: for thou art with me; thy rod and thy staff they comfort me. Thou preparest a table before me in the presence of mine enemies: thou anointest my head with oil; my cup runneth over. Surely goodness and mercy shall follow me all the days of my life: and I will dwell in the house of the Lord for ever.'

A marching song of a warrior, or the plea of a child?

———————

'With an AK-47 in my hand I felt powerful and invincible.' Adunfu's eyes twinkle. The former fighter of eighteen years plays nervously with a little latch on his copper watch.

'With that weapon I was on top of the world, I got everything my heart desired. People respected me. I saw it in their eyes. "Don't mess with him." I stood my ground, a free man. Now I'm a schoolboy again, dependent on others. My liberty has disappeared.'

Being a warrior in Liberia during the war caused traumas and created nightmares that will last some a lifetime. For others the experience was a peak they had never felt before nor ever will again. Adunfu tightens his bandana, taps anxiously on his thighs and speaks of the highs of a battle.

The adrenaline of a fight gave Adunfu a guaranteed kick. Every time. The tension, the sound of bullets whizzing past him, the smell of gun smoke. Fear-stricken voices, victims running away. He has no place for memories of atrocities.

Now, as a retired fighter in a time of peace, Adunfu learns how to put bricks on top of each other with a layer of cement in between. The excitement in his voice has given way to boredom. These hard wooden school benches are uncomfortable and hold nothing more than a vague promise of a meagre income after lots of sweating under an unforgiving sun.

Building walls, dead straight and level.

'I despise him for it,' says Robert King of his son. Tom had joined the warriors in the last round of fighting. 'I hated what those gangs did. No one likes having a son who is a rapist, a brutal killer, a looter, an arsonist. I don't want anyone to do any of those things to me, and I definitely don't like the thought of my son doing that to someone else. That's not how I raised my child.'

King's clothes are covered in mud. Just outside Harper in the hamlet of Hoffman's Station, he is building himself a new home of twigs and loam. Tom is seated askew behind him, huddled up.

'Just look at this house, my dear friend. Don't you see how we're suffering? My brother, if I were to tell you all the stories of the things done to me during the war, your notebook would be filled and still not everything would have been said. No work. No food. No money. No market. Everything I had was taken from me. I had to flee. Hell – that's what life was. And my beloved son stoked the fires. Can you believe it?'

How things could go so badly awry is a mystery to King. He handed down the wisdoms to Tom that he had received from *his* father.

Work hard.

Respect others.

Turn your back on evil.

'The moment you stop listening to your heart, and you refuse to listen to what your spirit tells you, things will go wrong.'

'Maybe that's where things made a turn for the worse,' King speculates, searching for an explanation. 'The younger generation no longer listens to their own hearts, their own spirits.'

He glances around to look at Tom. 'I honestly, genuinely hope that, even before I die, the youth will be able to taste the fruits that Liberia can provide for them.' And King turns back again. 'Be respectful, go to school, learn a vocation. We, as elders, gave them these words but they refused to heed them. My father already warned me. He used to say, "The youth no longer hears. Their hearts are not like ours." They are in a rush, always in a rush. They even demand money when I ask them to fetch water from a well. Imagine that, my own children!'

Irritation and despair have overtaken father King. He stands up, wipes the sweat from his forehead and barges off, leaving his son behind. Tom shifts on his stool, disquieted. His father's words echo in the room. Tom's eyes travel around the space, looking at nothing in particular.

I offer him my bottle of water and ask, 'When you yourself have a son, what would your most important advice to him be?'

Tom takes his time. 'War leads to nothing; it gets you nowhere. We destroyed our own future.'

He fought, Tom says, because his friends had joined the fighting. He had just turned sixteen and the school had closed. He lived with his father and stepmother – he was still a boy. His friends wore nice clothes and sunglasses. They took care of themselves.

'You're a boy for as long as you live in your parents' house, for as long as you have to rely on them. A man has his own home where he has a wife who takes care of him.'

A weapon hanging from his shoulder turned him into a man, instantly. 'Fighting is not a boy's thing. You need to be unflinching to fight a war.' However, he was shit-scared most of the time. He often found himself too nervous to load his gun. 'Maybe you could say I was a boy-man, somewhere in between the two. Although I was afraid, I did take care of myself after all.'

And now, back at his parents' home?

'A boy again, dependent on the man who fathered me.'

Tom has gone back to school. He is learning how to be an electrician and a plumber, in a country without electricity or running water.

'When a man fails,' he says, 'fate is against him. Or he is only half a man.'

Which values and customs can stand the test of time during a war? What are the raw materials for Liberia to construct a new foundation? Traditions point the way, remind you of where you come from and hint at where you need to go. But which traditions still make sense after years of brutal war?

The waves of destruction did not only tear down houses and wipe away families and roads, but also blasted an entire system of ethics to smithereens.

For years, only one law was valid: those with the strongest fists and the biggest guns will take whatever they can lay their hands on. The warriors of Liberia did not only level their own future, as Tom pointed out, but also razed their present and their past to the ground.

———————

'Most of our heritage and our customs have been obliterated,' says Jacqueline Collins. 'And we have turned away from whatever remains. We stumble along without any sense of direction.'

Collins is a social worker, involved mostly in 'rehabilitating' former fighters. She had just turned fifteen when the civil war broke out. Her nickname is Diode, meaning 'mother of a conscious daughter'.

The collapse of everything familiar in Liberia is both cause and effect of the civil war. The raging hordes of youths, out to get their hands on a piece of the pie, seem only the latest manifestation of a direction that was already visible in the 1920s, when the two anthropologists, Sibley and Westermann, visited Liberia. Slowly, Liberians began to get a distaste for everything genuinely Liberian. They wrote in 1928: 'Occasionally a youth of native parents who had assimilated the culture of the colonists [the former American slaves who settled in Liberia], came into prominence, being judged by his ability to conform to Western standards.'

The former American slaves who took hold of Liberia in the mid-19th century, opened a channel into the heart of Liberia's people, through which Western values, ideas, customs and beliefs could freely flow. It is as unrealistic to try to stop that flow now as it was a century ago.

Collins: 'But you know what? It is so hard to incorporate them.' She herself deeply desires an attachment to 'things' that are hers, that give a sense of belonging, of being home in her own Harper. Rituals. Ceremonies. Stories.

Collins draws my attention to a bell in the distance. 'Not too long ago, I heard the bell again for the first time in many years. Someone had died. This is how women call everyone to come and pay their final respect. They dance, while the men beat the drums. I remember it from my youth, and I'm pleased it's returning. I need to learn to dance again, like I saw my mother and grandmother dance.'

A young man thumps a metal rod on an old tyre rim hanging from a branch. The sound reverberates deep into the forest around Hoffman's Station. A call to all the men who can hear the gong to assemble and palaver. Liberians appreciate conversation and have dedicated special buildings, called Palaver Houses, to this art.

One by one they trickle in, young men and old men. The clan's chief, Wah Prawd, takes his seat below his own portrait. Next to him sits the village chief, Tibli Dickson. They wait silently. Prawd ignores my impatient stare.

Waiting is still not one of my strong points. And I have a chopper to catch back to Monrovia. I do my best to be polite when I ask Solomon, the man who brought me here, what is holding up the meeting. I simply want to have a chat with the village elders about traditions, customs and this strange thing called 'progress'. 'Do we really have to wait until the entire village has gathered?'

Solomon whispers in my ear while smiling at the chief. 'Please be patient. Time is only time. We are waiting for the kola nut – a symbol of hospitality. You will be offered a piece first, after which you will explain your reasons for coming. Then everyone else takes a piece too. And then the palavering can start.'

The minutes slide away. The men around me all remain silent. They stare, wait, breathe and stare some more until the kola nut arrives, cut into small pieces and laid open on a metal plate. I pick a piece and wait until everyone has taken his. As I bite, I become aware that some stories are not told in words, but through the acts of fellow men.

Wah Prawd clears his throat and raps on the table, commanding everyone to stop speaking. 'Respect is shown in little things. By saying "good morning", by helping others, by addressing people with the title they've earned. The youth don't know these things any longer.'

The wisdom and serenity that Prawd initially exhibits in his tone, quickly disappears. The topic clearly touches a raw nerve. His speech turns into a tirade.

His own children don't offer him the honourable label *Bobo* but call him *Papie*.

School children ignore the cry for help from a bedridden, elderly man who desperately needs water.

Adolescents ignore the advice they are given, and don't move a muscle when their father needs their help in chopping down a tree to clear the forest and make a field.

'Culture and civilisation start with a word which leads to a story – a living story. You listen to the story and learn from it. "That's how my father lived, and this is how I should do it." The story leads you by the hand through existence, tells you how to find your way. That's how it had always been, even when I was young. But these days it seems like all of that is dead and buried.'

I hear the muttering of an old man not unlike that of my paternal grandfather. He could belly laugh like few others, and he could grumble. He told me never to set foot in his house after I had had my ear pierced. When I went to visit him shortly before he died, I took out the stud. 'Your parents must be proud of you,' he said as his farewell.

Every generation clashes with the one before, and will do so with the next. It is the same in Liberia. Here, however, there are no subtleties to that clash. The younger generation literally fought their way into nihilism, tearing down everything old and established.

Village chief Tibli Dickson gestures for Prawd to take a sip of water and takes over. 'The war changed everything. Warlords showed the youth a way of life that promised to be without complications. Their lifestyle was based on nothing but raw strength, the power that comes through the barrel of a gun. It gave them access to everything. "It's your right," said the commanders. "Grab what you can grab." And that's what they did. They took it all and left nothing.'

It is this mentality that the elders and the chiefs find impossible to swallow. The impatience, the desire for instant gratification at the expense of others, and the illusion amongst the youth that entitlements come without duties.

The palaver house of Hoffman's Station is still. Prawd looks around and speaks to all who are keen to hear.

'What really, really angers me and at times makes me loose all hope, is when I come across those youngsters who want it all. When I try my best to explain to them about boundaries, about fellow human beings and a community they're part of, they answer me, "Don't talk to me about anything, I am standing up for my human rights." Those so-called human rights these young men are on about have caused a lot of trouble here. Other people's rights are secondary to their own, and they have no respect for them.'

Prawd slams both his arms on his chair. Loudly. He takes a very deep breath, and looks me straight in the eyes.

'Nothing, no tradition whatsoever, can withstand the terror of such a perception of human rights.'

Post Script

The war ended in August 2003 with elections held in late 2005. Despite national peace, a battle continues in bedrooms, behind bushes, near the water pump. That's where some fathers rape daughters, and some granddads abuse grandchildren. Some uncles, their nieces. Some friends of the family, a teenager. Shame stops women and girls from reporting the crime. On the day of her inauguration, President Ellen Johnson-Sirleaf broke Liberia's taboo on rape: 'I know the struggle because I have been a part of it. I recall the inhumanity of confinement, the terror of attempted rape.'

Rape was widespread during the civil war and has remained a huge problem in the post-war era. 'Not only are the terrible consequences of this still felt by many Liberian women today,' said a study released early in May 2009 by ActionAid, a British development organisation, 'but violence against women and rape continue unchecked.'

'You are not a man if you are not a father!'

Doctor Peace throws his statement in my face. He has no interest in a debate, and he doesn't allow for doubt.

Doctor Peace is one of ten herbalists who practise their trade in tents along Monrovia's main road. They originate from Ivory Coast, Nigeria and Benin, the only country on earth where voodoo is an official religion.

'Voodoo is dead,' proclaims Doctor Peace, whose real name is Hassan Mustapha. These days he believes in Jesus. 'The ways and sciences of the West have changed our lives and beliefs. The old is gone. We live in the 21st century.'

Apart from Jesus, he also believes in the medicinal power of his own herbs. He has them flown in from Nigeria. Doctor Peace keeps his potions – yellow, orange, purple – in plastic bottles on shelves inside his tent.

The herbalists write their specialisations on huge pieces of cloth which hang at the entrances to their tents. Their blends, elixirs and creams cure 'rheumatism', 'weakness of organs', 'pains of ears', 'noise of the stomach', 'piles' and 'male power', to name but a few.

Doctor Peace is the self-proclaimed King of Infertility.

'I teach men how they can improve their sperm. Thick sperm doesn't work. You need to dilute it. My potions help to do that. But that is not enough. I also teach men how they can improve their relationship with women. I tell them: "Conquer your woman's heart first and her uterus will follow".'

'Male power' seems to be the number one ailment against which the herb doctors use their skills, followed closely by 'barrenness' and 'women who cannot produce'.

Creating descendents is the *raison-d'être* of life in Africa. The continuation of the species, the nation, the tribe, the clan, the family, the name – that is what matters.

Everything else is minor detail.

A spouse and descendents: until a man has attained these goals he has not yet lived a complete life. The single person will be challenged by friends, family and even strangers to do what everyone does for the well-being of the community. Marriage is a social contract that gives each person his or her place in the group. Having children takes that one step further: a man changes from being 'the son of' into being 'the father of'.

I am yet to become a father. I am past forty, older than people expect to live in many parts of Africa. I have no guaranteed future for my genes. I still have to rescue my name from oblivion.

I smile when I think of a question my watchman, Lemaata, asked me in Nairobi, years ago. Is my seed up to par, he wanted to know. Why else would I, in my mid-thirties at that time, still not be a father? He had just married a thirteen-year-old girl. Consummating the marriage on the wedding night had been impossible – she had just been circumcised that afternoon.

I answered Lemaata: 'I come from a place where things work differently. Not better, not worse. Differently. And even though my cradle was rocked here in Africa, I took in life though my mother's milk in Europe.'

Once I had almost been there, on the doorstep of fatherhood. After that, the time was never right. How could I combine the urge to travel, to see, and to learn with being a modern, caring father?

I am the son of a father who was hardly ever around when I grew up. He was out working to fulfil his professional aspirations and pay the bills. I choose not to be such a father. The species, the family, the name – they have all already been guaranteed a future, even without my input. More importantly, the woman with whom I can take on the impressive project of parenting has not crossed my path, yet.

Doctor Peace listens to me intently as I explain the reasons for my self-inflicted 'barrenness'. His eyes cloud with incomprehension. The corners of his mouth rise; I hear a soft chuckle, which quickly becomes a hurricane of laughter. He slaps his thigh and then rocks with mirth.

Never in his life has he heard so much gibberish.

The heroes of Bisesero wear hats. Beige or dark yellow hats, black or dark grey. They also carry walking sticks made of branches with the bark scraped off. They dress in suit-jackets, sometimes with holes, sometimes patched up, which help to keep out the chill, high up in the hills of Rwanda. Green gumboots, with the trousers tucked in. They chew on long, thin blades of grass.

One by one we climb up onto the hilltop from where the views reach far over the surrounding landscape. Each man wants to visit their monument, the only one dedicated to heroes in Rwanda. Dark clouds come in from the east. It's nearing noon.

The men sit on the grass; searching glances observe each other briefly, and then wander out again over the hills. It's dead quiet. A magpie flies overhead, chattering. Another answers from afar.

The path to the mass grave zigzags from the dirt road to the top, passing newly constructed buildings, painted white and purple. The buildings are empty still, but will eventually house the remains of thousands of victims of the bloodbath that took place on the hills of Bisesero in May 1994. Those bones are laid out in neat rows in a temporary shed made of corrugated plates. Skulls neighbouring skulls, thighbones next to thighbones, ribs beside ribs. From one skull protrudes the nail that took its life.

The mass grave holds an estimated fifty thousand corpses. Death visited them when the *Interahamwe* militias attacked. The men with their hats and their suit-jackets, their green gumboots and their walking canes survived the slaughter. They defended themselves with sticks and stones.

'Bisesero was the only place in Rwanda where the Tutsis defended themselves.' Siméon Karamaga (60) pulls a pipe from his pocket, plucks a bit of tobacco from a pouch and fills his pipe. 'That's what happened in 1959, when Hutus first came at us, and that's how we responded again in 1963, and again in 1972. Bisesero has this reputation. "That's where you find people who won't be trifled with."'

The slaughter in Rwanda started on 7 April 1994, in the capital, Kigali. In the west of the country, tens of thousands of Tutsis managed to escape roadblocks and searches, and ran for the hills of Bisesero. For weeks on end, the men, women and children were able to fend off their attackers.

They managed to defend themselves despite the call of *Radio Mille Collines* to all Hutus to 'squash the cockroaches'; despite the state's creation of a killing machine consisting of tens of thousands of volunteers to wipe out all the Tutsis in Rwanda, a group comprising 15 per cent of the whole population. And despite an impotent United Nations mission, disempowered by its own headquarters in New York.[*]

Karamaga lights his pipe and turns his gaze on Narcisse Kabanda (45) and away towards the hills. Kabanda: 'We survived by eating the roots of maize and sorghum; we drank water from a swamp. The *Interahamwe* had destroyed all our wells by throwing in corpses. They burnt homes as far as you could see.'

He sweeps his arm 360 degrees around.

'The *Interahamwe* worked in groups, and so did we. The moment they attacked, we scattered. This strategy always cost lives, but most of us managed to save ourselves. They fought with machetes and guns. We defended with stones. I saw a few attackers drop dead.'

Hutu-extremists realised they could not 'cleanse' the hills of Bisesero on their own. Back-up came in the second week of May. The first round of attack took place on 14 May, the second one a day later. Tens of thousands of Tutsis perished. Kabanda: 'The attacks started at around four in the afternoon, and ended just after the sun had set.'

The events of 1994 have left deep scars in the daily life of Bisesero. Karamaga explains how the decimation mostly took the lives of women. 'Men were better able to defend themselves. Most of the survivors here are men. Their wives and kids were butchered.'

Both Karamaga and Kabanda lost their families. Karamaga had four sons, Kabanda two boys and one girl. 'What were we to do? We were unarmed.' He pulls a new blade of grass from the soil, sticks it in his mouth and gently chews.

Their families are dead, their cows have been stolen. Both men have slid into abject poverty. Kabanda: 'A cow costs a hundred and fifty thousand Rwandan francs [230 euros]. Where do I find that money? There's no work in Bisesero, no trade. I eat what I grow, and grow what I eat.'

---

[*] The Security Council refused to acknowledge that genocide took place, and so dodged the duty laid down in the UN Charter to intervene.

For a peasant in the hills of Rwanda, his wife, children and cattle make up all his wealth. Without cows or children a man means nothing. Cows are walking investments to be cashed when circumstances dictate. A family means care for the old and fragile. A man lives on through his descendants who carry his name, his memory and his face. Without children, oblivion awaits.

Where are you from and what will you leave behind? These are the two questions I am asked most often, once I've closed my notebook. My nieces and nephew in Holland will, after my death, slowly but surely forget their uncle in the southern hemisphere. A balding man, who popped in once a year for coffee and a chat.

Try explaining *that* in Africa. 'No, I have no children.' Eyes reveal the pity others feel for me, judging my barren life to be useless. Futile.

My life and that of Narcisse Kabanda have nothing in common. I lived in four countries, travelled through many more. I am single and live an urban life. He grew up in these hills where he got married and had children with his wife. They were killed while he was powerless.

Yet, I feel a weird sense of connection.

Both childless men, with one major difference.

He feels a hole where once he felt whole.

The first drops of rain fall down as Kabanda leads the way over the crest of a hill to his home. Inside, he brings a stool and a chair from his bedroom to the front room. Maize cobs dry on top of the wall that separates the two spaces. The bowl on the floor contains beans and maize, waiting to be sifted. His luxuries are a kerosene lamp and a radio that needs repairing.

Kabanda points at a poster on the wall of the political party that ended the genocide in 1994. 'As long as they are in power,' he says, 'I don't need to fear the Hutu extremists.'

Kabanda waits for a woman. 'Who will care for me when I'm old? Look at Karamaga – how much longer can he work his land and grow his food?'

Kabanda's problem has a clearly defined cause and a myriad of impossibilities in finding a solution. He's not to blame for not having remarried, he insists. 'Almost all the Tutsi girls have been killed. The dowry for those still alive has risen beyond my reach.' And marrying a Hutu woman? 'I've thought about it, but I am not that desperate yet.' He would only consider marrying a Hutu woman who can prove beyond doubt that her family's hands are free from blood stains.

The genocide ended one hundred days after the slaughter started. The memories are alive and kicking. Memories of days in which neighbours became rapists, looters and killers; of a time when cousins became enemies because their respective mothers had different ethnic labels in their ID-books.

Although men did the killing, insists Kabanda, it was women who searched the hamlets and hills for Tutsi hideaways. It was women who brought the killers their share of food and banana beer so that the murder machine could rage forth.

Kabanda is only willing to chat up a woman if she can claim innocence or, if that is too much to ask for, offer a confession. But a *mea culpa* is hard to come by. No one dares take responsibility for atrocities committed during those one hundred days in 1994, in which an estimated one million people were eliminated.

Three hundred years of tensions between Hutus and Tutsis culminated in several waves of 'culling' in 1959, 1963 and 1972. Distrust and hatred between members of the ethnic groups had grown deep and wide. Many different theories attempt to explain the animosity between them. According to radical Hutus, the Tutsis are newcomers to Rwanda, with their native grounds probably in Ethiopia.

More independent experts point to the social aspect of the differentiation: 'Tutsi' was the label given to those who had a certain number of cows, as well as those who formed the aristocracy. Hutus, on the contrary, were those who tilled the land. Up until the 19th century, expanding wealth could turn a Hutu into a Tutsi, while a slide into poverty would make a Tutsi a Hutu.

German and later Belgian colonial rule used the separation between Tutsis and Hutus as a means of governing the colony. Tutsis were given privileges unattainable to Hutus.

In the course of the 20th century, increasing numbers of Catholic priests objected to this class system. They chose to educate the Hutu majority on their rights as citizens equal to the Tutsis. When the Belgians prepared for their departure from Rwanda in 1959, Hutus revolted against the Tutsi aristocracy, to prevent princes and royals from taking power once the colonisers had left. They caused a bloodbath amongst ordinary Tutsis, most of whom were as poor as their Hutu neighbours.

A mass of Tutsis fled to neighbouring countries like Uganda. It was from this country that Paul Kagame united many of the refugees, and inspired them to go back home. The Rwandan Patriotic Front (RPF) invaded Rwanda in 1991, the start of a civil war. An international peace process opened the way, late in 1993, for a power sharing agreement between the ruling elite and the RPF.

The governing dictatorial elite of Rwanda, run by a Hutu clique from the north-west of the country, fought back. Apart from resisting the RPF, they had to counter growing pressure from international donors to introduce multi-party democracy. Extremists pointed fingers at the Tutsis as the sole cause of all Rwanda's trouble, and stirred the Hutu population to spill blood. A genocide was the strategy of choice for the elite to remain in power.

Behind closed doors, Hutu leaders designed the plan to wipe away all supposed opponents, including the entire Tutsi population. From a British company, they imported tens of thousands of machetes to hand out to volunteer killers. They hid arms caches all over the country. And they drew up a list of moderate politicians to be assassinated because they might otherwise spoil the orgy.

When the presidential jet was shot down by unknown assailants on the night of 6 April, the slaughter started. 'Mow down the high trees,' were the coded words on *Radio Mille Collines* ordering the leaders of the *Interahamwe* militias to sharpen their machetes and start hacking.

———

The search for a woman with clean hands and an innocent family might take both Karamaga and Kabanda the remainder of their lives Out of decency and politeness, both men claim to feel no resentment towards the Hutu women in the village. Still, their distrust trickles through in off-the-cuff remarks, some openly hateful.

Karamaga is about to give up the search. At age sixty, he doubts he has the energy to start all over again. 'A new adventure? At my age?' He fears he'll die before his second 'first-born' is able to pronounce his name, a curse he doesn't want to inflict upon either woman or child.

Kabanda, on the contrary, does have the time but his hope is running thin. Just like Karamaga, he only wants a woman with a clean conscience, someone whose family confessed. But he knows his people in these hills. 'Even if ten people saw a man split open someone's head with his machete, he would still deny it.'

Denial rules the hills of Bisesero. Elias Mungankiko (46) is one of thousands who were once jailed. Kabanda knows him as one of the killers. 'He confessed in jail. However, since he returned, his memory has blank spots.' Most of the guilty refuse to acknowledge their roles, much to the survivors' distress.

Karamaga: 'There are too many perpetrators to know all their names.'

Mungankiko lives a short walk from the village. The path leads through fields of tea. The wind chases fog along the ridge of the hills, along meadows and houses. Some of them are about to collapse, because families have perished. Others belong to absent owners who pass their days in overcrowded jails.

It's cold and grey. Men wear sweaters and women are wrapped in cloths to protect against the elements. Passing cows drink from a hollowed-out tree trunk. A diesel engine inside a home chuffs away, blowing out black fumes, while grinding maize.

Mungankiko washes his hands in a basin. 'I didn't do anything during the war. I haven't killed anyone.' Smoke fills the courtyard of his farmhouse. His son brings him grilled cobs prepared by his wife, Jurida Nyarabako- meza. She does her kitchen chores, while her husband speaks. A walking stick and a sickle lean against the wall, near the door.

The former prisoner professes his innocence again and takes his claim one step further. None of the killers are guilty of what they did. 'The real culprits are the leaders who incited the people with their propaganda.'

Mungankiko was jailed between 1995 and 2003. In the comfort of his courtyard, he gives his version of reality, the story as he has chosen to remember the events of 1994. None of those listening can tell a lie from the truth. His heart is locked away.

'No one is to blame,' he keeps saying, 'apart from the leaders.'

'On 11 April the authorities came to warn us that the war had started. The mayor arrived, as did the director of the tea factory. They brought the police with them. We were told to resist the Tutsis, to fight them with all we had. They had killed our president.'

Shame, guilt and despair have brought many suspects to the brink of self-destruction. It was estimated that hundreds of Hutus committed suicide in 2003 and 2004, when they heard they were being charged in the popular courts of Rwanda, the so-called *gacaca*. Villagers gathered in these courts to condemn those amongst them who were guilty of complicity.

Suicide is a rare phenomenon in Africa. The ties between relatives and villagers almost always offer a way out of material or emotional distress. However, the traumas in Rwanda run deep. Children killed their own parents, men their own wives; cousins raped aunts or nieces.

More importantly, however, those hundred days in 1994 severed the ties people had knotted over the course of centuries, ties that had enabled them to survive collectively. Families were shredded, the bonds that bound the hills became undone. And the end of the massacre did not stop this process of unravelling.

Parents lost their children; children lost their siblings. Afraid of retribution, massive numbers of Hutus fled to Tanzania in 1994, Zaïre (present day Congo) and Burundi, losing each other as they tried to march away from the bloodbath.

And this happened again in 1996, the moment Rwanda invaded its neighbour Zaïre to hunt down the militias that were still causing trouble. The invasion shattered many more ties of clan and family. Most displaced children were too young to know their own family names, or the villages they were born in.

In the first few years after the genocide, almost a hundred thousand Hutu men were jailed on suspicion of involvement in the wave of violence. Male candidates suitable for wedlock became as scarce and valuable as gold. Women therefore had to improvise to become pregnant. The wealthiest among them paid young men for sex, others they coaxed with charm.

Pierrine Mukammurenzi (28) is quick to laugh. She is a proud woman. Her second child takes refuge in her lap. He is ten months old. No husband in sight. 'His father has a wife. What do I care? I only needed him to impregnate me. He gave me two children and is no longer of any use to me.'

Bystanders, mostly women, cackle and giggle.

What would easily lead to expulsion from the community in many other rural areas in Africa, has become a habit in the countryside of Rwanda. In the village of Gishala in the east, it's the women who chase men, more so than the other way around. After a night together, it's the woman who kicks out the guy.

'He came, he slept with me and I bore a child,' Mukammurenzi recounts in the shade of banana palms. 'It's all very simple.'

In some parts of Rwanda the ratio of men to women is one to four. 'Women bear the consequences of all these men being behind bars,' states Sam Abbenyi of the National Aids Campaign. 'They lead a life without intimacy, and so – more importantly – without children.'

A life without descendants means a life without honour or respect. No woman is seen as a full woman for as long as she is without a child. Children are the link between past and future, a connection to ancestors as well as eternity.

'Shared husbands' is the solution for women to have their needs met in these conditions. Before the massacre of 1994, *kwinjira* was the custom in which widows were taken in by their brothers-in-law, Abbenyi explains. 'But when entire families have been butchered, there are simply not enough brothers-in-law available for the task. Women have had to broaden their horizons.'

Immediately after the genocide, AIDS spread to around 11 per cent of the rural population. Rape had been used as a weapon of war, which extended the virus's grip on Rwanda. However, in the late 1990s, the prevalence of AIDS kept increasing, long after the killings had ended. One hospital in the western town of Gitarama found that over half of all women tested had caught the HI-virus. The new-style *kwinjira* is one of the reasons for this.

Safe-sex campaigns could not make a dent in the trend. Pierrine says, 'If I want a child, what purpose is a condom? And having no children is simply not an option. I can't afford to fret about AIDS.'

The hamlet of Kinazi is an hour's drive from the tarmac road, west of the capital of Kigali, hidden deep in the hills. Kinazi would be some men's definition of paradise, where women carry the burden of life on their shoulders. It's the women who till the land, trade the goods and run the school. The few men around are found on verandas and inside bars, where jars of banana beer pass hands. They enjoy their privileges for all to see. They know that if their wives complained, they would easily find someone else to share their nights with.

The richest of the women of Kinazi hire men for their labour. In exchange for food or money, the men help in the fields. Their services are extended into the bedroom.

'Finding a girlfriend is easy,' Felix Buterise (40) smirks. 'Once in a while I even earn a bit of cash. What else could I hope for?'

Nurse Marie-Josee Shema (27) laughs when I ask her for her opinion about this male paradise she finds herself in. 'Women have needs,' she murmurs shyly. 'Of course, women would prefer their husbands to tend to their needs, but they are not around. We have all had to scale down our demands to fit the freelance lovers we have at our disposal. You have to be flexible and realistic, you see.'

She herself has sworn off *kwinjira*. The number of patients with sexually transmitted diseases she cares for has shot up rapidly. 'Some men have five or more semi-regular partners besides once-off flings here and there. It takes only *one* infected partner to destroy, in just a few years, the lives of everyone involved.'

Freelance fatherhood does not sound appealing to either Karamaga or Kabanda. Sinful pleasures are wasted on these men; they've had to endure too much to be able to find relief that way. Of course, Kabanda enjoys going out for an *urgagwa* (banana beer) in the tavern, a few minutes from his home.

One beer, that's it. Just to shake off the looming sense of loneliness. 'I'm back by seven; I know how to behave.' He smiles a wide smile with a hint of bitterness at the corners of his mouth.

'Only once I have money again to buy a few cows, enough to afford a dowry, do I stand a chance of happiness.' Slowly, however, Kabanda and Karamaga make peace with the fact that they will no longer produce offspring; they will have to make other arrangements for their final days, without the care of a daughter and the muscles of a son.

The moment earth falls on the lids of their coffins, memories of them will fade. They are men, heroes even. But neither is a father anymore.

The dark clouds in the sky have broken open. A thundershower pours down on Kabanda's roof. Standing in his door, he stares out over the hills, one hand tucked away in a pocket while the other holds his hat.

'The rains will be good.'

He turns around, takes a step inside and closes the door.

Years of wind have torn at the fabric and the sun has bleached its bright colours, but the Zambian flag flies proudly. An eagle soars above the dark green field, with three stripes at the bottom: red, black and orange. The cloth dances to the rhythm of a stiff breeze, blowing freely over the empty space of Lusaka International Airport.

From my seat near a window in the plane, I see men dressed in animal skins outside, dancing to a rhythm I can't hear. Others beat on huge drums.

Lusaka receives the body of Anderson Masoka, the opposition leader who died in hospital in South Africa. His son has brought the body home, and Zambia is ready to embrace it. Photographers take shots of the son and his wife – both dressed in black.

Hands are shaken, hats taken off – a homecoming.

'When last were you in Zambia?'

The immigration officer doesn't look up from the documents I have just given him. I was here briefly a few years ago, chasing Zambia's founding father, Dr. Kenneth Kaunda. Even in his eighties he tends to be on the road most of the time. I popped in and out of Lusaka then.

'I guess my last long stay ended in 1969,' I reply. 'The purpose of my visit is to find the place where I was born.' The officer looks up from his desk. I smile, 'I'm curious to see where my journey started. In 1969 we moved to Nairobi; I was two at the time.'

His eyes soften. 'Welcome home.' A stamp.

My last visit had been in 2002. I had spent less than thirty-six hours here, trying to locate Kaunda. I was to interview Zambia's first president in an attempt to better understand his peer, President Robert Mugabe of neighbouring Zimbabwe. Mugabe had chosen to rule his country with an iron fist, and by doing so steered it straight towards the abyss. Without any reasonable explanation.

Kaunda and Mugabe go back a long way. They share memories, anecdotes and opinions. Kaunda was instrumental in arranging the Lancaster House Agreements which, in 1979, set Rhodesia/Zimbabwe on a course to peace and independence. He was there when history was written. Maybe, I reasoned, Kaunda could explain what Mugabe refused to explain.

Despite our appointment, His Excellency Doctor Kenneth Kaunda was away. In the words of his office: 'The Old Man is gone.' Kaunda had suddenly left for Johannesburg. If I caught the afternoon flight, I could meet him in his hotel in Rosebank.

My visit to Lusaka in 2002 had been too short to do what I have now come for: a quest for my roots. Somewhere in this city, I was born and baptised. I almost drowned in the pool in the garden of our home in the suburb of Woodlands.

In my backpack I carry a copy of the New Testament my parents were given on the day of my baptism by the Lusaka Presbyterian Church. My father has drawn a map of Lusaka as he remembered it. He made two crosses on it: one for where he thought the church must be and another guess for the hospital where I was born. I also took with me two letters, one from my mother, the other from my father. My mother wrote:

When I close my eyes, I can still see the colours of the first hours of the day during which you were born. The night before, we had been dancing till the wee hours of the morning. It must have been at four in the morning that I felt the first signs. Half an hour later I told Dad he had to call the doctor and the hospital. At sunrise we raced through Lusaka. The contractions increased and I felt you were about to slip out.

I still keep the tiny Bible in the cardboard box in which it had been given to my parents. The snowy white cover has collected dust over the past four decades. The gold-coloured varnish on the margins has faded.

The first page carries a date (14 May 1967) as well as three names: the church's, mine and the reverend's. His name I can't decipher. The first character is an 'S', but what follows has been scribbled in characters too small for me to read. According to my dad in his letter, the *dominee* was a progressive Afrikaner. 'He baptised you in Afrikaans: "Ek doop jou Aernout Gert".'

As a boy, I could never get past the opening page, with a colour image of Joseph, Mary and their son. Being raised in my mother tongue, Dutch, the English words did not made sense to me. However, every time I moved to a new home, a new city, a new country I would carefully pack it, a relic with a meaning I do not yet comprehend.

_____

Kenneth David Kaunda led his country to independence in 1964. Twenty-seven years later he voluntarily left power after having lost a democratic election – one of the first of Africa's heads of state to ever do so. These days Kaunda is one of Africa's most respected elder statesmen, and one of the leading campaigners against AIDS.

'Self-restraint purifies the mind,' he said at our first meeting in his hotel room in Rosebank, in February 2002. Kaunda (then 78) wore pearly white sneakers, a pair of black, sporty trousers and a dark sweater. His lively eyes have observed the world for over three quarters of a century. His demeanour is, without a shadow of a doubt, distinguished.

'Can I get a drink?' the 'Old Man' asked his assistant.

'What would you prefer? Fruit juice?'

'Yes, that'd be nice. For today the fasting may end. I may have juice.'

Kaunda is a deeply spiritual man. He became a vegetarian when, as a youngster, he saw a white butcher sell his worst rotten meat to a black woman for a crippling price. It was on that day that he decided he would not consume luxuries that were beyond the reach of the poorest in his country.

For Kuanda certain values and norms are non-negotiable. As long as the vision is humane and holistic, one can cut to the heart of any problem with the scalpel of analysis.

I had once heard Kaunda speak at an international AIDS conference in Addis Ababa, broadcast by the BBC World Service. His voice had been fragile, yet unwilling to yield. Kaunda, a lover of music and especially of the guitar, sang a marching song. 'Sons and daughters of Africa: fight. Sons and daughters of Africa: shine. In the name of great Africa, we shall fight and conquer AIDS. Always forward, never backward.'

In the 1960s and 1970s Kaunda had been a leading international politician making a stand for an independent voice from 'the South'. Countries like Zambia, India and Brazil had no need to take sides in the Cold War, he believed. Injustice happened on all sides, and it was against injustice that Kaunda fought.

Repression in Africa, Kaunda explained to me, showed its ugliest face in the limiting of ordinary people's access to land: the most important resource to be able to simply survive. 'The pain of being without land in Africa...' Robert Mugabe addressed this pain, Kuanda emphasises, and so built up credit amongst many Africans. It is this credit that never seems to run dry.

Kaunda tries to find the right words, carefully, to convey the essence of Africa's deepest scars. 'The pain of being born in your own country and seeing how all the privileges are reserved for those who rule you. You are a nobody. At best you are an underpaid labourer. You are banned to the worst places in your country… An outsider will not understand this pain. It goes very deep and cannot simply be wiped away or forgotten. Reconstruction – and this is crucial – is not just about material things like infrastructure. The real reconstruction needed in Africa has to take place in people's heads, hearts, and souls. Even after so many years of independence, Africa still has to regain its self-confidence. We still have to rebuild our pride.'

Taxi driver Matthew looks intently at the tiny map I've laid out on the roof of his car. 'This is what my father has been able to draw from memory. I need to find a church, a maternity ward and a house. In the next few days we need to find Kaunda as well.'

Matthew's fingers meander across the map. 'The Lusaka Central Hospital of those days must be the University Teaching Hospital of today. The church should be easy too. Glastonbury Road in Woodlands does not ring a bell, though. Maybe that street has been renamed?'

We leave the airport and drive into Lusaka. Wide avenues, blossoming trees, homes hidden behind high walls. The city is spotless. People have gathered along the road into the city, waiting for the convoy to bring the body of opposition leader Masoka back home.

It's a Saturday morning and Lusaka feels cold. I feel like something's missing inside me. Normally when I've landed in a new place, a sense of curiosity and excitement fills me. But not today.

'Home' – what's that supposed to mean? I'm neither familiar nor comfortable with being tied to one particular place. The most appealing sentiment is 'Let's have a look around the corner and experience what life is like over there.' The sounds in a different neighbourhood, the views from that particular garden on that hill, or from a balcony in another suburb.

I open my notebook and read some of what I scribbled down months ago on a dirty piece of paper.

'Where is your home?'
The man asking this has a long beard which adds to his aura of wisdom;

his eyes don't just look, they see. 'My home is where I am.' I quickly glance away from his eyes and look at the back of Table Mountain.

My slick answer slides off his shoulders rapidly.

'That is bullshit.' He tries again. 'Where is your home? That place where you can go in silence. That place where your roots stretch into the soil, deeper every day. Where you sense who you are, without knowing.'

I stub out my cigarette in an ashtray on the cast-iron table. 'I can't afford to grow roots – that would stop me from learning, from journeying. I don't want to anchor myself.'

He remains silent. Looks at me. Plays with his beard. He points at some of the trees and bushes in his garden, and emphasises the beauty of the rays of light at this time of year. He tries to find his question.

'When you travel, do you go towards something or do you go away?'

I roll a new cigarette, observe the sunrays as they cascade over leaves and look the man in the eye, acknowledging the sincerity of his question.

What do I need to do with it? What can I do with it?

I request a minute or two to listen for insights from inside me.

Only while interacting with others, a West African philosopher once wrote, do we learn about ourselves. Africa taught me the beauty of the grey scale, the subtle boundaries – always in flux – between pain and happiness, between accepting fate and the curse of apathy, the smell of rotting human corpses and the sound of whizzing bullets. Africa taught me about me.

'When I travel, I leave a place where I can't find answers and go to a place where I might find people who will possibly recognise my questions. And yet these travels no longer feel sufficient.'

The usual bright colours, the charming chaos, the playfulness of existence – they are all missing in the first few miles into Lusaka. But once we've driven the Great East Road all the way into town we find ourselves in a city that is very much alive. People do their weekend shopping at the mall of Manda Hill, open till sunset, hidden behind a mean looking fence and guarded by men with bats.

I inhale deeply through my nostrils and smell urban Africa: smog, puddles with rotting leaves, the flowers of flame trees and the smoke from smouldering fires.

Is this 'home'? Lusaka – the place where I was born, but cannot recall.

Unless, perhaps, it is this delectable smell playing with my nostrils, bringing back my earliest days.

'You are a child of Zambia, young man,' Kaunda said when I told him about my place of birth at our first meeting. A stunning compliment which, coming from the Founding Father of a nation, still feels like a blessing.

The years have been kind to Kaunda. His near ascetic lifestyle has kept him safe from many an affliction. Even after sixty years of marriage to Betty, he will still pick up a guitar and play her the love song he sang her six decades earlier, when he was still courting her. *'I remember the night, in your arms...'*

Kaunda speaks as energetically nowadays as he did as Zambia's leader at independence. His enthusiasm was as infectious at our meeting as it had been over forty years ago. Kaunda's eyes sparkled when he spoke of the days in which it was perfectly okay to dream and be an idealist.

Nations were being built on hope and on the Great Stories of the era. Formerly illiterate people were being educated, wealth was being redistributed. Prices on the world markets for Africa's products were good. Copper, Zambia's main export product, financed investments in education, health and infrastructure development. It was an age in which it was realistic to dream.

'When I became president in 1964, Zambia counted a hundred people with a university degree, and 1120 people who had finished secondary education. Scattered about the land we had a handful of clinics.

'We built schools all over the country and added two universities. We constructed clinics for primary care, we opened district hospitals and even two academic medical centres. We trained doctors and educated teachers by the thousands. Of course, we are human beings, we made mistakes. But when it comes down to education, Zambia led the pack.'

Kaunda has an undying faith and belief in the malleability of life, and in the potential of human beings. His book *A Humanist in Africa* (1966) – once a bestseller and now no longer easily available – resonates with those convictions, which he still carries today.

'We were humanists,' he explained. 'Some thought we were anti-Christian, anti-God, anti-religion. They were wrong. We chose to put our efforts into creating the best possibilities for our fellow human beings. The moment you co-operate with others, you improve everyone's well-being. Everything we did evolved from that one principle: "What can we do to improve the lot of our people?"This principle of solidarity was and is the essence of Christianity.'

Despite all the efforts of Kaunda and his government, as well as the support of international partners and foreign governments, Zambia couldn't get onto a track of sustained development. The models failed, the market for copper collapsed many times – and South Africa bombed Zambia's infrastructure to intimidate the 'frontline state'. The average income in Zambia in 1964 was twice that of the average South Korean. In 2002 however, a South Korean earned twenty-seven times more than a Zambian. Something had gone seriously wrong.

Kaunda pointed out two destructive tendencies of the contemporary world economy: the issue of debt and the issue of trade. 'In the mid-1980s I decided Zambia's development had to play first fiddle. We used money reserved for paying off our debts to invest in agriculture. Our economy grew 6.5 per cent, that year. The World Bank was enraged. "Mister Kaunda meddles with our game." Because Zambia couldn't find other countries to join our campaign against the debts, we had to give it up.

'Jesus said, "Whoever has will be given more; whoever does not have, even what he has will be taken from him."That says it all. Everything Africa produces we cannot help but sell for next to nothing. And for everything we import, we have to bleed. This system of globalisation is unbeatable. We grow poorer because of it, and who gets the blame? Us. We are being portrayed as people "who can't develop themselves". That really makes me very, very angry.'

———

The fingers on my watch seem to have done a sprint. I want to take pictures during daylight to email to my parents for a response. My quest isn't served by going to the wrong maternity ward or the wrong church.

My father wrote, 'The church was built from natural stone, and had a tiny tower and a big parking lot.' He describes where to find it. Matthew recognises the description, but not the names. 'Why don't we just ask around where to find the Presbyterians?' At our first stop, we find clues. 'Saint Columbo's' is the name of the only Presbyterian Church in this neighbourhood. Once Ken Phiri opens the gates and hears my explanation, he smiles a broad smile. 'Welcome brother – welcome back!'

The building my father described has metamorphosed. Ken: 'The building was first widened and after that broadened.' The floor of the church still has marks where the walls stood previously.

Of the whereabouts of a baptismal register Ken knows nothing. He advises me to attend the service the next morning. 'I'll make you coffee as you browse through the books.'

Before I leave the church, I glance around the prayer hall one more time. Between the altar and the pulpit an opened Bible stares into space. The drawing is the splitting image of the picture I have in my baptismal Bible.

Glastonbury Road is my next destination. 'Go past State House,' my dad writes. 'Follow that road to the end and go down a hill.'

The roads in the suburb of Woodlands are nothing more than a memory of good times gone by. Potholes everywhere. No name signs anywhere. 'All the European names were changed to African ones, sometime in the 1970s,' Matthew explains. These days, no one knows of Glastonbury Road.

'The beautiful suburb of Woodlands' is a labyrinth of damaged roads and sandy paths. We drive past a school with gates that are about to collapse. This is where it should be: 'A house with a little pool and a separate cottage with two guest rooms, built to accommodate the many guests passing by.'

Untraceable.

Kaunda stepped down after he lost the first free multiparty elections in 1991. Zambians had been fed-up with the one-party state, and even Kaunda had taken to locking up his opponents. Rumours spread about high-level corruption.

However, the most important reason for Kaunda to open up the political landscape came from the radical changes in South Africa, where the racist regime freed Nelson Mandela and cleared the way for democracy.

'As long as racist Afrikaners were in power in Pretoria, Zambia could not afford democracy. Remember, they were bombing our bridges. Had our political system been open, the *Boere* would have bombed our politics.'

Union leader Frederic Chiluba beat Kaunda by a comfortable margin. After twenty-seven years in power, Kaunda left State House. 'In my last presidential speech, I said, "Sometimes you win, sometimes you lose".'

A quiet transition was not on the cards. Chiluba was out to discredit Kaunda, and accused him of having tortured people in a secret room in State House as well as stealing tens of millions of dollars from the state coffers.

'It was ridiculous,' Kaunda told me. 'My so-called "torture room" was a safe place in case of a coup d'état. It had a radio transmitter and food to last a few days.' Scotland Yard, the elite British police unit hired by Chiluba, could not find any proof of money stolen by Kaunda.

Kaunda retorted. 'The day I left State House, I had two million kwacha in my bank account [about ten thousand dollars in those days]. Some people become president in order to enrich themselves. My parents raised me with one core message: Whatever you do in life, you do for God and for humanity. I don't regret not having raked in millions. Honesty towards God, my Creator, and towards His people, that's what's important to me.'

Afraid of a resurrection of Kaunda's popularity, Chiluba went all out to destroy him. He attempted to take away Kaunda's citizenship, and once even gave soldiers the order to fire shots at his car. But the new head of state of Zambia didn't stop there.

'My son Wezi was a promising, young politician. Chiluba recognised that, and so Wezi had to die. You have to understand, my successor is a scaredy-cat. A little, fearful human being in whom God forgot to put a heart.'

Wezi was not the first son Kaunda lost. On 21 December 1986, Masuzyo died due to liver failure caused by AIDS. This loss sparked a re-direction in Kaunda's career.

Devastated by the death of their son, Kaunda and his wife decided in October 1987 to come out publicly with the cause of Masuzyo's death: AIDS. Only years later did Bakili Muluzi (Malawi) and Nelson Mandela (South Africa) follow Kaunda's example – they too each lost a son to the epidemic.

Kaunda, now in his eighties, still campaigns. 'A disaster is taking place in Zambia, in the whole of Africa. AIDS destroys human power needed to carry the future of our continent. As long as Africa's leaders remain quiet, the epidemic will continue to wreak havoc. We *have* to talk; we *have* to change our sexual behaviour.'

Where is Lusaka Central Hospital? Matthew can only think of one hospital in the heart of Lusaka: the present-day University Teaching Hospital. He drives me straight to the maternity ward inside a modern building, with all the characteristics of 1970s architecture: it's ugly, it's made of concrete and it is falling apart.

A sense of huge disappointment washes over me when I enter. The hallway is dark. Broken windows, once meant to keep out the blistering heat of midday. Men sit on benches, staring into nothingness. Behind the grille of the reception, a woman listens to the radio. The wall behind her consists of nothing but old files.

I translate bits of my mother's letter, hoping she'll recognise the descriptions.

I can still clearly envisage the stairway leading to the entrance, with lights behind the door and coming from windows on either side. The doctor, I remember his name as Dr. Hodges or Hodskin, had already arrived. I had to keep my belly with both hands to prevent losing you as I walked the steps. The moment I lay on the bed and the doctor broke my water, you glided out and made a yelp. The doctor sighed. 'You almost lost him on the doorstep. It is a beautiful, healthy son.'

The receptionist points at the stairway behind me – cold concrete.

'Maybe those were the steps?'

I shake my head. 'That's not the way British settlers built – they had a more imperial style. Do you know of buildings from the colonial days?'

She knows of one such building, tucked away in the corner of this complex. 'Go out the door here, follow the road, go right, go left, go right.'

As I follow her description and turn around the last corner, I find what I'm looking for. Pillars carry a white roof, red bricks form high walls in which tiny windows are placed. The stairway is red. I know intuitively that this is the place.

A torn and bleached flag waves high above the entrance. Numerous mothers with young children wait in the shade of trees for treatment.

A nurse walks out of the building, her grey hair packed neatly in a bun. Mary Mlenga listens intently to my story and grabs my hand. 'Yes, my boy. This is certainly the old Lusaka Central Hospital. This is where women delivered, behind these doors. I gave birth to my daughter in 1969, in the private section. If you were born in 1967, you were born here.'

On the doorstep I am suddenly frozen with doubt. Do I enter or do I turn around? What is it I am searching for? What do I hope to find here? Once I find what I don't know I'm looking for, what happens then?

I grab my camera from my backpack, take a few snaps to send to my parents. Only when Willem and Bertie recognise the facade does it make sense to step inside a memory I myself can't recall.

Both my parents write about their period in Zambia shortly after independence. My father's assignment for one of the main Dutch development organisations brought them to Africa, after they had spent years in New Guinea. The young Kaunda, leader of a young nation, inspired both Zambians and foreigners alike. My mother was one of them.

> *His humanism. Everyone experienced that as something special. Here stood an African leader, trying to find a way for his own young nation to achieve a situation where all could blossom. Kaunda was in those days an example to Africa.*

My father met Kaunda every month at State House to discuss, in confidence, topics of development. Kaunda: 'I see great beauty in listening to advice; especially if it comes from people one can respect because they are people of integrity. However, it is crucial to take that advice to heart, otherwise you're just wasting everyone's precious time as well as the chances given along your path. I see honour in learning, and acting according to what you learn.'

The books Kaunda wrote are not easy to find – neither in the book shops of Cape Town, nor on the Internet. I try my luck in Lusaka, but seem to be at a dead end. Even a biography of the Founding Father is not to be found on the public shelves of the capital. Zambians no longer seem interested in the life and times of their first president.

One bookseller remembers how, not too long ago, he cleared up his stock room and stumbled upon a few copies of *Letter to my children* (1973). Kaunda wrote it as an apology to his children for his continual absence from family life. The man disappears into the back of his shop and returns with a second edition from 1974, wrapped in cling foil.

'Let's say this letter is a kind of public apology for neglecting you all so badly by putting my political career before my family. [...] It is fatally easy to serve mankind in the mass and neglect those people under one's nose. [...] The fancy business of being a President's children is no substitute for a father who is there when you need him – to play with, talk to, or just to love.'

In his book, Kaunda describes what he sees as the essence of life, the core of being African; something he would like to see embraced by his children. 'The African-ness which has its roots in the soil of our continent rather than the lecture rooms of Western universities is basically a religious phenomenon; we are who we are because of our attitude to the mysterious depth in life, symbolised by birth and death, harvest and famine, ancestors and the unborn.'

That night I read Kaunda's book, preparing for a third interview, scheduled for 'anytime soon', according to his office. Our first interview in February 2002 focused on history and politics; our second meeting in May 2006 evolved around issues of AIDS, life and death. During our third meeting I'd like to ask Kaunda for the meaning of 'home', 'heritage' and 'identity', and ask him about his personal life of which he wrote so beautifully:

[E]very man has a secret history which is more than just a recital of events. This is the side of a public figure which the historians cannot investigate – the inside. They can examine his papers, read his speeches and record his recollections but they can't climb into his head or explore his heart. It's just as well. Who wants to be shown the rust on the inside of the shining armour of one's heroes?

I believe that the true measure of a man is not to be gauged by the state of his bank account, the size of his popular following or the grandeur of his titles or degrees. It is a mark on the soul which represents the point at which he finally harmonised his achievements with his ambitions, where he settled for what was possible as against what was desired; not so much a mark perhaps, as a scar – a scar made by his dreams coming to earth like falling comets.

Eileen Bender receives me with open arms outside the church. She is an elder at St. Columbo's. 'You're re-tracing your steps; of course I understand that.' Her steps go back to 1787, when a Dutch ancestor settled in Cape Town, on the Heerengracht. She arrived in Zambia in the 1950s, from 'Zululand' in South Africa.

'Have you remained faithful to the Church?' Her tone indicates that I have to tread carefully.

'To be very honest, I haven't visited churches for any other than professional reasons for a long time,' I stutter, and wonder if maybe silence would have been better. Bender's friendly eyes seem to ask for an explanation. 'The images of divinity in the Christian religion don't appeal to me anymore; they've lost their power of persuasion.'

Sadness in her eyes, as if my soul has slipped away from a salvation so close at hand. 'Come inside, the service is about to start.' In her presence I feel it impossible to decline the invitation.

The reverend preaches passionately. He is convinced that Jesus will return soon, admitting that no one can say for sure when it'll happen. He asks his congregation, 'Are your prepared? Are you ready to die, unexpectedly, and face your Creator? The day you were born was the day you started to die. Every day you live brings death closer. Are you ready?'

My thoughts begin to spin; my levels of irritation rise. How can anyone prepare for something he will never, ever grasp – even with all the knowledge and insight available on the planet? How does one prepare for the Big Unknown, other than practising faith and trusting in blind uncertainty?

The modern style of the church – its corrugated roof, the tasteless decorations, the sermon and the hymns; it all touches my psyche, soul and spirit less than a fly would tickle my skin.

Before I came, I had no idea what I would encounter on my journey to the world of my earliest days. I was too young to store the memories that I now, almost four decades later, would have liked to tap into.

I know rationally that this is the place where, with a few splashes of water, my spirituality was supposed to have been awakened and my soul cleansed.

Alas, that is as far as it goes: my frontal lobe. My presence here does not open up a secret reservoir inside.

No dramatic breakthroughs.

No climax.

All grey.

Bender hands the copy of my Bible to the other elders. No one is able to decipher the name of the reverend. Maybe the register can provide clues?

Where on earth is the register? Rumour has it a reverend took all the paper-work with him when he left for Tanzania.

After the service, members of the congregation walk towards me, shake hands, ask me for my name and want to have a quick look at my Bible. They tell stories of who they are, where they came from and how they ended up here in Lusaka.

An accountant from the Scottish Highlands. A verger from Tanzania. A singer from the Kenyan coast, with an angelic voice. 'Will you return here?' someone wants to know. 'Will you stay?' Or: 'How good of you to come and visit us!'

For a while I feel at home, but not because of any memory.

I feel welcomed by the warmth others give me.

'You are an internationalist,' Kaunda once teased me. 'Internationalists feel at home everywhere.'

That night I find a short message from my mother, replying to the photos I sent her via email. 'I remember those steps as if I'd walked them only yesterday; you have found your place of birth!'

A day later I head off to the old colonial building. I tread on the clinic steps. In the hallway a man armed with a polishing machine works the linoleum. Children play with wooden toys.

Sitting on a bench in a deserted area, I close my eyes. I scan my body, my head, my spirit, my soul.

Zilch. I feel absolutely nothing.

Again I take out the letters my parents sent me. My father: 'You simply rushed out – whoops – on a bed, thrashing about. A grand little boy.'

My mother: 'The nurses were too sour for my taste. We took you home to your brothers, who were chuffed they had another sibling.'

My parents were younger then than I am now. I was the fourth son; one more would follow a few years later. Four decades later I can still taste the joy and happiness they felt.

Only when I descend the stairway do I feel a rush of excitement. The last time I went down these steps was just over thirty-nine years ago.

Then in the arms of my mother.

'Please, repeat your first name again...' Kaunda fiddles with his white handkerchief. We are seated in a small office in a suburb of Johannesburg.

The calendar indicates a day in May 2006. 'The Old Man' had been too busy to meet in Lusaka.

The topic for our meeting is his dreams, of which a few have 'crashed to earth like comets'. An introduction to Kaunda, the man, the human being, the father who had to endure losing two sons.

He tells me the story of his youth in Lubwa Mission in what is today known as Malawi. His father was a missionary, his mother a teacher. 'My father travelled through landscapes where in those days you could still be caught by a lion or a leopard and where cobras, pythons and puffadders writhed in their paths. There were no bridges; he had to wade his way through wild rivers. He ended up at the home of a local ruler who appreciated my father's stories about Jesus. After three months he told my father, "Go back to where you came from, find a woman and then come back here to settle. I want you to keep telling these stories of yours".'

Kenneth David Kaunda was the last of eight children, three of whom perished. His father died while on a tour – Kenneth was eight. He thinks back to his parents with nothing but affection.

'They taught me the two pillars of life. The first one is "Love the Lord your God with all your heart, with all your soul, and with all your mind". The second is "Love your neighbour as you love yourself and treat him as you wish to be treated". The next question then: who is my neighbour? For me, my neighbour is every living creature, beyond the boundaries of states and nations, and beyond the divisions of religion, skin colour, persuasion and the like. We are all God's children. This has been the foundation for everything I have done in my life, and for everything I still try to achieve – to improve the space for all individuals so each can shine.'

Kaunda is known for being a sensitive man. As president he easily embarrassed diplomats and executives when he, the nation's leader, would weep during a speech, or while listening to hymns.

Books, music and debates are the loves of his life – apart from his wife Betty. 'Learn to love words,' he wrote to his children. Only through learning the art of communication are knowledge, insight and wisdom worth pursuing. Observing, hearing, learning and practising what was taught. Otherwise you could 'just as well be the village joker.'

Masuzyo's death in 1986 confronted Kaunda in harsh ways with this new disease called AIDS. 'Only a few people in Africa in those days had heard of this animal. People were dying, yet no one spoke about it. "Please, don't say a word." But I couldn't stay quiet, not as a father and not as president. People were silent because they fear death. AIDS kills; if you are infected, you keep quiet. People lied to others and to themselves.

'I howled, cried and wept when my son died. Until weeping was no longer possible. Maybe I can prevent others from having to experience this pain, I thought. That is the day one starts to act.

'I had no idea how many more children I would lose to this "thing", this animal. In those early days I had no idea where it came from, or how my boy had become infected. There was this deep-seated urge to understand it all, so I knew what I was dealing with.'

The former campaigner for independence chose to resort to old, proven tactics. He set out to campaign again, this time to create awareness amongst his citizens of the threat of AIDS. He had himself tested for HIV, and announced the results.

'We had to do everything we could to break the taboo, to break the silence. Now, twenty years later, there is no doubt whatsoever that my decision to go public with my son's cause of death was the right course of action.

'It has helped me enormously to speak about Masuzyo's death. I climb the stages of the world. I talk. I assist others – use my own pitiful circumstances to assist others.

'Some put all responsibility in God's hands. I can't. Of course, it would have made my suffering easier to blame Him and put my fate in His hands. It would have lightened the burden. The thing is: I don't believe in such a God. AIDS is neither an experiment nor a punishment from God. We, men, need to accept our responsibility. There are still a great deal of men out there who honestly think they can go about seducing women, as if AIDS hasn't knocked on our doors. We, men, carry a huge chunk of the blame.'

I ask Kaunda to lift the veil covering what he called the 'rust on the inside' of his heart. What does it do to a man when his child dies?

Kaunda leans back into his chair. On his lapel he carries badges of his political party, as well as the international logo of the campaign against AIDS: the red ribbon. Kaunda breathes in deeply and serenely, pulls his handkerchief with one hand through his other slightly closed hand. Looks me in the eye, and comes forward.

'Aernout, it is a gruesome experience when your child dies. You feel as if you're covered by something that you can't take off by yourself, not in an easy or safe way, that is. The way in which some people express their sympathy sometimes only increases the pain.'

He takes a short break, stares at a wall.

'You feel as if someone or something has framed you into this irrepress-ible pain. Recovery is next to impossible. It's as if the world has stopped exclusively for you. You feel hopeless, helpless. The deepest desire is for some-thing bad to happen, simply to eradicate the pain. You wait for something, but nothing happens. So ...'

Mr. Godwin knocks on the door. 'You need to wrap up, lest we are too late for our next appointment.'

Kaunda looks at me in a friendly way, and slowly rises from his chair. 'Next time you're in Lusaka, will you come visit me?'

On the pavement outside, he steps into a waiting car and waves his handkerchief. A smile.

His eyes yet again leave a mark on my soul.

Bright, strong, lively. Honest.

I am unable to meet Kaunda a third time; he is needed at the funeral of opposition leader Masoka, and I have a flight scheduled to Southern Sudan.

A few weeks later I hear snippets of an interview with 'The Old Man'. Again he condemns, in the strongest possible words, leaders' irresponsible behaviour regarding the lethal issue of AIDS.

A man with a mission.

A lone voice in the desert.

A father, with rust on his heart.

A *ZWERFKEI** BEHIND A DIKE

My father is called Willem. In the memories I have of my childhood, he is conspicuous by his absence. He was always either travelling or working.

I can still visualise him sitting behind his desk in the living room. A modern, grand table it was, with a white top and black sides. A very old map of Africa hung above it, with many blank spots.

As a teenager, I imagined where on that map my conception could have taken place, sometime in July or August of 1966. It surely must have been during a holiday. Maybe they were on leave in Holland. But I prefer to imagine a merger of my mother's x chromosome with my father's y chromosome somewhere on a dusty savannah, or otherwise in a tent on a warm tropical night.

Maybe it was there where huge territories north of Lake Kariba were blank spots in the perception of European explorers; places that meant 'home' for Africans. Or maybe it happened along the shores of that same lake, during a night in which 'natural family planning' was too drastic a dampener for the passion between my parents.

When he was a teenager my father dreamed of becoming a missionary. Following his own father's advice, however, Willem attended a prestigious business school and was appointed colonial administrator in one of the last Dutch colonies: New Guinea. He ploughed through mud on weeks-long hikes through uncharted territory. He gallivanted to hear stories. He listened, and wrote reports.

As an administrator, he recorded one of the dilemmas of the non-Western world, dominated by a small, European country in the latter days of its global aspirations. One conversation in particular stayed with him, in which an elder in a Papua village made a remarkable request.

---

* There is no suitable English equivalent of the Dutch word 'zwerfkei'. A 'zwerfkei' literally means 'wandering boulder' or 'roaming rock'. These huge boulders are found in the north of the Netherlands; however, the country has no mountains to explain their source. The rocks were in fact carried south by glaciers from Scandinavia, during the last Ice Age. The Dutch phrase 'een kei van een mens' refers to a person with a strong, charismatic character, aware of his or her purpose in life.

This man pleaded with Willem *not* to build a mission school. There, the children of the village would be told of a certain Jesus, or so the elder understood. This *tuan Jesus* would clear the way for them to a paradise which holds no seats for the elders and the ancestors who did not believe in him. The problem was, he explained, that when the elders were growing up, they'd never been told stories of the man Christians believe to be the son of God. The mission school, therefore, would create a great divide in the after-life between the elders and the ancestors on the one hand, and the younger generations on the other. That would be wrong. Therefore, it was a kind of school the elder did not want.

This conversation became a fundamental building block for my father in more than forty years of development work. 'It taught me that even with all the might of the colonising power behind me, I could achieve nothing of my so-called "civilising mission" if what I did was not rooted in the convictions of those I was supposed to "civilise" – a word that makes my stomach turn these days. I learned: Listen to what people say, what *they* want and how *they* analyse their own circumstances. Be guided by *their* stories.'

During his entire career, until his retirement in 1999, my father was a man with a mission. His last posting was in the town of Bonga, in the southwest of Ethiopia. For three years he and my mother lived just outside this village, on a compound without power or phone lines. At times she felt deeply unhappy, thousands of miles away from friends, children and grandchildren.

To facilitate my father's last assignment, she had to leave everything she held dear, and everything she had excelled in at home. In Ethiopia she had to find new benchmarks to spend her days usefully, abandoned by a husband who slaved away at his office.

Just before Willem Zevenbergen retired and my parents returned home, I travelled to Bonga for an interview with my father. We spoke of Africa, of development co-operation, hope, despair and the malleability of life.

His shoulders askew, a head of salt-and-pepper hair and pouches under his eyes. The old development worker gazes from his veranda deep into the south of Ethiopia. Mist slowly rises from the forests and fields in the distance. Wind plays with an Aeolian harp. The man speaks deliberately. I last visited my parents two years ago. In those days they still lived in a house made of shipping containers. They wore gumboots unless it was a Sunday, and they showered with collected rain water. My mother has turned the chaos of those days into a neat yard where cows and sheep graze. Coffee bushes do well on this fertile land. A gardener mows the lawn.

Development workers. White Heroes flying in progress with water pumps? Or Lords of Poverty, profiteers sipping cocktails by the sides of pools?

In the man opposite of me I see neither a White Hero nor a Lord of Poverty.

A slogger. I remember the evenings at home. He would return from the office late at night, with a bag full of reports, files and documents. On his own he would eat his warmed pot of food, often with my mother opposite him. He would talk shop, think of new strategies; she would make suggestions.

Or maybe an optimist. Giving in to fate is not an option for him. Life can always be improved upon, and once you set your mind to it, nothing can possibly stop you. With only three fingers and a stick stuck inside a fake arm he plays complicated organ pieces – even in Bonga. In 1944, aged ten, he had lost his right arm and two of his left fingers in an accident in Rotterdam. His life, or so it seemed, was destined for failure. 'He would have been better off if he'd died,' an uncle once remarked.

Poverty alleviation in the Ethiopian province of Kaffa is Willem's farewell performance. I had heard him ask my mother years ago, 'Will you come along, Bertie? It looks a lot like where we started four decades ago.' Half a year later they had set off.

Now they are packing their suitcases again. Destined home this time.

Although he started his career as a colonial administrator, Willem spent most of his working life as a development worker. After the last Dutch colony 'in the East' (New Guinea) gained independence, Willem was given an opportunity to retrain. He chose to study human geography, and was appointed head of a Dutch development organisation in Lusaka in 1965.

As the years passed, he climbed the career ladder and eventually became Head of Quality Control at the ministry for Development Co-operation. He resigned from this job when his then minister suggested providing India with three huge fishing trawlers with the sole purpose of preventing the closure of Dutch shipyards. That donation would threaten the livelihoods of thirty thousand Indian fishermen, who would be unable to compete with the industrial fishing ships. Willem was ordered to find a way of providing alternatives to the thirty thousand victims of Dutch development co-operation.

'Sheer madness,' he thought. 'That is setting the cart before the horse.'

Willem resigned. At his farewell the same minister labelled him 'the conscience of this department'.

For the next ten years Willem travelled the world as a private consultant. However, at age 62, with his retirement in sight, he wanted to start up and run a programme one more time, to prove that poverty alleviation is possible.

Bonga hardly seems changed since I last set foot here. Most people still walk barefoot along muddy roads. Youngsters roam around, unemployed. The village generator is still switched on at six p.m., and is still switched off at midnight.

I notice a new clinic on one of the hills, and I am told a boarding school for girls is being erected. I also hear of new water points having been installed. Within the province of Kaffa, three hundred and fifty farmers have planted just over a million coffee shrubs. Is this the harvest of three years of my father's work?

'Development takes generations. We have only started. What did you expect? Those one million coffee bushes will eventually be sold to thousands of farmers. They will be able to harvest two million kilos of beans. That will provide them with more money than I have invested here on behalf of the Dutch tax payers.'

The province of Kaffa is, according to the inhabitants, the birthplace of coffee. It is as big as the Netherlands and has a population of eight hundred thousand. The province could be prosperous thanks to the coffee that grows in the wild, but Kaffa is one of the poorest places on earth.

According to the inhabitants, Kaffa suffers from a spell cast by its last king. The Ethiopian emperor defeated him in 1897. The king was convinced his own circle of confidants had betrayed him. When he was deported he therefore threw his royal ring in a river and cursed his people.

'This curse is alive and kicking – regardless of whether or not it actually *exists. A great deal of people in Kaffa feel cursed, which takes away almost all motivation. If someone is convinced his work will be to no avail, he will not invest time, money or energy in his own future. The core of what I do aims at stimulating and challenging people to go the extra mile, to invest in tomorrow.*

'No, that has nothing to do with feeling pity. I do not pity anyone in Africa – no matter how poor he or she is. Why not? Because I see that your average African lives relatively cheerfully amidst his circumstances. He survives through his strategies of endurance. The only ones your mother and I give alms to are the hunchbacked paralysed who drag themselves through mud on their hands and feet.'

Neither is my father bothered by a 'moral obligation' to help Africa. Decades after its independence the continent owes a lot of its problems to itself. Bad leadership, especially, has harmed numerous nations.

Willem does development work first and foremost because of the numerous challenges of the job. He slogs away in Bonga's muck because he thinks it's useful and captivating.

'Already in New Guinea I learned we can improve the lives of men and women who, measured by our standards, live in poverty. We, as outsiders, can contribute our own forces and energies, input that does not come from within those societies themselves.

'That is what has frustrated me often in the past and still frustrates me now. Initiatives taken by people to improve their own lives are, I think, few and far between. I notice only a tiny spirit of enterprise and little inclination to save and invest. Many see poverty as God-given, as a fate you cannot walk away from. Few think of tomorrow and even fewer of the day after tomorrow. The focus is on making it to the end of the day.'

In the rainforest of Ethiopia, I notice the first signs of a gap between my father and me. What I admire in Africans – their talent to laugh despite it all and the perseverance to start all over again every day – are brakes on progress in my father's eyes. To perceive poverty as an inevitable fate seems to me a necessary trait not to go berserk in the absence of prospects.

'I am stubborn enough to think there are enough chances around to create a better life, even here. And I think the African is nuts if he doesn't grab them. I am here to help him grab them. Understand me correctly. I do not have a magic formula to achieve great wealth overnight. The majority

of the unemployed youth roaming around this village went to school thinking they would never ever have to dig in dirty soil. My work passes them by. I offer support to those who realise that development is a process of blood, sweat and tears. Fighting hard for living conditions that will be better tomorrow than they were yesterday.'

His recipe for poverty alleviation reads like the reports he wrote four decades ago in New Guinea. Encourage people to go the extra mile, to take a risk. Hammer the message home that citizens as well as governments have to pick up their responsibility. Choose unconditionally for the ordinary man in the fields. *'That in itself is very un-African. African leaders hardly ever take the side of the ordinary man or woman. Most of them only take care of themselves.'*

Most Africans are brought up on the principle of subservience to authorities – the chief, the communal elders, the civil servant. The village will give you all you need. Do not rebel. The progress of one threatens the delicate balance of the community.

Ethiopia's history has always seen farmers as the first in the food chain. A peasant was no more than a serf of the feudal lords or the emperor. The 'communist' revolution of the early 1970s at best only replaced the lords and left the system intact. Even the 'democratic' government of Meles Zenawi (in power since 1991) has difficulty breaking old patterns.

Its constitution explicitly states the liberty of all subjects. Yet, citizens trying to improve their own lives continue to be plagued and harassed by all-powerful civil servants and dignitaries.

'Civil servants desperately fear every success of every citizen. All progress made by a peasant nibbles away at the power and influence of the employee of the state and makes him more useless. However, that civil servant does not want to be expendable. On the contrary, he seeks status and power.'

The obstinate refusal of many of the African elite to create space for ordinary people to do what is required to improve their livelihoods, forms one of the biggest obstacles to progress. That is why Willem perceives the refusal of villagers to construct a water point for the benefit of another town's dignitaries as one of his biggest achievements during his time in Bonga.

'The dignitaries of that particular town wanted to use the money this

programme offered to get their own access to water to the exclusion of everyone else. They had already told a group of peasants to start the work. However, the villagers stood up and refused to slave on behalf of the wealthy and powerful. That spoke of empowerment of the powerless – which is exactly what my work is all about.'

In the eyes of traditional African leaders, this kind of behaviour is pure blasphemy. Whoever dares to criticise the corruption or dictatorial tendencies of African leaders will quickly be named a racist or, if he or she happens to be African, 'a puppet of outside forces'. Statesmen like Robert Mugabe of Zimbabwe and the Kenyan former president, Daniel arap Moi, despise anyone who attempts to really empower their subjects. They are quick to throw labels around: 'Interference' or 'Neo-Colonialism'.

'You have to make sure you do not end up being pedantic. We, outsiders, have to be modest enough to admit that we have no precise knowledge of where Africa needs to go or what it needs to do. We do know where to go in Europe – let's face it, the troubles and afflictions there are less than they are here.'

'A measured amount of pedanticism is okay, especially if you have been around the block a few times. For me this job is easier now that I am in my sixties than it was when I was in my twenties. I think I have earned the right to speak up. This is not my first visit to Africa, and people I work with know that.'

Slowly, step-by-step, the image of the 'development worker' in front of me becomes clear. That image has nothing to do with either a White Hero or a Lord of Poverty – not for me anyway. The outline of a 'benevolent colonial' of days gone by shines through when we speak about corruption in Africa. Do not walk away, he believes. Do not pull out. Stand next to those who want change, who seek good governance. If needs be, look over the shoulders of those you suspect of missing the point, and risk being seen as 'politically incorrect' for doing so.

For decades the motive of 'taking responsibility for Africa' was nothing more than a cover-up for Europeans ruthlessly chasing their own interest on the continent. The West would bring 'civilisation' to the natives. In the 1960s the same motive was the driving force behind the first attempts to do development work. Sometime in the mid-1990s 'taking responsibility' had become taboo. Political correctness, combined with spillage of billions of euros, had eradicated all desire in large parts of Europe to have anything to do with Africa's future. Still, my father shamelessly uses the term 'take responsibility', and does not apologise for his desire to be involved.

I realise, though, that the phrase 'benevolent colonial' does not do justice to my father. He continuously spells out what Africans need to do themselves. It is, after all, their continent, their future. 'All I do is to make suggestions, and to induce people to act. If they are not willing or able to take it from there, I will catch the first plane out of here.'

Perhaps he's a kind of missionary from Spijkenisse, who voyaged the world not with a Bible under his arm but with a mixture of 'the best of liberal and social-democratic thinking' running through his veins. He thinks for a while and then shakes his head.

'The missionary will feel disappointed if he is unable to find converts. Not me. My attitude is: It is all up to you. If you want to live an easier life, you'll have to take the first steps and do your bit. If you do not want to do your bit, I will not do anything for you. If you prefer to die, you are free to do so. It is your right to die.'

According to some, Africa's future looks bleak. They believe the continent has already lost the fight. Frustration and anger linger, waiting to burst. Where does Willem find the energy to do what he does so relentlessly? How does he come up with the unfaltering trust that his work will be fruitful?

As a journalist, I travel through a different Africa to the one my father meets day-to-day. For three years he lived in a village where everyone knows everyone. A village where children played in the streets, women gave birth and elders were buried.

I, on the other hand, rush through hamlets, drive to frontlines.

He chats to people about the weather; I talk about war and abuse of power. He receives written requests for support, well argued and well documented. He encounters glimpses of hope while I encounter vistas of despair. I meet enraged youngsters, demanding prosperity and demanding it fast.

Our conversation scares me. Here I am – young. Was I not supposed to be limitlessly optimistic? I realise I am more of a cynic than my father who is about to retire. Was he not supposed to be bitter about evaporated illusions?

'Many in Africa have indeed missed the boat – development that has taken place elsewhere, like in Asia, has not yet happened here. But that should not stop us from doing what we can do to turn things around. It should not prevent us from creating possibilities with and for the poor masses. In this area that means using the potential of coffee. It means creating facilities for women to have caesareans when a baby lies breach. It means assisting with the provision of clean drinking water – as long as those who will use the service add their energy and money to the exercise. Nothing is a gift – gifts do not work.

'Of course, these tiny steps will not rescue Africa. Still, they do make life for ordinary people a bit better, a bit more enjoyable, a bit more humane – and, most importantly, they strengthen people's self-esteem.'

'Who are we to imply we can solve Africa's problems? Who am I to suggest I can?'

March 2005 – Close to the Rhine River in the back of beyond

Willem and I have tightened the laces of our hiking boots. Weeks ago we agreed to go walking on this Sunday morning near the riverbed of a dead branch of the Rhine River. Shortly after he moved into the old house on the dike with my mother, he started researching the area.

He knows the old stories and gossip about the dukes and barons who ruled here centuries ago. He shows me the new bicycle track. He can pinpoint the exact location of castles that have turned to dust, and he can trace the old meandering river. He shows me the hidden nest of a beaver and the track of a deer.

I still have to get used to him talking so passionately about 'wildlife' in the Netherlands. Once he proudly explained how beautiful it is to bump into a heron in a Dutch field. Having just flown in from Kenya I smirked at his joy. The pleasure he got from seeing a wild heron seemed like a joke, coming from a man who has traversed the globe and had had his boundaries challenged in every possible way.

Here, in the midst of a tame Dutch landscape, my father reminds me of a caged leopard pacing up and down. But he is serious.

When I grew up, my father played his role as a man according to the morals of his time. He provided. With my mom he debated his work, his mission and the battles he had to fight 'at the office'. He would have similar conversations with my oldest brother, who would follow in his footsteps.

My admiration for my dad in those days knew no limits. The strength with which he lived his life, the perseverance which pushed him to learn to play the organ better than peers with ten fingers, his conviction of the necessity and the potential of his work – all this combined to make him intimidating to me.

Being a son of Willem is no easy thing. He is his own worst critic. What he demands of himself he also demands of his loved ones: the same conviction, the same perfectionism.

His compliments are rare. At best he hands me his friends' praises. 'So and so read a text of yours, and he liked it,' he might say.

Once he called me in Kenya, just to draw my attention to an article he liked in the newspaper for which I wrote, about something in Africa. 'It is a marvellous story. Read it, Aernout.'

My father encouraged me to write like this unknown author had done, in a way that appealed to my father's heart. He could not have known it was my article. An editor at the paper had accidentally deleted my name in the by-line.

While we are walking through the muddy grass fields bordering the Rhine, I realise that I have been waiting for too long for his approval. It is futile to hope he will one day voluntarily stop blocking my sunlight.

It is *me* who has to step out of *his* shadow.

As the link between ancestors and offspring, my father has played his role immaculately. His name lives on in a new generation. My father lives on in me, in my urge to travel, to see what is beyond the horizon – in the desire to sit on a fallen tree trunk and ask questions.

Our hike along the river this Sunday soils his hiking boots. He has zipped up his thick winter coat and closed all the buttons to keep out the chilly breeze.

'You guys had Mom who did a perfect job raising you. I genuinely felt there was not a lot I could add to that.' In the way he speaks, I realise he is still in the process of formulating his thoughts. 'I am now aware that I cut all of us – including myself – short.'

He glances away, observes the river and then investigates the dirt under one of his nails. Black soil from his garden. 'I cannot undo the past. I am conscious of it. That must surely mean something, mustn't it?'

I vaguely hear a knot of shame overshadowing his regrets.

We amble along for a few hundred metres, silently.

Over the past couple of years my father has become a different man. The moment he retired there seemed to be no more space for the man-with-a-mission. These days he plays with his grandchildren as if he were their age.

'Strangely enough, when I look back on the highlights of my life,' he told one of my brothers, 'it's not the times when my career peaked that I see. Instead, I remember the moments I spent with you – my family. I recall the holidays in France, our overland trip to China and Mongolia, building boats together ... Those were without a doubt the best periods in my life, so far.'

My dad has spent a lot of time since his retirement to prepare for what he calls 'the next big project in my life': his death. During our hike we talk of the cosmos, of God and 'those damned church fathers who trashed everything of value'. He tells me how he would prefer his ashes to be dispersed because 'man's earthly frame has no relevance whatsoever'.

His boldness has changed. These days he has opened the door to doubts, thoughts, worries and musings – about life as well as about death. His vulnerability gives him a new strength.

He too has questions. He too is not as sure of things as he once was. Time is eating away at the old fortress.

25 December 2005 – another remote corner in the Netherlands

This time, my stay will be short. Christmas with my relatives, and that's it. I stand outside the home of my youngest brother in a wintery landscape and admire my parents' new car. My father shows me his gadgets playfully. Pots and pans with some of the dishes for a Christmas meal wait in the boot.

My parents will be here today, as well as my brothers, their spouses and their children. My youngesr brother lies in bed with a serious temperature. His partner comes running outside, a phone in hand.

'Willem, your oldest son. He sounds extremely serious.'

He takes the phone.

'Tell me, Kees.' A worried look.

I walk towards my father and lay my hands on his shoulders.

'No, it cannot be... NO!'

Silence.

'We are coming over now.'

He hands me the phone and places his hand on his mouth.

'We have to catch your mother, to keep her from falling.'

He does not look me in the eye, but instead glances over my shoulders into nothing.

'Dad, what happened?'

He takes a deep breath.

His eldest grandchild has died.

Wisse Amani Zevenbergen was born in Kigali (Rwanda) on 4 May 1992. On the day of his birth extremists killed the head nurse of the maternity ward in the run-up to the genocide of 1994.

He loved people, adventures and travelling. Eight years old, and sitting on the roof of my Land Rover in the arms of my watchman, Lenompony, he sang *In excelsis Deo*, while enjoying the nature reserve Amboseli, in Kenya.

Wisse accidentally asphyxiated himself on Christmas Day, in his bedroom in an old farmhouse in a Dutch river land.

He was thirteen.

26-31 December 2005 – the land of Maas and Waal

Every morning since Wisse's death, Willem wakes up and repeats to himself, 'Wisse is gone – he will never return.' Without those words my father finds it impossible to grasp the scope of the event.

A family mourns the loss of a child, and a village grieves with them. Hundreds of condolences arrive on the doorstep of my brother and my sister-in-law. Neighbours assist Kees and his wife Jeske where and how they can.

Wisse's relatives choose to organise the funeral themselves. Kees makes the coffin for his son himself with the assistance of Wisse's uncles. With Martijn he takes measurements and cuts the wooden boards. Gys burns a crest on the cover, designed by Jeske's sister – a crest which combines a Tuareg sword with cowry shells and the wings of a dragon. Wiebe and I cut the cushions on which Wisse will lie.

In the attached barn my mother and my sisters-in-law create an atmosphere suitable for a dignified farewell.

'You are in all aspects a clan,' people will comment weeks later. 'A family in which a person can tumble and everyone else helps soften the blow.'

31 December 2005 – The land of Maas and Waal

Wisse lies in state in the barn of an old farm, behind a Dutch dike. His coffin of unprocessed pinewood stands on a Tuareg king's bed from Mali. He lies in unbleached cotton cloths, a Rwandan custom. A *djembé* drummer calls for the village to gather. Hundreds have arrived

A poem of Khalil Gibran is read, a song by Youssou N'Dour is played. Stories, legends, memories.

Kees wraps the cloth around the body of his firstborn, caresses his face and folds over the last bits of cotton. He takes the cover and closes the coffin. Jeske leans in the arms of a brother-in-law. Wisse's brother Niels and his sister Hannah watch silently, their faces stricken with grief.

My father embraces my mother. Wisse's other grandmother stands in a circle, hand in hand with his aunts, uncles and nieces, and closest friends of the family.

Once he has closed the coffin, Kees leans forward in a cramp of profound pain. He lays his hands on the corners of the cover. His silence cuts deeper into my soul than the loudest bellow would have done.

My father observes. On his face I can read the sorrow of a grandfather. His own pain, the pain of his firstborn, and that of his oldest grandchild who felt to him like his sixth son. Three generations bear down on his shoulders.

We stand in front of the oven in a crematorium somewhere in an industrial area. Those who choose to, stay. Others leave the room. The coffin leans on a steel fork on wheels. One flower, a Zimbabwean flame lily, lies on the cover, put there by my mother. My brother Gys and I push the fork into the oven. Flames embrace Wisse.

Late 2006

Sometimes my father sits and ponders near a *zwerfkei* behind a dike in a river landscape – a monument to Wisse. With the death of his oldest grandchild my father lost his own fear of dying. He leafs through letters written by Wisse's friends and siblings, collected in a box with the inscription 'Mailbox to Heaven'.

'Will you help me?' Niels wrote to his brother.

'Help me to grow up?

'Tell me – are you comfortable?'

A hint of sarcasm in his voice. The kind of sarcasm that speaks of ruthless compassion. He knows exactly that the least comfortable place is the one he has me sitting in.

He blows into the flames. Adds some more wood. Stirs a bit.

'Hot enough?'

I am cooking. Seriously cooking.

And he knows it.

The pot is hot. The water is hot. The steam is hot.

I feel snails crawling out of my skin. One by one. Black snails. It feels like I'm covered in them.

'You need it hotter? This is not a holiday, don't forget that. You're here to work.'

I recall a sentence I recently heard: 'Whatever is fully experienced becomes love itself.'

My life so far has confirmed this wisdom. Endless dodging and diving is not possible. Nothing stays buried forever, it will always pop up eventually, in whatever disguise. I deeply desire a thorough cleansing.

'Heat it up please – I'm not there yet…'

As he throws more wood onto the fire, he tells a story.

'Centuries ago, alchemists experimented with matter, trying to create gold. Their inspiration came from mystical texts, while the confusion originated in their own minds. In mythology the processes of alchemy were not aimed at turning physical lead into physical gold. The metaphor was taken too literally. Alchemists were supposed to work with souls.'

Malachi 3:3 – 'He sits as a refiner and purifier of silver.'

Silversmiths heat silver in the heart of the flames, where it is hottest. The smith must remain absolutely focussed.

One second too long, and the silver is destroyed. Too short and the silver is not pure yet.

When is silver 'just right'?

When the smith sees his own reflection in the material.

Again his question:

'Are you comfortable in the heat?'

'That depends,' I reply.

'When you look at me, can you see anything appearing slowly?'

'I can't tell you what death is. The only thing we humans can do is to accept the fact of death. That is hard, I know. It's hard for everyone. I think though, that for a European it is even more difficult than it is for us. You think, much more than we do, that you can somehow control life, and therefore death.'

King André Nicoles (71) sits cross-legged in his palace, built from wooden poles and covered with reed mats, in the seaside town of Mananjary. In one corner I see pots and pans, dented and covered in soot. In another corner, Nicoles keeps his wicker baskets.

As the evening progresses and darkness descends outside, a few families of chickens with their chicks find refuge in the reed cradles. Drums hang from the ceiling. A torch dangles from a nail. A whiff of roasted coffee beans enters through the windows of the office of the *mpanjaka*, a local king in Madagascar.

'The most important lesson in life is this: we are mortals. We cannot but surrender to what is bigger than we are. If I have trouble doing that, I have a problem. My power and strength as a human are not enough to turn back the clock, or even understand the "why?" of most events. As long as you fail to accept that existence comes with a string of realities you can't change, you will not be able to grasp what lies beyond the horizon of reason.'

Nicoles weighs his words serenely. While he listens to my questions and my explanations, the king plays a game of *solitaire*. He has another game, a wooden box containing blocks of different sizes. The purpose of this one is to 'liberate' the biggest block by moving the others.

'When a person dies, that is the wish of the ancestors. They either need his or her spirit, or they feel that is has been enough. Usually though, in my belief, a human dies because the ancestors call upon the spirit to pass on.'

King Nicoles is a humble man. When his rice fields demand labour, then that's where he'll be. If the hallways of the clinic need a thorough scrub, he'll scrub the hallways. 'If you want your hospital to be clean, why not extend a hand yourself?'

His shirt is torn. His pants end at his calves. To protect himself against the sun, he wears a ragged straw hat during the day. His office is his palace;

it probably measures five by eight metres. On a small table in a corner lies a chaotic stack of paperwork through which only *he* will be able to find his way.

Nicoles administers a region that is rapidly losing inhabitants. Cyclones that hit the area in 2003 and 2004 destroyed too many livelihoods, too many homes. No one in Mananjary is wealthy – this is a town where the roads are full of potholes and grass grows from brick walls. Men earn a living with the *pousse pousse*, a cart pulled by humans. I see them pass by outside with sweat streaming over their torsos, while I listen to the king.

———————

The body. The brain. The spirit. The soul.

What fades? What stays?

Wisse's death has brought to the surface a wide variety of questions with which I have never before been confronted so directly and so intensely. 'Not death itself, but the way we dance with death defines our lives,' a wise man once wrote.

I smelt death in Rwanda, where swarms of blue-green flies rested on the leaves of banana palms a few metres above the rotting corpses of rebels.

Bullets whistled around my ears in Mogadishu, Somalia.

I followed a trail of destruction in Freetown, Sierra Leone, shortly after a so-called 'rebel movement' had come to town.

On Africa's dangerous roads I encountered blood, brains and body parts, and saw my own death pass by a few times.

Despite those flirtations with mortality, dying always remained strangely distant – always far away, no matter how close-by I stood. The stories were always those of others, some heart-wrenching.

Most of my own emotions bounced off my notebook – the journalist's shield. Or else they were channelled away through my fountain pen.

A few times I received phone calls or e-mails from friends or relatives who had read my stories on some of the excesses of existence.

'How are you, Aernout?' they'd ask. 'Are you still standing?'

'I was fine, until you asked. Now I've started shaking like a leaf.'

The death of my nephew gave sudden urgency to my musings on life and death. For my trip to Madagascar, I packed books on relativity, space-time, Newton's curse and the riddles of quantum mechanics. I added books on ancestors in Senegal and Ghana, on *sasa* and *zamani* in Eastern Africa, on spirits and on souls.

The hodgepodge library I carried on my back was a mirror of the mishmash in my mind – a mind exploded into chaos on that pivotal Christmas day, only a few weeks ago.

I keep re-reading a poem by Birago Diop:

Listen more often
To things than to beings
The voice of the fire can be heard
Hear the voice of the water
Listen in the wind
To the sobbing bush
It is the breath of the ancestors

Science in the 20th century has come to the boundaries of human intelligence, 'reason' and 'logic'. Mathematicians already play with riddles in dimensions most people will never be able to understand. 'Magic' and 'science' extend invitations to each other to come to the ball and dance.

Magic has never left Africa. Spirits roam around inflicting damage or bringing blessings. Beyond the smoke and mirrors of simple superstitions, the most talented shamans are able to pop in and out of different levels of reality. The town of Mananjary still embraces these different realities, as if Western Enlightenment is but a dust particle in human evolution.

All of the nineteen ethnic groups of Madagascar honour their ancestors, and celebrate life and death in respectful ways. Some dig up their dead once every year, wrap the remains in new cloth, sprinkle rum all over them and parade them through the village, after which the dead may rest for another twelve months.

However, modernity is settling down in Madagascar as well, especially in the cities and in the north of the country. Traditions are fluttering away.

But not in Mananjary. Not just yet.

Nicoles: 'What's the purpose of a car if I myself am not grounded, if I have no clue what my life is about or why it is I am here?'

———

Nicoles and I sit opposite one another, both cross-legged. As ruler of this area he is seen as one of the liaison officers between mortals and ancestors.

After I have laid down the reason for my visit to Mananjary, he slowly gets up, starts pacing up and down his palace, grabs a cloth from a hook and wraps it around himself. A vague hint of nervousness.

'I can't. To assist a white man to converse with *our* ancestors... I've never heard of it before; not here, not in Mananjary.'

Nicoles advises me to learn how to listen to the world around me. 'Spirits are everywhere. They're housed in the trees, they live in animals, they nestle in stones and rocks. They are here with us now. They listen, observe, look. They only speak when we ask their advice, or when we are about to do very silly things. They have tapped me on the shoulder a few times, when I was about to make decisions that would negatively affect the community. They've shown up in my dreams and told me, "Stop what you're doing. This won't work out well." But talking to an outsider? A white man?'

Nicoles asks me what it is I want to know, what advice it is I am seeking.

'I want to understand death better. What it is. I want to hear what the ancestors can say about this issue of masculinity and of male identity. I'd like to hear news of Wisse who, just like me, was born in Africa – I assume his name must appear somewhere in the register...'

I smile carefully. It feels strange to long for the jokes he and I shared, to desire contact with a soul beyond my grasp.

Nicoles shakes his head. 'We can't talk to Wisse. Even though he was born in Africa, his culture is not ours – we are not familiar with the rituals that would invite his spirit.'

The king notices my disappointment, presses my hand and goes out to search for a woman a few blocks away. 'Wait here, don't leave.'

As Nicoles leaves, I see the village idiot lean against a wall outside. On his head he carries a pot without a bottom. Wrapped around his waist is a black garbage bag. Tucked under his arm is a piece of scrap metal, which he guards as if it's solid gold.

Nicoles returns with two bottles: one rum and one tonic water. 'You're welcome to see her at seven-thirty in the morning. The minute you wake up, you need to retreat into nature. Go to the beach, into a forest, or walk along the rice paddies. No eating, drinking or smoking. No working. Only breathe. Observe. Be.'

He puts two glasses on the wooden floor in front of his desk. Carefully, he pours three shots onto the reed mat. 'Spirits, please come. Bless this man who has come here to ask my assistance. If he really needs it, then come, help.'

He pours a shot of rum in my glass, then in his own and adds the tonic. 'Let the impossible become possible: a white man communicating with our forebears.'

———————

The tropical shower comes down hard on the corrugated roof of my 'beach bungalow'. My bones ache after a night-long fight with the bumps and pits of my mattress. Through the curtains I see the day has started without me; I've missed sunrise. My watch points at six o'clock; I still have an hour and a half left. Out of respect for the living I shave my unsightly stubble – for the woman who will be my guide, as well as the king who'll bring me to her. I leave my tobacco on my nightstand and skip breakfast.

Seated on the beach, I browse through my notebook and re-read a piece of text I wrote a few years earlier. The story I wrote after meeting a *laibon* (a Masai priest) just before I left Kenya for South Africa.

Ole Ntoika wore a thick, knitted cap and had his red cloth wrapped around his shoulders. He covered the corners of his eyes with white powder and spoke incantations. From the fringes of his cap protruded silver hair. Jewellery dangled from his ears and wrists: white beads, orange beads, green and black. A sheepskin lay on the grass, covered with a black piece of cotton. From a plastic bag he took the calabash and tapped rhythmically. Before he strewed the left-over powder in his hand, he saluted the corners of the earth.

'What the future holds for you, is that what you'd like to know?' The laibon stared at me intently, silently, as if he looked straight through me. His right hand started shaking the calabash he held there. He mumbled words and phrases. In one throw he spilled some of the contents of the calabash onto the black cotton.

Marbles. Stones in a rich variety of colours and structures. A snake's tooth. Bolts. The laibon read what he threw and looked at me, grinning widely.

'Twenty-nine – a throw doesn't come any better than this. Your future invites you.' He started shifting through the stones, studied the snake's tooth, put it aside.

You will travel. You will leave your home here to build a new home far away. That's good. Pain. You will experience pain there – I can't tell you what will cause it. It's not a pain you can't deal with. You'll survive and you'll gain from it.'

Ole Ntoika selected the pebbles with negative energy, and gave them to me, after he spat on them. I had to undo their negativity by rubbing them over my forehead, my chest and my lower arms. After that, he put them back into the calabash.

A second throw.

Again marbles, stones, grit.

A dented bullet.

A scare ran through me.

'Where is it you're heading off to? I see a country with weapons and lots of violence.'

I answer: 'South Africa – it's time for change.'

'The bullet won't hit you, don't worry. Know that it is there; that's sufficient.' Again he gave me the stones I had to purify.

A third and final throw. This time, I asked the question and put my mouth on the calabash.

'Will I be content in that faraway place?'

The answer poured out in a rich collection of objects, one of them a toy airplane.

'You will travel often.' Ole Ntoika fiddled with the objects, looked at some of them. Again his friendly grin. 'You will have many friends. And offspring even. Your seed will be fertile in the land you're heading to. A family awaits you.'

Before he wrapped up the objects, he had a final glance.

'The most important thing of all is: learn to have faith; let life happen. It'll be good to you.'

Restlessness sweeps through my body as I look out over the fishermen reeling in their nets in the surf. My head refuses to surrender to fortune telling. Voices tell me it's all a waste of time, superstition. And even if it were anything more than simple nonsense, I would surely be playing with fire.

I grew up with fresh peppermint sweeties on Sunday mornings – a Dutch reformed delight for enduring a sermon. Only when the seven Zevenbergens had arrived could the service begin.

In my early teens, Bible studies were obligatory – until my parents relieved me of the burden of listening to peers for whom God was a man on a white cloud, in a white robe, with a white beard, on a white throne, with a wand in his hand. That god never came alive for me; he seemed a human invention, and I had no need for yet another grandfather.

Spirituality as I have come to know it in Africa has directed me back to the roots of the religion I grew up in. Those same roots I find in Zen Buddhism, in Daoism, in the works of Sufi poets and Gnostics, in the writings of mystics and in the lives of shamans. Everyone uses different images and tells different stories for what is, essentially, identical.

At the heart of the spirituality of the Mande in West Africa, for example, lies an appreciation of the vital connection between spirit and matter and the laws that weave them together. Each part of the cosmos is connected to every other part – an insight shared these days by scholars of modern physics. Nothing you do remains without effect.

'Be careful what you throw into the "pool of life",' notes the Senegalese dancer and drummer, Adama Doumbia, 'because of the ripples that inevitably result.'

Doumbia and his wife Naomi describe in their book, *The way of the elders* (2004), aeon-old African insights and wisdom that essentially do not differ from the wisdom and insights of Buddhism, Sufism and mystic Christianity.

Or modern-day scientific cosmology, for that matter.

'Everything that has life speaks; everything that speaks tells the story of Spirit. This is the language of our ancestors, the language that teaches us how to live in harmony with our surroundings and with one another. Many of us have lost this language, though everything around us continues to speak.'

New truths have entered. New gods and idols. New rules and habits. When I close my eyes, I see a continent slowly forgetting its own stories. I see storytellers without an audience.

In the farthest outbacks, Vin Diesel and Arnold Schwarzenegger have become the new heroes. Materialism is the new bar against which people measure each other and themselves. Just like everywhere else on the planet, life is dumbing-down; instant gratification is silting up the river of existence.

For some in East Africa death used to be nothing more than a shell's demise, with the spirit moving on. In their cosmology, time is no more than a collection of random events that, collectively, have led to the present. Everything that once existed has left its mark. Great events have simply left bigger marks in the memory of more people, and grand characters have remained longer in memory.

For as long as there was even just one mortal around to remember an event or a person, that event or person was still part of existence. They would only fade out once the last memory of the last living person had been taken to the grave. Only then would a spirit move from the 'now', the *sasa*, to the *zamani*, the big unknown that preceded and transcends us – the mystery, eternity.

Slowly, however, this *zamani*, with everything it embraces, is inching its way towards that collection of stories once told, but now forgotten; a memory without a mind to hold it.

'Real wealth is to know who you are deep inside,' king Nicoles told me last night. 'To be conscious of where you come from and where you are going. Everything else is just a side issue, a frill, a decoration. But the frills have become the main ingredient of existence.' He looked dejected and worried.

Waves crash onto the sandy beach. Far away on the sea, little canoes bob up and down. Behind me, cows low as they roam around looking for grass.

I am ready to meet the ancestors.

––––––––––

King Nicoles leads the way through a maze of pathways past huts and laundry. Chickens run around; children play in the dust. From a radio comes the Abba hit *Knowing me, knowing you*.

The *pänelanëlani*, Gertrude Baomazava (53), awaits our arrival inside her hut. Her hair is combed back, wrapped in tightly plaited strings. 'The ancestors watched you this morning on the beach; you're not playing games. Please enter.' A shy smile.

I leave my shoes outside, next to the single step up to a wooden floor. A reed mat lies in the centre. On a table waits a bottle of rum. A small stove contains glowing coals. Other objects are unfamiliar to me. Baomazava has stuck a comb in between the banana leaves that make her roof, next to a strip of pills and the feathers of a bird.

She asks me for an offering, 6 000 ariary (2.50 dollars). From under her side table, she takes tiny blocks of arabic gum and throws them into the glowing coals. They immediately start melting and produce a strong, sweet scent.

In her next ritual, Baomazava takes a plate holding the horn of a zebu and a thin layer of water on which floats a leaf – all elements of nature in which spirits can house themselves, if they so choose. She adds a drop of rum, stirs, takes a sip, and spits it out into a corner of her hut. Another sip: this one goes out through the door facing east. She closes a curtain in front of the door facing west. A spirit, once entered, won't leave too easily.

'Bring me the forebears – let me speak to ancestors.'

Her tone of voice changes. Her eyes transform. She unties her plaits and pulls her hair down. With her hand she does her best to iron it flat. She stands up, throws off her outer skirt and pulls on a white robe. She pours herself a glass of rum.

Gone is the gentle, shy woman. In comes a character with raw, angry masculine energy. Rough. Undaunted. No one seems to understand her accent. Another woman is called in; she will translate the words.

'Are you prepared?'

The voice thunders through the hut.

'Prepared for what?' I stammer.

'To hear the ancestors, to follow their advice?'

I move about uncomfortably and answer as honestly as I can. 'My soul is not for sale. Apart from that, yes, I am prepared.'

The spirit – his name is Tsimeloka, I am told later – is satisfied with my answer. The female body in front of me convulses in hectic ways on her tiny stool. Fidgety. Looks left, looks right. Into my eyes. Into the eyes of Nicoles. And Tsimeloka starts speaking.

'A great deal of people will not like your book. Not at all. They don't want you to write this. They think "men in Africa" are none of your business. Many of them silently think to themselves, "I am my own God. I don't need anyone commenting or asking questions." That's how the white man taught them; to think of himself as master of the universe.'

Tsimeloka grabs a knife and starts scraping off tiny bits from the zebu horn, from different pieces of wood, from a bone. He catches it all in a minute piece of paper.

'You'll find many an obstruction. Wash yourself with this every Friday and the obstruction will recede. We will protect you.'

My brain starts playing tricks with me. A voice inside objects strongly, Wash myself every Friday with a powder? Yeah, right! What's wrong with a stiff debate, a conversation?

I swallow my doubts and objections. His recipe I find less interesting than his story.

'What is death?' I ask.

He stands up, exchanges the white robe for red pieces of cloth.

New eyes. A new voice. This character orders the king to give him a cigarette.

Kotovola takes a few drags, grabs the rum and pours himself a glass. A big gulp. With legs opened wide he sits down on the stool, his lower arms resting on his knees. Machismo re-defined.

'You enquire about death. I won't tell you much. The body stops moving and feeling. The spirit continues ... Ah, what am I doing? I can't explain death to a mortal. You wouldn't understand any of it. It's not your task to *understand* death. A human has to die. It's not his role to ask the "why?" of it.'

Seated opposite me, I see the ultimate alpha male – the way he moves, orders people around, does not accept a dissident sound. After the seance, Baomazava will explain that Kotovola first sent Tsimeloka to test the waters. He had no desire to waste his time on clowns.

'Listen!

A demanding field of energy.

Definitely not a joker, this Kotovola.

Doubts keep welling up in me, until he starts talking about aspects of my past, of many details far too personal to guess. Of a long-lasting love that crashed just before the harbour of marriage.

Of my life in Africa.

My work.

Just like Tsimeloka, Kotovola acknowledges the many doubts I have about this book, and encourages me to not lay down my pen.

'Africans are losing sight of their roots, their origins. Change is normal. It is part of life, of existence. What I fear is that many are losing their way along the track.

'It is not at all necessary to go back to how things were in the old days. The past has passed. At the same time, a tiny bit more respect for one's own identity, one's own rituals – that would be good, even if people themselves no longer practise those rituals.

'Africans are, deep in their heart, still Africans. However, more and more tend to forget what that means. It seems that you're inviting people to reach into their past and salvage what is useful and good. It is this endeavour we, on our side, support.'

When Kotovola reaches out for the knife to scrape off his powders for me, I again start to doubt. I have little to no faith in powders or potions. For me, the chain between cause and effect becomes too blurry the moment powders play a role.

A powder doesn't hand me any clue as to what *I* can do through my *own* chain of thoughts, speech and actions. No matter the amount of affection, goodwill or wisdom that has gone into producing the powder. What is left of my freedom to accept my own responsibility?

I am yet again aware of my 'reasonable' background. At the same time, Kotovola has told me too many truths about events and trends and people thousands of kilometres away from Baomazava's hut to be able to dismiss what is happening as 'rubbish'.

The pieces of incense are burnt. We have been working for over an hour. Kotovola pours himself another stiff glass, lights another cigarette. Looks at me.

'It's time for a woman, my man. Are you listening?' His eyes stare, but again seem to go straight through me.

'I see two children. Two sons. Good-hearted sons. However, before you can find a woman, you need to make a choice. One of your feet is still firmly planted in Europe, the other one stands in Africa. Choose! Your time to play has ended. Stop keeping your options open. You belong in Africa, not in Europe. This place is better for you.'

The eyelids of the *pänelanëlani* drop, her straightened back loses its posture. Kotovola seems to vanish. Silence.

After a while Baomazava gets up and takes off her red robe. A deep sigh. She wraps her flower-covered dress around her waist. Gone is the macho. Before me I again see the woman in her early fifties, shy and toothless. Slowly she regains her composure, grabs a few bank notes from the 'offering' I have given her and hands it to her daughter. 'Go get me a rooster to slaughter.'

She turns towards me and says, 'Phew – you want to know so much...'

Baomazava takes a ribbon and binds the rooster's wings. Her son will cut its throat on the western side of the hut, just outside the door through which only shortly before the spirits came and left.

I am asked to take a sip of the mixture of rum and water from the plate that contains the leaf and the zebu horn. The son will use the same plate to catch the blood. Slowly he cuts the throat.

The rooster's life juice is a deep, dark red. It slowly mingles with the transparent fluids on the plate. Thick drops glisten on the razor-sharp blade of the knife.

Before I leave Mananjary, Nicoles wants to take me to the royal graves in the burial grounds of his town. Crosses are placed higgledy-piggledy and some have fallen down without any attention paid to them. Under and in-between the crosses placed in the front of each building, lie metal plates, hats and cups. Behind those crosses are a few square metres of open space. That's where the remains are buried.

'The only reason we use crosses is because the horizontal bar allows for our tradition of giving people long names. Here in this part of the country, Christianity has not been able to convert many souls. Missionaries did not allow us to honour our ancestors.'

A chilled breeze blows over the cemetery. Birds whistle and frolic in mid-flight. From the corner of my eye, I see a man undress to bathe himself in the creek between the village and the burial grounds.

The paper leaves of my notebook dance in the wind to a tune I cannot hear. My right hand itches like crazy. Scratching doesn't help. It feels as if words need to come out urgently.

What am I to make of the stories told by Kotovola and Tsimeloka? What am I to do with the words of wisdom shared by the king, seated not far from me under a tree?

Life and death, death and life. Inextricable concepts.

The itch will not go away. Until I start writing. A long list of words that seem unconnected, unrelated – but they always come in pairs.

Life, death.

Cold, warm.

Growth, decay.

Destroy, construct.

Light, dark.

Masculine, feminine.

'When a person dies,' goes an African saying, 'it is said of him, "His feet are in agreement".' A riddle – until I come across another saying, also from West Africa. 'Man can only walk through the disparity between his feet, because all disparities are complementary. Such is the great law of dualism.'

I continue jotting down concepts.

Zero, eternity. Full, empty. Compassion, revenge. Sacred lust, saintly celibacy.

The itch in my hand slowly fades away.

I browse through old notes and decipher a scribble I jotted down from Joseph Ki-Zerbo, the philosopher from Burkina Faso:

'Without identity we are an object of history, an instrument used by others, like a utensil. Identity is an assumed role; it is like being in a theatre where everyone is given a role to play.'

Identity. Masculinity.

What is theatre?

What is real?

I look at king Nicoles, in his royal rags and trodden-down sandals, seated under a tree in the burial grounds of his town.

He radiates a pride that is increasingly rare. Honour and respect come naturally to him.

André Nicoles knows who he is.

Knows where he comes from.

Knows where he is headed.

He does not play a role from a soap opera.

He is himself, in the shadow of a tree, chewing on a blade of grass.

EMPTINESS

2009 – Devil's Peak, Cape Town

Africa has been emptied of its content
And what has been imported is empty too.

These two lines of Joseph Ki-Zerbo pull at me. They goad as much as they vex. Is that because they seem so dark? Or because they resonate with a simple and undeniable 'truth'? Do they constitute a charge, a call-to-arms, or are they merely a description?

The two lines are impersonal; no one gets the blame. To minimise the risk of an eternal 'yes/no' debate, Ki-Zerbo purely zooms in on the result: vacuity.

Not the desolation of the open plains, but a growing purposelessness deep inside the soul of Africa. His words challenge and seem to say, 'Awake! It has happened. Whereto from here?'

'Do you have a happy ending for your book?' a friend once asked me while I was still slogging away. 'Are you optimistic or pessimistic?'

Strolling over a gravel road on one of the slopes of Table Mountain, I still have no answer to her question. A recent bushfire has scarred these slopes of Devil's Peak. My quest into contemporary masculinity in Africa started in October 2001, when I was told about exploding testicles and the need to plant seed.

Since then, I've fired questions at others, and questions were bounced back at me.

Sometimes people responded in a curious fashion, almost surprised that some of their own life's riddles were identical to mine. Other people reacted without any attempt to hide anger, mistrust or contempt.

'Who do you think you are? A white man your age? Without children? Without a woman? Who are you to talk about fatherhood and loneliness, romance and friendship?' In any conversation about intimate topics, suspicion easily intrudes. And any dialogue of this nature between a black man and a white man is further hindered by our mutual past.

Talking sex, love and romance in Africa is no easy feat, thanks in part to 'explorers' who marched into the continent in the mid-19th century, armed with their measuring tapes. They measured genitals to confirm the foregone conclusion of the 'primitive' nature of 'natives' who needed 'civilising'.

Yes, I am a white human being in Africa in the 21st century. A man in his early forties. With loads of questions.

The most important question on almost all of my journeys has been, 'What does it mean to be a man?' Of course I haven't found one simple answer to that question. Instead, I've encountered confusion, aversion, frustration, despair and nihilism, balanced at times by ingenuity, resoluteness, laughter and lightness.

Masculine honour all over the planet has become a stew of dissonant issues. The codes of old have lost their validity and their meaning. Circumstances that, in the past, provided men with opportunities to fulfil their roles have transformed, and have – in some instances – even faded away.

The result was scribbled into the stucco of the holding cell at the asylum in Freetown: 'To be a man is not easy.' The same phrase I saw written on the cart of a water seller in Monrovia, and on walls elsewhere in West Africa.

All over the world traditions have changed, as they have since time immemorial. Traditions are never rigid, despite a general belief to the contrary.

Rigid traditions lead to fundamentalism, an inability to move with the changes that form the crux of life, and are no more than a deeply romantic nostalgia for a past that will never return.

Most rituals have lost their meaning because they no longer echo the sounds of the present day, the realities of contemporary existence. But can a human being live without rituals? Is it possible for any person to meander from cradle to grave without clearly marked phases of transformation and metamorphosis? Can a boy really become a man without some sort of initiation?

Of all the spiritual streams that, at one time or another, flowed through our collective history to nourish our collective ancestors, not one has ever done away with the need for clearly demarcated stages in life. But we, modern human beings *have*. We've done this out of a misdirected arrogance and belief that reason alone defines where it is we go and how we should live our lives.

Modern man 'is asked to be a man when no one can define it except in the most trivial of terms,' wrote James Hollis in *Under Saturn's Shadow*. 'He is asked to move from boyhood to manhood without any rites of passage, with no wise elders to receive and instruct him, and no positive sense of what such manhood might feel like. His wounds are not transformative; they do not bring deepened consciousness; they do not lead him to a richer life. They senselessly, repeatedly, stun him into a numbing of the soul before the body has had the good sense to die.'

Do I, in some kind of reactionary response, suggest going back to what once was?

No, I don't.

The rituals of old belong in the past.

Men need new ceremonies, new rites of passage, grounded in today's soil, in today's hearts, minds and souls. They need pointers, valid and credible at today's crossroads.

Only a few dare to query a path for the future.

Are these men exceptions to the rule?

Lone voices?

Or the designers of desperately awaited new codes of masculinity?

––––––––––

My eyes are drawn to the slopes above me. The *fynbos* of the Western Cape needs bushfires to survive. The presence of too many shrubs and bushes chokes seedlings. Some seeds need the heat to sprout.

Each friendship that breaks or evaporates over time asks for self-reflection. A tumbling love brings a healthy dose of disenchantment. The death of a loved one creates, with a stupefying punch, space for renewal.

I feel the wind pick up as I walk below Devil's Peak. More traces of the past are blown away. More traditions dissolve. Pride fades. Foundations disappear under a layer of fine dust.

I have found it impossible to debate the roots, crossroads or musings of others without looking these exact same issues straight in the eye myself. The men and women I spoke to about their inner life in turn touched mine.

The ancestors of Madagascar who challenged me to take my second foot out of Europe, to choose unconditionally for a 'home', gave me the push I needed.

My confrontation with some of the hate-filled clergy of Uganda set alight a large part of my own spiritual background.

Being alone in godforsaken deserts brought simplicity and, more importantly, serenity.

Finally, I can formulate an answer to my friend.

A story is never finished. It moves, waves, breaks, slides, changes, loses all its meaning and sometimes regains it again in either the old or in something unknown and uncharted.

Sometimes emptiness is all that is left.

Is emptiness optimistic, or pessimistic?

Neither, I'd say.

Emptiness invites.

ACKNOWLEDGEMENTS

The features published in this book are the result of travels I have made through Africa since March 1996. A word of gratitude therefore goes to all the publications who made those journeys possible, most importantly AD *Newsmedia* in the Netherlands and *De Morgen* in Belgium.

I owe André Beijen a special 'Thank you!' – he has been my editor for most of my career as a newspaper journalist. He has the magical ability to make me laugh out loud at myself.

Publisher Jan Mets of Mets & Schilt in Amsterdam, who, in 2007, published the Dutch edition, *Vlekken van een luipaard*, recognised a theme where few others saw it, and gave his encouragement through an appreciation of silence. 'Let's not talk too much. Just write, and all will be well.'

Patrick Slavin in Liberia, Nico Pater and José Tegels in Niger, and Jean-Charles Rajoelisolo in Madagascar helped me find my way.

Gethwane Makhaye in Pietermaritzburg, Thami Nkosi in Soweto, Mbuyiselo Botha in Johannesburg, Jackie Greeff in Upington and Robert Morrell in Durban encouraged me when encouragement was needed.

Over the course of many years, Eric Miller in Cape Town allowed me to spy over his shoulder once in a while and learn the art of silent observation. Kim Stevenson provided pushes and kicks when needed. Amelia Carthy reminded me of the need to see the image in the mirror. Isabel Coello opened my eyes to the theme of patriarchy, and did so with passion and rigour.

Zoë Clifford and Stephen Beale gave solid, witty and light-hearted feedback on one of the final versions of the manuscript. The pencil marks left behind by Peter van Straten were nothing short of art. Dean Peacock has challenged my ideas non-stop and has shown himself a more than worthy adversary. Thanks for keeping me sharp.

Elzanne Roos and Nico Roos cleaned up the text, tightened it and made it run smoother than I could have done on my own. To *Judy Garland*: thanks for allowing me the use of your right brain! As always: the errors and mistakes in 'Spots' are my responsibility, and mine alone.

Manuela Dzionk remained, after all our adventures, an amazing friend.

Jane Eedes: thank you for allowing me glimpses of your soul.

My parents, my four brothers and their wives taught me a maddening love for perfection, for detail, for the bigger picture and for life outside the box.

With his roving eye my father Willem warns me of errors. My mother Bertie keeps pointing untiringly at beauty. Kees shows me, with a wink, the power of 'wiping the floor therapeutically'. Gys challenges me to lift even more of the veil. Wiebe tells me stories about polar bears and a man dressed in a leopard skin – a gift beyond reason. Martijn has the amazing talent to make one phone call, at the only time it really matters.

And Wisse?

Wisse wrote along with his pinky.

As he had promised.

Go well, audacious traveller!

Go well…

LITERATURE

A full list of the literature I read specifically for *Spots*, as well as other books I think might be of interest to readers, can be found on the website www. laughingleopard.co.za. The webpage 'Bookshelves' also includes books on cosmology, Daoism, Gnosticism, African history, as well as on the so-called mythopoetic men's movement, feminism and the works of pro-feminist male authors.

Here I limit myself to the books I quoted from in the previous pages.

Atuhaire, Bernard; *The Uganda cult tragedy – a private investigation*; 2003; Janus Publishing Company Ltd.; London; ISBN 1-85756-521-5

Clarke, P.H.C.; *A short history of Tanganyika*; 1965; Longman International Education Division; ISBN 978-0582602359

Conrad, Joseph; *Heart of darkness*; 1999; Könemann Verlagsgesellschaft GmbH; Köln; ISBN 3-8290-3003-7

Doumbia, Adama and Naomi; *The way of the elders*; 2004; Llewellyn Publications; ISBN 0-7387-0626-4

Ellis, Stephen; *The mask of anarchy – The destruction of Liberia and the religious dimension of an African civil war*; 2001; New York University Press; New York; ISBN 0-8147-2211-3

Falk Moore, Sally and Puritt, Paul; *The Chagga and Meru of Tanzania*; 1977; International Africa Institute; London; ISBN 0-8530-2051-5

Föllmi, Danielle and Olivier; *365 Days of African Wisdom*; Thames & Hudson; London; ISBN 0-500-54311-9

Faludi, Susan; *Backlash*; 1993; Vintage; London; ISBN 0-09-922271-X

Hollis, John; *Under Saturn's shadow – the wounding and healing of men*; 1994; Inner City Books; Toronto; ISBN 0-919123-64-3

Iliffe, John; *Honour in African history*; 2005; Cambridge University Press; Cambridge; ISBN 0-521-54685-0

Iliffe, John; *The African AIDS Epidemic: A History*; 2006; Ohio University Press; ISBN 0-85255-890-2

Kapuscinski, Ryszard; *The shadow of the sun*; 2002; Penguin Books; London; ISBN 0-14-029262-4

Kaunda, Kenneth; *Letter to my children*; 1974; Longman Group Limited; London; ISBN 0-582-10128-X

Reid, Graem and Walker, Liz (ed); *Men behaving differently - South African men since 1994;* 2005; Double Storey; Cape Town; ISBN 1-919930-98-1

Sibley, James and Westerman, D; *Liberia - old and new*; 1928; Doubleday, Doran & Company, Inc.

Somé, Sobonfu; *The spirit of intimacy*; 2002; Quill, New York, ISBN 0-688-17579-1

Stanley, Henry; *Through the dark continent* - Volume One and Two; 1988; Dover Publications, Inc.; New York; ISBN 0-486-25668-5

Turyagumanawe, David; *Sexual fulfilment*; 1997; Faith Communications Ltd.; Rukungi.

LAUGHING LEOPARD PRODUCTIONS
inspires debate about masculinity through the art of storytelling.

We create journalistic productions for a global audience with,
as our focal point, the humane and the human.

We adhere to the highest quality standards, and work only with talented
photographers, writers, designers and other media professionals.

We let principles of journalism prevail, and therefore approach reality
with a great deal of folly and a dash of madness wherever and
whenever we can.

We are based in Cape Town, South Africa.

More information can be found on
www.laughingleopard.co.za

For questions, enquiries or comments, please contact us on:
info@laughingleopard.co.za